The new, must-have handbook for the modern family! Get ready to chuckle at the familiar challenges facing "lunatic" moms and dads. Thank you, Dr. Palmiter, for showing us how busy parents can become better parents!"

— Mindi Ramsey
Morning News Anchor, WNEP-TV

Better than David Letterman's Top 10 List. Dr. Palmiter provides his Top 10 List of clinically based strategies for effective parenting with warmth, wit, wisdom, and practical tips. Destined to become a go-to book for caring, busy, and confused parents for years to come.

— Michele Novotni, PhD
Author, *What Does Everybody Else Know that I Don't?*

A new kind of self-help book for parents that offers 10 strategies for effective parenting, which actually rely on scientifically based research to guide and empower parents. What's also fresh and exciting is the humorous and respectful approach taken toward parents. The author is a child psychologist, who also uses his own clinical and personal experience as a father to illustrate his practical and sage advice to parents. A wonderful, warm, and witty must-read for all fathers, mothers, and anyone who loves kids!

— Nancy Molitor, PhD
Clinical Psychologist in Private Practice, Wilmette, Illinois
Fellow, American Psychological Association
President, Division of Independent Practice, American Psychological Association
Assistant Clinical Professor of Psychiatry and Behavioral Science,
Northwestern University, Feinberg School of Medicine, Chicago, Illinois

Working Parents, Thriving Families is the "how and why to" book for parents who are looking for succinct answers, actions, and understanding for common and not so common behaviors presented by their children. Wearing both his psychologist and dad hats, Dr. Palmiter effectively normalizes reactions and thoughts parents often experience in their parenting adventures and equips them with an "I'm not the only one" empowerment and a proactive and practical skill set—valuable for overtaxed and busy parents who care about creating a happy and balanced environment for their children and themselves.

— Jana Martin, PhD

Chief Executive Officer, American Psychological Association Insurance Trust

Past President, Division of Independent Practice, American Psychological Association

Past President, California Psychological Association

Dr. Palmiter's book is perfect for busy parents who want tips on efficient and effective parenting. What's best is that *Working Parents, Thriving Families* is full of clear examples of practical suggestions that are based on research. This book is positive, yet realistic. Filled with real-life examples, it offers hard-working parents practical advice they can apply. And, it's based on some of the latest research on promoting thriving children. Not just another parenting book, this book by Dr. Palmiter offers parents clear, specific, and practical strategies that are based on research.

— Mary K. Alvord, PhD

Co-author, *Building Resilience: A Cognitive-Behavioral Group Program for Enhancing Social Competence and Self-Regulation*

This book is for good parents who want to be even better. In a practical, down-to-earth approach, Dr. Palmiter highlights ways that you can help your child develop confidence, responsibility, and a healthy outlook on life.

— Pauline Wallin, PhD

Author, *Taming Your Inner Brat: A Guide for Transforming Self-defeating Behavior*

President, Division of Media Psychology, American Psychological Association

Dr. David Palmiter is a highly regarded scholar and leading authority on some of the most important issues of our lives. This book reflects that expertise and provides crucial insights for today's over-stressed families—news you can use!

— Nancy Doyle Palmer

Journalist and *Huffington Post* Blogger

The wisdom, tips, and advice Dr. Palmiter offers in this book proves that he truly understands the lives of families today. As a psychologist and mom I appreciate the humor and down-to-earth style with which he presents his strategies. *Working Parents, Thriving Families* is a book I will recommend (and read!) often.

— Stephanie S. Smith, PsyD
Owner, Front Range Psychological Associates
Public Education Coordinator for Colorado, American Psychological Association

David Palmiter shares practical pearls and humor with parents striving to do well. The fundamental task of parenting—to produce a loving person using her or her God-given talents in relationships and service—is clearly and boldly stated. What follows are practical ideas to address that challenging task that are based on solid science, experience as a coping parent, and years of successful compassionate clinical practice. Any parent would be fortunate indeed to discover this book and use these ideas.

— Paul Kettlewell, PhD
Chief, Pediatric Psychology
Geisinger Medical Center

Working Parents, Thriving Families represents the integration of practical, everyday parenting problems with the best practices based on current scientific research. Yet this is no "ivory tower" book but a title full of practical problems and practical solutions. It speaks to parents who are looking to expand their parenting repertoire and to build more resilience and success into their kids' (and their) lives.

— Ed O'Brien, PhD
Professor, Marywood University
Co-author, *Multidimensional Self-Esteem Inventory*

Working Parents Thriving Families

Working Parents Thriving Families

10 Strategies That Make a Difference

DAVID J. PALMITER JR., PhD, ABPP

SUNRISE
River Press

Sunrise River Press
39966 Grand Avenue
North Branch, MN 55056
Phone: 651-277-1400 or 800-895-4585
Fax: 651-277-1203
www.sunriseriverpress.com

Edit by Karin Craig and Karen Chernyaev
Layout by Monica Seiberlich

ISBN 978-1-934716-14-4
Item No. SRP614

Library of Congress Cataloging-in-Publication Data
Palmiter, David J.
   Working parents, thriving families : 10 strategies that make a difference / by David J. Palmiter, Jr.
      p. cm.
   Includes bibliographical references and index.
   ISBN 978-1-934716-14-4
   1. Parenting. 2. Parent and child. 3. Work and family. 4. Families. I. Title.
   HQ755.8.P343 2011
   649'.1--dc22
                              2010052938

Printed in USA

10 9 8 7 6 5 4 3 2 1

This book is dedicated to my three children: Morgan, Gannon, and Lauren. I am exceedingly proud of both who you are and who you are becoming, and I love you more than my words can capture.

Contents

❖ Acknowledgments

I would first like to thank those who supported this book coming to life. I'm grateful to Dr. Julie Silver and her staff at Harvard Medical School's annual writing conference for giving me the strategies and resources I needed for this journey. I'm grateful to those who reviewed parts or all of previous drafts and offered helpful feedback: Karen Osborne, Dr. Lauren Hazzouri, Dr. Brooke Cannon, Dr. Lia Palmiter (my wife), and my wonderful and extremely effective editors, Karen Chernyaev and Karin Craig. I also am grateful to Dr. Ed O'Brien who forwarded useful materials and to Joseph Patterson, Tanisha Drummond, and Sarah Killian who assisted me with some of the leg work. Lastly, I am grateful to the administrators and trustees at Marywood University who granted me a sabbatical in support of this project.

I would next like to thank the people who inspired me to write this book. I am greatly indebted to my clients and students: So much of what I have written in this book has grown out of your questions, challenges, strivings, and beauty; I would not be half the psychologist I am today without you. Second, and most importantly of all, I want to thank my wife and children: Your willingness to let me love you, and to love me back, despite my bountiful limitations, is the top blessing in my life.

Raising kids is part joy and part guerrilla warfare.
Ed Asner

Every parent knows that children are a lot of work—a lot of really hard work—and although parenting has many rewarding moments, the vast majority of its moments involve dull and selfless service to people who will take decades to become even begrudgingly grateful for what we're doing.
Dr. Daniel Gilbert, *Stumbling on Happiness*

For most of the day, on most days, I deal with child and parenting issues. I'm a dad, a child psychologist, a psychology professor, a supervisor of budding child psychologists, a provider of child-focused professional workshops, an author of child-related articles, and a coach of youth sports. These experiences have taught me that three parenting-related factors are on the rise in our culture:

- The number of cultural demands and stressors that shrink the amount of time we have available for parenting
- The degree of confusion regarding how to parent well in our run-and-gun culture
- The amount of practical, scientific information regarding how we parents can help our children to thrive and be strong

My goal is to provide you with the best evidence-based strategies available for promoting wellness and happiness in your child while being sensitive to the demands on your time. I also review strategies keeping the more crazy parts of our culture from having a toxic effect on your child.

We parents are overtaxed. For instance, two-thirds of two-parent households are dual earners, and 70 percent of all mothers work outside the home. Here's what a typical working mom's weekday might look like:

Mom's Day

Early Morning: *Alarm goes off at 6:30. Wake from a dream of giving a presentation in my underwear. Weird. Put on CNN while doing a quick couple of miles on the treadmill (spouse is already on the stationary bike with iPod), glance at the personal organizer a few times to get a sense for the day. Finish with the treadmill, turn on the shower, shake the kids up from sleep, and tell them to get ready. Shower. Dry hair. Check kids' progress; mandate cease-fire between eldest two. Put on makeup. Go downstairs for first cup of coffee (thank God for automatic coffeemakers). Holler up to kids that their lives are at risk if they're late for the bus. Make instant oatmeal for middle child, unwrap two granola bars for the eldest, and slap milk on some sugar concoction for the youngest (no energy or time to try to get her to eat something healthy today). "Ask" husband to empty the dishwasher while he's checking the scores on ESPN (make mental note to call him at lunch to ask about the glaring look). Remind eldest two children that we're selling the mephitic dog if they can't take care of him without being reminded (no, they don't know the word "mephitic" but they get the point, and it's never too early to prep for SATs). Quickly scan children's homework for obvious errors. Give kids money for lunch, telling them not to eat pizza or pasta (this morphs into don't ask/don't tell later). Eldest child asks, for the first time, when we can get the clay for the map of the United States that she has to turn in tomorrow; avoid having a stroke by encouraging child to seek out father for answer. Phone rings; the fool calling at this hour deserves the answering machine. Tell kids to get into my car (to be taken to the bus stop) while I gather up stuff for work. Eldest comes back in and says that my car has a flat. Manage to keep swearing inside head. Tell kids to walk to the bus stop—ignoring eye rolls during good-bye kisses—and ask spouse if he can call the auto repair guy and I drive his car; he says yes as he has the time plus enjoys having the auto club guy get a look on his face that says, "Dude, it's just changing a tire." Out the door ten minutes late but make the time up in traffic and have enough time to spare to get a fresh cup of coffee going into work.*

Morning and Afternoon: *Boss out on vacation. Easier to get stuff done. Subordinates seem more cheerful and eager today. Call spouse to check about morning tensions; it's okay. Arrange to have lunch with best friend for first time in four months. Finish about 85 percent of what is on organizer to-do list; take the rest home. Great workday overall.*

Late Afternoon: *On way home grab three kids' meals from fast-food joint. Pick kids up from latchkey program at 5:30 and give them the meals between making unfinished phone calls from work. Drop eldest off at soccer practice ten minutes early; husband meets us there to pick up youngest and to take her to ballet class. Drop middle child off at soccer practice five minutes late. Stay and watch end of middle child's soccer practice while making a few unfinished edits to a report on the laptop. Spend a few minutes of quality time with middle child on the way to pick up eldest. Middle child asks if we can pick up ice cream on the way home as they have been good; my turn for eye roll, but I agree.*

Early, Early Evening: *Get home by 7:15. See husband's dishes in the sink but decide to ignore. Tell older two kids to finish their homework once they're done with the ice cream and bring to me and Dad for checking; tell youngest she can watch her* Arthur *DVD. Grab a glass of red wine, nuke some soup, and throw together a salad; swear to self while giving dog his dinner. Eat while finishing edits on report; interrupted by youngest who asks if she can have a sleepover. Take occasion of interruption to tie the beast outside (where's a dog-thief when you need one?). Tell youngest, for 106th time this school year, that sleepovers are not allowed on school nights but suggest maybe this weekend (note that this may be her way of getting a spot in the queue ahead of her sibs). Check on eldest two; eldest finished homework and has started U.S. map with Dad—helps me remember why I married him; watching further, it's unclear if the child or man-boy is doing more of the work. Middle child is caught playing favorite sci-fi video game with homework half finished on the floor: amount of blood on the screen mandates silent double check of rating on the box while boy is told he's grounded from his video games until the weekend (make mental note to figure out how to enforce that) and to finish his homework. Youngest asleep in front of TV. Wake her up, give her a quick bath, and tuck her into bed. Middle child has homework done and is on Internet playing video games; decide to ignore Internet play as I have no energy for the debate on the definition of "video game" in previous grounding. Dad and eldest working on project still (seems more of the project is on them than board). Warn all that showers are due in fifteen minutes.*

Early, Middle Evening: *Go downstairs to throw a quick load of laundry in; resist urge for another glass of wine. Let the beast in. Make two quick business calls. Holler upstairs, "Showers!" Back to report on laptop. Eldest comes downstairs, dripping wet, half naked, stating middle child has filled a water gun with toilet water and was squirting in the shower: tell her to tell her father but she says he's asleep. Stomp upstairs—this causes the dog to start barking and a mild sprain in my ankle; limp to son's bathroom and bang on the door, asking him if he is squirting toilet water. He says it's from the water from the back of the tank and that the science teacher said it's clean. Tell him he better be dry, in pajamas, with teeth brushed properly in fifteen minutes or find another place to live, together with his smelly dog (want to be sure he knows what I mean this time). Youngest comes out of room rubbing eyes asking if I'm okay. Tell her I am and to go lie with her father. Sit with eldest on her bed for a few minutes of quality time, while I admire her project in the corner. Come out of her room and note husband sitting on son's bed talking quietly; note youngest in her bed somehow. Go downstairs to finish laundry. Husband, now awake, comes downstairs and puts on TV, asking how my day was. I say, "Typical," and ask how his was. He says, "Same thing," but is into the crime drama thing he's watching. Ask him if he'd mind starting the dishwasher, hoping not to have to point out the dishes in the sink. Think there's a sigh, but he does it. Don't want to know if dishes are still in the sink.*

Late Evening: *Sit down in family room with husband and fold clothes. Finish report. Husband goes up at 10:00 to bed, kissing me on the forehead. I stay and watch the news and answer a funny e-mail from best friend. Decide to get a quick jump on work tomorrow while a sitcom plays in the background. Start having hallucinations of Smurfs dancing, laughing maniacally, and flipping me off; decide that's a signal that I should get to bed. Go upstairs. Check on each child, blessing them silently and kissing them on the forehead. Too tired to brush teeth so just rinse mouth with bacteria-killing stuff. Change into gown. Get into bed. Husband rolls toward me suggestively. Tell him only if he's into necrophilia. Notice clock says 11:30 as my eyes close.*

If your heart is racing, if you're chuckling, and if you're thinking that the pace of this fictional woman's life sounds familiar, this book is for you. Like millions of parents, you may be considering the implications of our culture's priorities and pace. You may be wondering if a very hectic lifestyle is compromising your family's wellness and how you can promote and maximize happiness while everyone is so crazy-busy.

Is this just another self-help book for parents? Before I answer that question I want to mention two well-reasoned concerns about parenting books. The first is from economist Dr. Steven Levitt and his writing partner, former *New York Times Magazine* editor Stephen Dubner, in their book *Freakonomics:* "The typical parenting expert, like experts in other fields, is prone to sound exceedingly sure of himself. An expert doesn't so much argue the various sides of an issue as plant his flag firmly on one side. That's because an expert whose argument reeks of restraint or nuance often doesn't get much attention. An expert must be bold if he hopes to alchemize his homespun theory into conventional wisdom. His best chance of doing so is to engage the public's emotions, for emotion is the enemy of rational argument. And as emotions go one of them—fear—is more potent than the rest . . . how can we fail to heed the expert's advice on these horrors when, like that mean uncle telling too-scary stories to too-young children, he has reduced us to quivers?"

The second is from psychiatrist Dr. Alvin Rosenfeld and his writing partner, award-winning freelance journalist Nicole Wise, in their book *The Overscheduled Child:* "The problem is, in seeking out the experts . . . to solve the problems inside our homes, we parents give up important creative control . . . buying into a set of standard behaviors authored by an expert, a person who doesn't know us, our child, our lives, our aspirations, and our dreams, [which] makes it easy for us to relinquish a sense of unique ownership—and with it full involvement and responsibility . . . is it really worth it if, in exchange, you lose the opportunity to feel pride in working it out yourself, to forge your own unique connection based on understanding, and communicating with a child you are passionate about?"

These concerns are both fair and wise. So, is this a self-help book for parents? Yes, but with four important qualifications.

First, I base my recommendations on research findings and let you know when I'm deviating into personal intuition and experience; likewise, I don't overstate a recommendation when the research supporting it is scant.

Second, I acknowledge that you will need to adjust each of the parenting strategies in this book for your family and your child. You are one of the world's leading experts on your child. My goal is to partner with this expertise, not supplant it. Moreover, once you've seen one child, you've seen one child. We're all created as one-of-a-kind beings, from the minute and measurable building blocks of our genetic code to the deepest and scientifically unassailable recesses of our souls.

Third, I'm not trying to produce perfect parenting nor act like I'm a perfect parent. Believe me (and as I'll illustrate), I can be as big of a parenting idiot as the next yuck-a-buck. We all have bad days and weak moments. Instead of striving for perfection, or acting like it's possible, my goal is to provide specific and effective strategies for you to use when you are acting intentionally toward your child.

Fourth, we parents are shepherds, not sculptors. When I was in graduate school we were taught developmental models suggesting that a child's personality is like a lump of clay at birth and that it becomes sculpted by his parents and environment. Those theories must have been authored by men who weren't around babies very much. Because, and as many seasoned parents take for granted, infants are very different from each other from birth. (I know my three kids could not have been more different from one another, well before my wife and I had any opportunity to mess them up.) So, a great deal of our children's outcomes has to do with the spin of the genetic roulette wheel.

For instance, and as happiness researcher Dr. Sonja Lyubomirsky argues in her book *The How of Happiness*, each of us has an internal happiness "set point," which seems to be mostly determined by our temperament (i.e., biologically based personality attributes). This set point explains about half of how happy we are. However, parenting plays a critically important role. First, we parents help favorable temperamental dispositions (e.g., to be sociable) to flourish. Second, we try to keep unfavorable temperamental dispositions (e.g., to be afraid of novelty) from becoming impairing. Third, and perhaps most importantly of all, we help our children to think and behave in ways that will most likely garner them success in areas that define the other 50 percent of the happiness pie (e.g., thinking adaptively). We cannot sculpt our child's temperament or innate abilities, but we sure as heck can shepherd them in ways that best promote their well-being and resilience; *Working Parents, Thriving Families* is designed to be your shepherding guide. So, read on, Bo Peep!

What Is the Primary Goal of Parenting?

Of the good in you I can speak, but not of the evil. For what
is evil but good tortured by its own hunger and thirst?
Kahlil Gibran, *The Prophet*

We must begin to love in order that we may not fall ill, and must
fall ill if, in consequence of frustration, we cannot love.
Sigmund Freud, *On Narcissism: An Introduction*

An interesting exercise is to try to summarize the primary goal of parenting in a sentence or two. Sure, it's easy to say, "for her to be happy." But, what does it take for that to happen? Is the primary goal for him to be wealthy? Is the primary goal for her to obtain a level of education that will allow her to be independent? Try to specify, in only a sentence or two, what you're trying to accomplish as a parent.

A basic assumption in this book is that the degree of wellness in a person's life can be ascertained by gauging how effectively that person loves; this is the single best measure of someone's psychological wellness. A person who effectively and consistently executes love is self-actualized. Likewise, the degree of illness in a person's life is correlated with limitations in how well he or she loves. The loving person is generally fulfilled, happy, well, and sane; the unloving person is in pain.

I propose that a fundamental goal of parenting is to produce a loving person who works hard to exercise his or her God-given talents in relationships and service. This is a short script for happiness and self-actualization.

The consistent application of the strategies in this book are designed to help you help your child become as loving, happy, and self-actualized as possible; that is, to become an effective human being. Much of this book's content is designed to help you in this regard as well.

Resilience is a related concept and refers to a child's ability to remain well, and even improve, in the face of stress and adversity. Resilience is not Arnold Schwarzenegger as the Terminator, taking attack after attack but still surviving in a marginal form and pressing on. Resilience is about taking the hit and coming out stronger and better because of it.

Two things are remarkable to me about research on resilience. First, it's striking how short the list of resilience-promoting variables is. Quoting developmental psychologist Dr. Emmy Werner: "The frequency with which the same predictors of resilience emerge from diverse studies with different ethnic groups, in different geographic and sociopolitical contexts, conveys a powerful message of universality." Some of these resilience factors cannot be influenced much by parenting (e.g., if a child is physically attractive or has an extraverted temperament), but others can be. Second, it's noteworthy that the same factors that promote a child's resilience also appear to promote wellness.

A primary goal of this book is to transform this research into specific strategies or techniques that can be efficiently and effectively delivered within a hectic family schedule.

Of course, parenting doesn't occur in a vacuum but within a social context. Thus, I also review those cultural forces that seem to promote insanity in our lives. While our culture abounds with blessings, structures, and processes that support and promote love and wellness, it also suffers from forces that interfere with love in a very specific context—child rearing. In this book, you'll learn how to identify and protect your child from some of these powerful and toxic forces.

Who Is This Book For?

I see no hope for the future of our people if they're dependent on frivolous
youth of today, for certainly all youth are reckless beyond words . . . When
I was young, we were taught to be discreet and respectful of elders, but the
present youth are exceedingly wise [disrespectful] and impatient of restraint.
Hesiod, eighth century BC

Children today are tyrants. They contradict their parents,
gobble their food, and tyrannize their teachers.
Socrates, fourth century BC

This book is for parents of children ages four to twelve who possess common sense about child rearing. These parents understand that children should not be subjected to physical or sexual abuse, use substances, be deprived of proper medical care, view pornography, and so forth. Parents who lack such understanding, or who cannot apply it consistently, are likely suffering to a degree that cannot be helped much by this book.

Most of you already know how to meet your children's basic needs and can apply this knowledge most of the time. But, you are also overextended and confused. You feel confused about how to promote wellness and strength in your children, given the cultural forces that impinge on family life: Should I make him go out for sports? How can I get her to open up to me when she acts like she hates my guts? Should I let him play video games whenever he wants to as long as his homework is done? Do I have her scheduled for too many activities? How can I possibly keep track of what music she listens to or what Web sites she views? Am I hurting him by only feeding him what he is willing to eat? What can I do about the fact that he won't do his homework? On and on it goes.

The strategies outlined in this book are meant to reduce this confusion. I say reduce because it never goes away altogether. Indeed, we wouldn't want it to, as a manageable dose of confusion motivates us to become better parents. But, by eliminating some confusion we increase our confidence in how to think about, avoid, and respond to the many common challenges and struggles that arise as we shepherd our children.

Parental Lunacy

Making the decision to have a child is momentous. It is to decide
forever to have your heart go walking around outside your body.
Elizabeth Stone, *Village Voice*, 1985

I worked with parents and their children in a clinical setting for about ten years before I had my first of 3.0 children (were I to count our Portuguese water dog I'd say 3.5 . . . though my wife says 4.0 as she counts both me and the dog). Until I had my first child, it seemed to me that the parents with whom I was working would, from time to time, temporarily lose their minds. This temporary insanity would occur in the context of us having established a good working relationship. The parents seemed to realize that I cared about them and their child. They also seemed to view me as competent and appeared invested in our shared goals for healing their child. Yet, despite all of this, they would occasionally distort something I said and become angry or hurt. They recovered quickly enough, usually by the next session, but this temporary "insanity" confused and troubled me. I usually didn't see it coming and had no clue what was causing it. Then I became a father and it became instantly clear: The average parent loves his child so much it makes him crazy.

My wife and I suffered from infertility for three years before our first child, a girl, was conceived. When she was born it was like crawling out of hell and into Eden; we were instantly healed and indescribably elated. During the nine months of pregnancy, my wife and I were obsessive in how much we studied, prepared, hoped, and worried; during the latter part of the pregnancy I would calm myself, and imagine what she would be like, by listening to the Elton John song "Blessed."

My eldest ended up being delivered by emergency C-section, which was maddening in itself. After she was delivered, I accompanied her and the nurse to the neonatal unit. As the nurse was prepping, I was allowed a few moments alone with my new baby. I offered her my little finger, which she began to suck on as the song "Blessed" played over the intercom (a gift from the Master Lover). In that moment I felt so much love that it hurt, and I found it difficult to breathe. While I had had experiences of intense love before, I had never experienced anything like this. Other loves in my life felt like some combination of exciting, gentle, and soothing waves I could either float on or swim in as I chose. This love felt too powerful and big for me physically and mentally, like a huge and powerful wave that knocked me knees-over-elbows and carried me where it would. I still cannot describe or write about this experience without tears.

Later in the week, when my wife and I were readying for the discharge, we were filled with peace and patience. We also realized, and understood, that the discharge nurse had to review a number of things with us that were obvious: "Yes, when our daughter is crying we should consider feeding her, as that may mean she is hungry. Good health tip. Thank you."

"Make sure to change her diaper routinely."

"Yes, a good hygiene strategy. We appreciate that." And it went on like that for about twenty to thirty minutes. No problem because, as I said, we were in Eden.

Then, in the evening of our first night home, we found blood discharge in our baby's diaper. The madness that descended upon us was intense. Here we were, three years trying to have a baby, and there was something seriously wrong with her. It took me about forty-five minutes to get the on-call pediatrician on the phone—forty-five minutes that felt like two days. After hearing the problem, the pediatrician immediately tried to be reassuring. He adopted a soft tone and said *exactly* this: "Dave, your daughter has just been born. She is still going through a lot of hormonal changes. Blood discharge from the vagina is common and not to be worried about."

My first-ever bout of parental lunacy—and I've since had hundreds of them—was to respond: "Well, if it's so blankety-blank common, how come that blankety-blank nurse at that blankety-blank hospital didn't mention this on that long list of blankety-blank obvious blankety-blank guidelines that she gave us!" Except I wasn't saying "blankety-blank."

Sensing that the real emergency was a psychiatric one, he tried to calm me with a joke: "Dave; relax, man. Just think of it as her first period." At that point I lost consciousness.

Three years later, while driving to the hospital to deliver our third child, my wife brought up the pediatrician's comment and got red hot about it all over again. Yes siree. Becoming a dad helped me to understand why my parent-clients sometimes act like lunatics; and, should I forget, I need only monitor myself for a week or two.

As I write this book for you, my fellow parent-lunatics, I remember my own parental vulnerabilities and try to cast my words in an empathic manner. I'm also a parent fan. While there is too much ineffective and abusive parenting going on, I firmly believe that the average parent would sacrifice his or her life to save the life of his or her child. Is a greater love possible?

Knowledge Deficits versus Performance Deficits

Let me state the obvious: We all demonstrate performance deficits as parents. There are times when we know what to do but don't do it. These are moments when we're too run down to be the parent we would wish and plan to be. Whenever I give a talk to a group of parents, I find it important to stress this, because I don't want to sound as if I'm lobbying parents to be perfect, trying to pile on guilt for errors a parent knows she has made, or infer that I'm some sort of holier-than-thou know-it-all. To this end, I often tell a story that demonstrates the typical sort of performance problems I'm capable of.

At the time of this story, my wife and I had two children. We had had an exceptionally busy weekend and so got out of our ritual of shopping for groceries together on Saturday morning. Instead, we went late on a

Sunday night. Because we were all tired, we were in a regressed state of mind. This included our two children, who were sitting in the grocery cart tormenting each other.

I tried a number of my fancy-schmancy child psychology techniques on them, but they failed thoroughly and quickly. As the kids continued to torment each other, I raised my voice and declared, "I'm going to spank you both if you don't stop it right now!"

First of all, this was a bluff (first performance problem), as my wife and I believe that corporal punishment, or undisciplined discipline, is ill advised. Second, I was doing a parenting intervention after I had lost my composure (second performance problem). But, my son proceeded to punish me by crying out loudly, for about sixty seconds, "Don't hit me, Dad! Please don't hit me!" I thought, with my luck, I would run into a client or graduate student if he kept it up. So, I told him I would not hit him and would give him an ice cream sandwich if he would just stop saying that (third performance problem).

Follow me around with a video camera and you will see evidence of me showing other performance problems as well. But, I'm very proud of my parenting game when I'm acting with intention, as I believe I do most of the time, employing the strategies I review in this book. I'm also very proud of how my children are turning out—as I write this they're ten, thirteen, and fourteen. (However, and in the spirit of full disclosure, I need to share that my dog is neurotic. Portuguese water dogs have been bred for centuries to aid fishermen, including to the point of having webbed feet and a rudder-like tail. Mine, however, is afraid of the water. He also is a chronic flatulator and has an ingrained habit of greeting humans by burying his nose deep in their crotch, lifting and sniffing.)

This book is not about performance deficits but about knowledge deficits. It's an evidence-based manual for effective parenting when your time is pressed and limited but you are able to act with intention.

Efficiency and Guilt

My second favorite household chore is ironing; my first one
being hitting my head on the top bunk bed until I faint.
Erma Bombeck, *I Lost Everything in the Post-Natal Depression*

I can just *feel* your ambivalence in picking up a book like this. On the one hand, you're interested in learning how to promote your child's happiness and wellness. On the other hand, you're already overtaxed with responsibilities, so how could you possibly be expected to do anything else, such as the strategies I review in this book? I understand this concern, as I live it too. But the ten strategies in this book are highly interdependent: The more effectively you do one, the easier it is to implement the other ones. Moreover, the strategies in this book are designed to free up time while improving your effectiveness as a parent.

As a child psychologist, I cannot tell you how often parents tell me that their top stress and time drain is dealing with their child's behavioral problems or psychological symptoms. After these problems are healed, these parents report that life is *much* easier, even though they're often required to employ a collection of strategies that we've created together. Preventive strategies take a little time up front. Symptoms take much more time later. It is this way across all domains of health.

Consider me to be your parent-efficiency expert. By following these strategies, you'll stand to be more effective and save time.

As overtaxed and overextended parents, we often have guilt-provoking thoughts such as "How is our crazy pace affecting my boy?" or "Maybe if we weren't always running around like crazy people she'd be doing better." We parents are already disposed to feeling guilt; we intuit that it's somehow our fault when bad things happen to our kids. Heaped onto this is a concern that we may not be investing our time wisely. *Working Parents, Thriving Families* tries to help with these sorts of concerns.

Implementing the ten strategies can be like soothing "medicine," alleviating some or all of the parent-induced guilt you may be feeling. In practicing these ten strategies, you're taking some of the most important steps you can—other than providing basic necessities such as food, shelter, and medical care—to promote your child's wellness and to create evidence-based conditions for a thriving family.

Strategy One

Complete One Hour Each Week of "Special Time" with Your Child

*Happy families are all alike; every unhappy
family is unhappy in its own way.*
Leo Tolstoy, *Anna Karenina*

Parents often tell me that it's difficult to make time to do healing interventions with their child. This is not because they want to make more time to watch *American Idol* or because they're not deeply committed to parenting. It's because *life's obligations feel so overwhelming.*

Here's what a typical weekday of a working dad might look like:

Dad's Day

Early Morning: *Where's a hammer to crush that *&^% alarm? 5:45. I'm a slave. Ask wife if she could live with me quitting my job and declaring bankruptcy. She chuckles and says, "Sure." Roll out of bed. Put on the Tivo'd* Who Wants to Be a Millionaire? *Shower. Do a quick mental checklist: Do I really need to shave today? Better shave; getting too old for* Miami Vice *look anyway. Get dressed, checking with wife to see if tie matches other clothes* *(she's beaten me out of the idea that I can manage this). Go downstairs, almost tripping on evil-seed cat. Make coffee. Put out bowls for kids. Check e-mail. Read how the lowly Mets are doing; why do I punish myself? At least the Giants stand a decent chance this year. Wife comes downstairs telling me she wants to put the kids up for adoption: I say, "Go, girl!" Kids argue over who gets to pour which cereal into which bowl. I put on my iPod and remind my wife we agreed to let the kids settle their own disputes unless there is blood or property damage. They seem to work it out. Oldest boy asks if he can have a popsicle. I tell him that his next dad will probably let him have popsicles for breakfast. Youngest boy asks if they'd have to move if that happens. See wife checking homework with a frown. Asks if I can make sure to fill out and mail the registration forms for basketball. I say yes. Ask her if she can call the bank and find out what the miscellaneous charge is on our checking: She says yes, but complains (something about how it would be nice if I didn't have to ask her to do something whenever she asks me to do something), but I'm busy gathering my work papers. Boys come by for a good-bye kiss. I remind them that we're to go fishing this weekend; puts a smile on their face. Drive wife to metro. She spends the time in the car talking to her mother: Can't grasp the molecular structure of light photons nor how those two can entertain each other by talking about curtains. Drop wife off; ask her if she'd like one of my special massages tonight. Puts a smile on her face. Deal with rush-hour traffic. Keep thinking I should get one of those blow-up dummies so I can drive in the express lane; conversation probably wouldn't drop off much.*

Morning and Afternoon: *Get to morning meeting with boss and work group ten minutes late. Should be okay because I landed a new account yesterday. Boss still has to say, "Glad you could join us, Brad." What a *&^%-head. Back to bankruptcy fantasy. Rah-rah speech boring. Ted interrupts meeting when his forehead hits the table because he nodded off; we all start to laugh but *&^%-head seems mad. Get assignments for the day. Our group gets the jobs done, plus a couple of things the *&^%-head didn't think of. Is Claire flirting with me? Bill asks if I'd like to golf on Sunday. Say I'd love to but can't (guilt over not being with the family plus wife would use as a club in our next fight); I'm glad Bill doesn't get impatient with me. Ask him if he's free for a happy hour on Friday; puts a smile on his face. Get a call from new account with questions. Get those cleared up. Leaving twenty minutes late, but learning to accept slave status. Call wife to check in; our usual cryptic conversation. Pretty soon we'll be reduced to sighs and grunts.*

Early Evening: *Traffic is killer. Gotta remember to get some books on CD. Get home to smells of pasta filling the house. I ask what happened to the boys' karate class: Wife says she had a bad day at work and was too tired to take 'em. She continues with a complaint that my mother got the boys to do their homework by bribing them with ice cream and that they still didn't get it done. I point out that she saves us thousands each year in nanny costs. Wife slams down pasta spoon and says that I always side with my mother against her. I give her space. Eldest boy tells me he finished his homework and asks if I want to shoot some baskets outside. I say maybe this weekend 'cause I'm too whipped now. Suggest he get his brother or a friend to play. Wife bellows, "Supper in ten!" I check e-mail and confirm time of start of the Mets game. Wife hollers, "Dinner!" We eat a rare dinner together. Wife and youngest boy keep their eyes on their plates while eldest and I talk about our fishing trip this weekend. Ask youngest boy if anything is wrong. He starts tearing up and says that another boy at school called him "fat" and other kids laughed. I get the details but feel lost how to help. Wife says she'll call the principal, but youngest begs her not to. Eldest says that if he didn't eat so much people wouldn't call him fat; they start arguing. I tell boys they're not allowed to open their lips except to insert food. Everyone finishes dinner. Tell boys to shower and get ready for bed. Wife asks if I can do dishes. Easier just to do them than to argue. Ignore boys' arguing upstairs. Wife goes up; hear her voice above theirs.*

Late Evening: *Can't bear watching Dodgers abuse Mets. Flip around TV watching ninety channels of nothing. Wife on the phone with her mother. Fall asleep. Wife wakes me up with word "Bed"; she's in her bedclothes. I check on boys, blessing and kissing them on the head. Get ready for bed. Wife has her back to me in bed. Set alarm for 5:45. Wife says, with her back still to me, "Thanks for the massage." I curse to myself. I'm annoyed, but I ask if I can make it up to her with a double massage tomorrow. She says "Sure," turns to me, and kisses me goodnight. Okay, she's not mad at least. Did a little good today. Ask God to help me do better tomorrow. Pass out.*

Today's Hectic Lifestyle

Does the day-in-the-life of the man above feel familiar? I had a book editor review one of these day-in-the-life accounts in a writing group I attended. A grandmother, she challenged, "Is it *really* that bad these days?"

All of the people in the group who were parents replied, "Yes, it's that bad, if not worse." For example, the 2008 *Sleep in America* poll indicates that "the lines between work and home life are blurred. More than half of Americans (58 percent) are bringing work home to complete at night. In fact, 20 percent spend more than ten hours per week doing job-related activities at home," even though 90 percent work outside the home. This same survey indicates that the average American worker starts the day at 5:35 a.m. and concludes it at 10:53 p.m.

According to economics professor Dr. Andrew Oswald, our pace leaves 46 percent of U.S. workers endorsing the statement "I would like to be able to spend *much* more time with my family." However, even when we're at home, we're equally taxed. For example, American families seem more likely to share a meal in a minivan than around a kitchen table. And, as we struggle to make ends meet, our kids often occupy themselves with sedentary pleasures. For instance, according to a national survey published by the Kaiser Family Foundation in 2010, our kids spend a little more than 7.5 hours per day consuming entertainment media.

A few years ago I noted that parents coming to my private office do not like the comfortable furniture, as it puts them at risk to nap while I'm meeting with their child. Many don't like it because they bring work to do. When I come out into the waiting area, most parents are not reading a magazine or staring off into space; they're either doing tasks or sleeping.

I speculate that the majority of family problems I see in my practice and clinic are either caused or worsened by the shrinking amounts of time we're making for each other. Here's a metaphor: Imagine that a person purchased a well-built car but rarely changed the oil, checked the air in the tires, or did repairs. It would not take long for the car to come into disrepair. The problem would not be with the vehicle but with its maintenance. How silly would it be for the car owner to say: "*&^%$ car! I got screwed on that one! Time to trade it in!" I know this sounds farfetched, but aren't we doing the same thing when we harshly judge our family members or our relationships, when we haven't invested sufficient one-on-one time? Of course, contemporary demands do not allow most of us to become the Waltons either (for you younger parents, just Google "Waltons TV"). But, what is the minimal maintenance needed for relationships?

The car metaphor seems farfetched because our culture educates us about how to maintain automobiles. Most of us do not suffer from a knowledge deficit regarding car maintenance. (If we do, we at least know enough to take our vehicle into the repair shop on occasion.) We may not do what we know, but most of us know what to do; should we forget, the car has indicators to help us. (Kids have indicators too, but they're more difficult to interpret.) Likewise, we have reasonably good awareness about how much physical activity we should be getting, how often we should brush and floss our teeth, and how often we should shower. We may not always do what we're supposed to do, but we know what targets to set when we're resolved to act with intention.

What about relationships? What is the *minimal* amount of time I need to spend, one-on-one, each week with each child and with those who matter most to me? The question seems foreign, doesn't it? *A minimal maintenance schedule for relationships? What?*

In so many American families, the one-on-one time given to relationships each week is the time that's left over after life's obligations have been met. For most families, though, that time is as mythical as the unicorn. We talk about *finding* one-on-one time for each other. But, there is no finding time, at least for most families across most weeks. The real or imagined demands on our time either eat it all up or leave us so exhausted that it's hard to actively invest in our relationships, at least in a disciplined fashion.

One father told me that he spends at least two hours of one-on-one time each week with his eleven-year-old son. Encouraged and surprised, I asked him what they do. He responded that they watch TV in the evenings together after he gets home from work; during this time they don't talk much.

It's easy to be zoned out in the company of family members. It's not so easy to be actively engaged with them on a one-on-one basis. According to research conducted by Claremont Graduate University psychology professor Dr. Mihaly Csikszentmihalyi, the average American father spends nine minutes per week one-on-one with his teenage child. This works out to about .008 percent of the week. I wonder how many childhood behavioral disorders would evaporate, or significantly diminish in intensity, if the dosing of harmonious one-on-one time among family members was sufficient.

In households where kids act defiantly, it's often the case that the kids get much more attention for behaving poorly than for behaving well. The parents do not intend for this to happen. They're certainly not lazy. Typically, they're running-and-gunning, trying to meet life's obligations. Thus, if the child is behaving, the parents are silently grateful and focus their attention on the tasks at hand. However, if the child acts defiantly, the parents give heavy doses of passionate attention. This attention then reinforces the negative behavior. Sounds counterintuitive, doesn't it? After all, what is rewarding about getting yelled at? Here's an analogy to illustrate my point:

Suppose you came to my office and I offered you a snack of raw, unwashed radishes? Odds are that you'd decline. But, suppose I offered you the same after you had not eaten for ten days? You'd likely tear into them like Scarlett O'Hara in *Gone with the Wind* (again, with the Google). Kids who act defiantly typically have high unmet needs for attention. Getting yelled at, though a raw and unwashed radish, is reinforcing. To say this is not to suggest that the parents of such children are acting neglectfully; it's to suggest that they're acting typically. In thousands of instances I have found that the more a parent has worked out the time–attention issue, the greater the odds are that her children are doing well.

Quoting Drs. Robert Brooks and Sam Goldstein from their book *Nurturing Resilience in Our Children*: "The importance of unconditional love in the parent-child relationship cannot be underestimated. When children feel that parents only love and accept them if they excel in athletics or sports, if they're socially adept, if they always meet their responsibilities, or if they look and dress in a certain manner, then those children cannot feel secure should they stray from the path of acceptance . . . Unconditional love is one of the foundations for helping their children develop a resilient mindset." This opinion is grounded in many studies indicating that a close relationship with a parent is highly associated with good adult adjustment.

One of my favorite strategies for dealing with this type of time-related madness is "special time." This is a strategy that I've adapted from a treatment manual for defiant children written by esteemed psychology professor and prolific author Dr. Russell Barkley.

THE STRATEGY

Love cannot survive if you just give it scraps of yourself,
scraps of your time, scraps of your thoughts.
Mary O'Hara, *Green Grass of Wyoming*

"Special time" accomplishes multiple agendas. It provides you with the opportunity to excel in the art of parenting; provides your child with a critically important gift; gives you the chance to capture more meaning and a deeper sense of purpose in your life; facilitates your child's wellness; and increases your child's capacity to cope with stress.

The technique sounds simple, but it's not. Summarizing, the technique is to spend one hour per week, one-on-one, doing *nothing* but attending to, praising, and expressing positive thoughts about and feelings toward your child; this works out to be about .5 percent of the time in a week.

You can do special time in one of two ways. First, you can wait until your child is doing some activity that you can praise her for (e.g., drawing, shooting baskets, playing a video game). Then move next to her, watch what she is doing, praise that which is praise-worthy, and express positive thoughts and feelings that you're having. If your child is watching TV, and this is the only time you can do special time, have someone else turn the TV off (if you are the only adult at home, turn off the TV forty-five minutes or so before you plan on doing special time; this will give your child time to transition to some other activity). The second way to do special time is to tell your child that you'd like to spend some special time with him, as he matters so much to you and you love him so; then ask him what he'd like to do so that you can watch him.

If you had a video recording of a parent doing special time well, only three verbs, and their synonyms, would describe her behavior: attending, praising, and emoting. If a parent is doing special time well, he ought to be able to have his hands in his pockets, except to maybe rub her back or tussle his hair.

Special time is different from "quality time." Quality time is a great thing. If there were more of it there'd be fewer prisons. But, when I'm sharing quality time with one of my children, something else besides my child is capturing my attention. For instance, my son and I have an annual tradition of going to Camden Yards on Opening Day; this is a very enjoyable ritual that involves heavy doses of quality time, but it's not special time. At this game I'm giving my son attention, yes, but I'm also giving the game and our surroundings attention. On the other hand, when I watch him shoot baskets or hit baseballs and both praise what goes well and tell him what he means to me, I'm doing special time. Quality time is 70 percent attention; special time is 100 percent attention.

During special time, a parent should avoid teaching, inquiring, sharing alternative perspectives, offering corrections, or moralizing. All of these are valuable parenting tasks, but they can be done during the other 99.5 percent of the week. Special time is just for attending, praising, and emoting—"I like your choice of color for that tree. Good shot! I could never advance through those levels so quickly. I love spending time alone with you. You're fast on those skates. Have I told you lately that no one matters more to me than you?" Start out trying to find something legitimate to say every two minutes or so; with practice, you'll find the right dosing of commentary.

It's also important to be truthful and to keep the praise in perspective. In their outstanding book *NurtureShock*, award-winning and bestselling authors Po Bronson and Ashley Merryman make a compelling argument that consistently praising a child indiscriminately (e.g., "You're smart"), instead of discriminately (e.g., "It was clever of you to figure out that level") can actually have a negative impact on a child. You also want to be honest and not say that some behavior is executed well when that is not true (see Chapter 2).

For some older children it may be harder to do special time while they're participating in an activity. Instead, special time may be completed through a conversation, but an atypical conversation. During this conversation, you would be listening and pointing out only that which you value, appreciate, or admire—"I never looked at it that way . . . You have a creative mind . . . That's one of the things that I most admire about you, your loyalty to your friends . . . I have a lot of respect for how well you handled yourself in that situation." If you hear something that you don't like, bite your tongue and wait until you hear something you can value. You can offer alternative perspectives, teach, moralize, and direct during the other 112 some odd hours of waking time during the week. Doing special time during a conversation is akin to being an effective in-law: talk about what you like and be quiet about the rest.

If you really want to hit the ground running, do twenty minutes of special time each day with each child for the first week. After that, the target is to complete at least one hour each week with each child; this can be done all at once (it's how I do it), or you can break it up into segments. I refer to this hour as the minimal, weekly attentional requirement for any healthy parent-child relationship.

Imagine what it would be like to have someone, whose opinion matters, watch what you do for an hour and tell you what he values about your performance. "I know it was hard for you to get up today. You were up late ironing our kids' clothes after a long day of putting them first. Not only did you get up without complaint, but you stayed patient throughout a trying morning and kept your focus on our son's needs. Have I told you lately how outstanding of a mother you are?" Imagine one hour of that each week. For most of us this would be like coming upon a crackling fire in the middle of a frozen tundra. For kids it's incredibly powerful. I have heard hundreds of stories in my practice about the power of special time. This is a typical example:

Jeff was a single dad of twelve-year-old Sophie. Jeff was a captain of industry. He was paid handsomely to solve problems for the international company that employed him. However, Jeff could not get Sophie to do her homework. He had "tried everything" and was so frustrated by his lack of results that he was in the process of emotionally divorcing her.

Jeff viewed bringing her in to see me as a desperate measure. After completing the evaluation, the first thing I had Jeff do with Sophie was special time. This confused Jeff. Being the problem solver that he was, he diplomatically implied that I was introducing an unnecessary delay in getting to the real problem. Though not totally persuaded by my explanation, Jeff decided to try special time on faith. When they came in the following week I asked him how it went. I could see that he was struggling to be polite when he answered "Okay." He followed up with, "However, I'm looking forward to doing the interventions that will deal directly with Sophie's homework compliance." (He had read his share of parenting books.)

I then turned to Sophie and asked her what special time had been like for her. She responded, as many twelve-year-olds do, with, "I don't know." I followed up by asking her to rate the experience on a scale from one to ten, with a ten representing how she would feel sitting in the front row of an Aerosmith concert (she was "in love" with Steven Tyler) and a one representing how she would feel eating a warm cupcake. I barely got the question out of my mouth and she declared, with a quivering lip, "ten."

Jeff opened his mouth so wide he looked like he was confusing me for a dentist. He had no idea that he had that kind of power in Sophie's life. We worked together for another six sessions or so until we reached our goals, but, with hindsight, we probably could have stopped our work right at that moment. I could have turned to him and said, "That's really all you needed to know, Jeff. Let me know if the homework problem doesn't resolve on its own in a few weeks."

After doing special time, parents have made comments such as, "Thank you for giving us our son back," and "I feel guilty because I see how much my child loves this and I haven't been doing it all along," and "Why isn't this taught on maternity units in hospitals?!" Parents who do the intervention over the course of a few weeks get it: What an apple is to the physician, special time is to the child psychologist.

I mentioned that I've adapted this strategy from a treatment by Dr. Barkley. I tell parents, when I'm administering that treatment for their defiant child, that special time is the most important module, even though it's not designed to reduce their child's defiant behavior. I rank it so because I believe we parent-lunatics most want to be close to our children, and special time is the intervention in the manual that best supports that goal. I also rank special time as the most important strategy in this book and ask all the parents I work with to do it with all of their children.

Make (Don't Find) Special Time

Special time sounds easy, doesn't it? I promise you that it's not. First, it's difficult to *make* (not *find*) the time to do special time. If a parent says she'll try to find the time to do special time, that's like saying she's not going to be doing special time consistently. Each of us needs to decide what other (seemingly) important activity will not get done so that special time may get done. Second, it's tough for us to *only* attend, praise, and express affection toward our children. Let me elaborate on each of these issues.

For years I ran parent groups that included special time. I would ask one parent to play the parent and the other to play the child. Before the role-play started, I asked parents to rate the imagined difficulty level of the parents' roles; I had them repeat the rating after the role-play was over. About 85 percent of the parents reported that it was more difficult to do special time than they had imagined. The top three challenges were spacing out; not doing something else other than watching, affirming, and emoting; or exaggerating or fabricating their praise. I've also seen special time easily morph into quality time. After all, I may be more entertained if I'm playing a game of chess or fishing than if I'm watching my child do something. Again, quality time is outstanding; it's just not as intense in its dosing of positive attention.

Regarding the prescription of one hour of special time per week, per child, Jenny, a mother of five, once said to me, "Are you asking me to make five hours a week to do special time?! Are you crazy?! Haven't you been listening to what our schedules are like?!"

I responded, "Jenny, let me change the challenge. Let's say you purchased a house on an acre lot, and the entire perimeter of the lot was adorned with beautiful rose bushes. You, wanting to maintain the roses, ask a gardener how to keep them thriving. The gardener answers that you need to consistently water, prune, fertilize, and weed all of them. Would you then say, 'Are you telling me that I need to make the time to water, prune, fertilize, and weed an acre's worth of rose bushes?! Are you insane?! Haven't you been listening to what our schedules are like?!'"

This is one of the problems we have in how we think about our relationships. We're not used to making decisions about the *minimal* amount of time we need to invest. Moreover, we're not used to thinking about our relationships as something that we need to be disciplined about. Dr. Erich Fromm, in his book *The Art of Loving*, argues that people living in modern Western cultures are used to being disciplined in their work lives but not in their personal lives. Quoting Dr. Fromm: "I shall never be good at anything if I do not do it in a disciplined way; anything I do only if 'I'm in the mood' may be a nice or amusing hobby, but I shall never become a master in that art." The consistent implementation of special time, and the other strategies in this book, affords you the opportunity to become a master in the art of parenting, even though your time is pressed.

So often it seems to me that what adults most value in counseling is the life-affirming and undivided attention I provide for them. I do more specific things than that when I offer psychotherapy, but so often I sense that my clients are starved for that level of human connectedness. If you consistently provide one hour of special time to your child every week, you're giving her an uncommon and critically important gift.

Consider Your Priorities

And ever has it been that love knows not its own
depth until the hour of separation.
Kahlil Gibran, *The Prophet*

You only see things properly when you're about to leave. Then it's
as if you're seeing for the first time. Everything seems to shine.
Alice Peterson, *How About You*

One of my favorite books is Stephen Covey's *The Seven Habits of Highly Effective People*, which helps readers find meaning in an overly scheduled existence. In the book Mr. Covey has the reader do an exercise that I've adapted below. (If you are in significant emotional distress, it may not be helpful to do this exercise.)

Get as comfortable as you can. I'm going to ask you to imagine various scenes. When you do so, try to engage all of your senses, envision the sights, sounds, smells, and touches of every scene. Mentally depict the interactions you'll have with other people in the scene. Proceed by reading one prompt at a time. After you read the prompt, put this book down and imagine the scene for about two to four minutes. Then, read the next prompt. If you read ahead, you won't get the full effect (you'll need about twenty to forty minutes to do the entire exercise).

Prompt #1: You are getting up in the morning to go to a wake. Though the person who has died is not one of your children, or a significant other, the person is someone you love a great deal. So, this is a very sad day. Imagine how you will get ready for the day, and help your family members to get ready, prior to making breakfast.

Prompt #2: Imagine getting breakfast for yourself and for your family.

Prompt #3: Now it's time to travel to the funeral home. It's sunny and warm. Imagine the route you'll take and the conversation you'll engage in on the commute.

Prompt #4: You are now walking up to the funeral home. It's a nice day, so some family and friends are congregated outside on the porch. Imagine whom you'll greet there and the brief conversations you'll have.

Prompt #5: You now work your way, with your family, into the funeral home. As you make your way to your seats, you run into other family and friends. Envision those encounters.

Prompt #6: Now it's time to pay your respects to the deceased. You decide to leave your family behind and go up to the open casket by yourself. However, when you arrive there, you are shocked to see your body in the casket. This is your funeral. But, you are lying there conscious, reflecting on your life. Give yourself a moment to realize that your life is finished. Then, let your thoughts turn to the things that you celebrate about your life now that it's over.

Prompt #7: What are your chief regrets now that your life is over?

Prompt #8: Your significant other or closest friend is going to get up to speak about you. What do you think he or she will say?

Prompt #9: Each of your children is going to get up to speak about you. What do you think each of them will say?

Did you find yourself thinking any of these thoughts: *I wish I could have done more laundry, too bad I didn't keep the car in better running condition,* or *I sure wish I could've worked more overtime.* Probably not; yet, these are the sorts of activities that interfere with doing special time.

When people know they're facing death, what goes through their mind? Recall accounts of what people say to each other when facing death. Study the dispositions of those on their deathbed. They all radiate the same disposition: People facing death wish to let those they love know that they're loved deeply. They wish they had made more time for their loves, and they celebrate the time that they had together.

Dr. Mihaly Csikszentmihalyi, when discussing his concept of "flow" (see Chapter 2), argues that we have two lists: One is the list of what matters the most to us, and the other is the list of how we spend our time. Few people have their two lists in total harmony. In our culture, life needs to be managed, bills paid, and residences cleaned. However, the more a person's lists are not in harmony, the more a person is likely to be leading Thoreau's life of quiet desperation. Likewise, the more the lists are consistent, the more a person's life is likely to be rich with meaning and lavish with purpose. I assume that you, like most parents, think of your relationship with your child as a top priority. Thus, the consistent use of special time has the added value of enhancing your sense of meaning.

I struggle to make the time for my kids, too. Actually, and I'm embarrassed to admit this, but I prescribed special time for hundreds of families before I started doing it myself. During those years I kept imagining a bright neon sign in my consulting room flashing the word "Hypocrite!" So, I either had to start wearing sunglasses to therapy sessions or begin doing special time. Given that I had already been providing steady doses of quality time, I didn't expect special time to have such a dramatic impact. But, I was wrong, and by a lot.

A Few More Comments

If you and your child have a history of sustained conflict, he may initially resist special time; this could tempt you to punt on second down. Before you do, consider two points. First, imagine you have a contentious relationship with your boss or significant other. All of a sudden, that person starts acting attentive and affirming. It could make you a little suspicious—*Is he trying to get me ready for a transfer? Is he having an affair? Is she trying to butter me up so we can have another kid?* But if the person persists, you're naturally inclined to give in and enjoy.

Second, when you come out of a dark movie theatre in the middle of a sunny day, you squint your eyes to adjust to the brightness. Ever have an adult, whose opinion matters, suddenly give you a heavy dose of praise while looking you in the eyes? It's divine, but it can make you feel uncomfortable. One of my graduate students recently said to me, "The standard for graduation from our program ought to be that the student can put things as well as you do to clients. You're a brilliant artist with words." I told her that she was both making my week and embarrassing me, so I changed the topic. (I wish I had said, "You mean like what you just said?"). It takes some getting used to, this praise that strikes at our core, so don't let your child's resistance weaken your resolve. (By the way, the longest I've had a child resist special time, who wasn't otherwise afflicted with a serious mental illness, was three weeks.)

I've seen special time fail only in three types of situations. First, the parent is not sold on it. This may be because the parent is uncomfortable with intimacy. (This is not to say that the parent doesn't love his child. But some of us, even though our hearts are filled with love, feel uncomfortable drawing close.) Or, it may be because the exercise doesn't seem potent enough to justify the time. In this instance the parent's reluctance becomes a self-fulfilling prophecy.

The second situation is when the parent has already begun emotionally divorcing her child. There has been so much pain in the relationship that the parent's heart has become hardened in order to avoid breaking into a thousand pieces. If this sounds like you, you might start by trying to recapture your feelings of love (e.g., watch videotapes of your child as a toddler, go through old pictures and mementos, view the video clips I've listed in the Further Reading and Viewing for this chapter).

The third situation is when the child is afflicted by a significant psychiatric problem (e.g., childhood schizophrenia, moderate to severe autism). If you're the parent of such a child, consult the mental health professional with whom you are working for suggestions on how to modify the approach (if you don't have such a person in your life, see Chapter 10).

If your child is especially resistant to special time, you can try any number of the following strategies:

1. Sit at your child's bedside at bedtime, when he's a captive audience.

2. Wait until your child needs a ride somewhere and do special time during the drive. This is not the pure form of special time. The lack of eye contact lessens the intensity of your focused attention.

3. Ask your child what movie she'd like to see. Assuming you approve of the rating, offer to take her and plan to arrive twenty minutes before the commercials start. Again, the lack of eye contact may make it easier to have a conversation. (I remember using this strategy when I first started dating female creatures.)

4. Offer to take your child to his favorite restaurant for a meal and do the conversation version of special time. I do this, rotating a before-school breakfast on Fridays among my three kids—they love doing this, even though it means getting up at 5:30 a.m. during the school year in order to get everyone to the buses on time. (I confess that I sometimes whisper to one of my kids, as I'm shaking him or her awake: "Would you rather go to breakfast or sleep some more and do special time this weekend?" I never had a taker until my eldest hit her teen years. Even I am still sometimes surprised by the power of special time.)

5. Offer to take your child out for some activity he's been longing to do: golfing, fishing, camping, whatever; then, at certain junctures, look down at your watch, tell yourself you're starting special time, and do nothing but watch, praise, and express positive thoughts and emotions toward your "baby" for that time period.

I hope that you will try this intervention. If you do, I believe your child's reaction will sell you on the value of continuing it.

Supportive Strategy

Write One Gratitude Letter Per Month

Every relationship could use special attention. In order to nurture the adult relationships in your life, and thereby uplift both yourself and your relationship with your child, try to write one gratitude letter per month.

1. Pick someone toward whom you feel significant but unexpressed gratitude. This gratitude could be recent or ancient.
2. Hand-write that person a letter of three hundred to five hundred words expressing your positive thoughts and feelings. Don't hold back, be specific, and write legibly (don't type it).
3. Schedule a face-to-face meeting with this person, but don't tell her or him about your gratitude letter.
4. At your meeting, take out your letter and read it to him or her. Don't chicken out by handing it over to the other person to read. If you start to cry, that's okay; don't stop yourself (you most likely won't be the only one tearing up).
5. Give her or him the letter after you're done.

Consistently writing these gratitude letters stands to enhance your happiness.

Strategy Summary

Spend one hour per week, one-on-one, doing *nothing* but attending to, praising, and expressing positive thoughts and emotions toward your child.

Avoid confusing special time with quality time. If some other activity is capturing significant amounts of your attention, you're probably doing quality time.

Don't let your child's resistance throw you. A medical reality is that we need oxygen. A psychological reality—assuming average-or-better brain functioning—is that we need doses of unconditional positive regard, or unconditional affirming attention, from those who matter to us.

If you've accounted for the weekly dose of special time, get in as much quality time as you can. Your deathbed self will likely be happy with you for it.

The Skeptical Parent's Challenge

Parent: You act like this spending one hour a week giving attention will have this miraculous effect on my child. How can that be?

Author: I don't think this will create any miracles. But, over time, it is likely to create a closer relationship with your child. And, the scientific literature indicates that a close relationship with you is one of the mightiest protective shields your child can possess against the world's slings and arrows.

Parent: You differentiate special time from quality time. Given how much you've emphasized this, what research study can you cite that demonstrates that an hour of special time a week, over time, is more potent than an hour of quality time a week, over time?

Author: You've got me. As far as I know such a study has not been done. Listen, quality time is excellent. I find that my relationships with my children are stronger the more of it that we have in our lives. And, some of my favorite memories with my children occurred during quality time. But, doesn't it make sense that 100 percent attention is more potent than 70 percent attention, or less? Which would be more intense for you: a loved one enjoying your company while you watched a baseball game or that same loved one sitting you down and telling you what he or she most values about you? I've had so many families come to me who were already doing quality time, but the addition of special time significantly ramped up the quality of their relationship with their child.

Parent: I'm sorry, but I have too much going on. I can't make the time to do special time.

Author: Wow, you sound overwhelmed. Without knowing more, I'm guessing much of your busy lifestyle is organized around service. If so, you're to be saluted. However, have you fully recognized the impact of your stress on both you and your child? Moreover, how many of these competing activities will matter on your deathbed? Please, just try it. If you absolutely can't pull it off, consider the counsel I offer in Chapters 7 and 10.

Parent: Might my kid get a big head if I praise him too much?

Author: As in most things, extremes are to be avoided. So, yes it is possible for praise to be harmful to a child if it's excessive, vague, or tied to behaviors that are really not praiseworthy. Moreover, there appears to be value in intermittently praising a child throughout the week, instead of calling his attention to all that is praiseworthy. However, keep in mind that special time is one hour per week. So, if you make sure that the praise during special time is specific, honest, and proportional, it's difficult to imagine an undesirable outcome.

Discover, Promote and Celebrate Your Child's Competencies

*The mass of men lead lives of quiet desperation and
go to the grave with the song still in them.*
Henry David Thoreau, *Walden*

God gives every bird a worm, but he does not throw it into the nest.
Swedish Proverb

In Chapter 1, I cover the value of providing unconditional positive regard. This chapter is about the value of *conditional* positive regard.

As this chapter is about promoting child competencies, and so many of us do this by coaching our kids in sports, I would like to take a moment to offer homage to such efforts.

Coach's Day

Before game: *Work up lineup and field positions on the metro ride home from work. Get home fifteen minutes late. Change into clothes in laundry room. Holler up to son to get in the car for the game. Holler up to wife asking her if she's seen my baseball cap. No answer. Call the house phone on my cell phone. Daughter picks up from her room. Ask her to give the phone to Mom. She says Mom is not home yet. Ask teen daughter if she's seen my baseball cap; she chuckles and says she put it back in the closet after she got done using it as a security blanket (if only there were an SAT test for sarcasm!). Call wife on her cell asking her where she "cleaned" my hat to. She asks me if I left it in the van. I say, "No, never mind," privately thinking it's probably there. It's there.*

Boy is in the van and properly dressed. Get four blocks away and think to ask him if he has his glove. He said he thought I put it in the back. Give him lecture number sixty-two for the one-hundreth time regarding his gear; look in his eye suggests he's thinking about how to get past level six in Halo 3. *Go back home and get glove. Have to drive faster now to get to the field on time; hate to get there late because of sermons I've given to parents about punctuality. *&^$! Cop lights. Going forty in a twenty-five-mph zone; not braking hard enough down this alpine hill. Officer's manner suggest he thinks I'm running cocaine from Colombia. Get ticket. Get to game fifteen minutes late but still fifteen minutes before start time. Hustling with bag and son in tow. Laces on shoe snag on the gate door, giving me a dirt sandwich and spreading balls across the field. A couple moms rush to see if I'm okay; assistant coach laughs.*

Most of the boys are looking sharp today. Spread out equipment, arrange for five parents to help during the game with various tasks. Consult with coach on opposing team about the rules for the game. At first he seems friendly but then starts complaining about how other coaches have "screwed" him over by being unfair with the rules. "Here we go," I think privately. This guy is a trip, talking about "cleanup hitters" and won/loss records (if these six- to eight-year-old boys field a grounder, somehow get it to first, and somehow it's caught while the boy's foot is on the bag, that's a W). Too many "losing is for losers" coaches at this level.

Game: Starts ten minutes late, but world keeps spinning. It's very hot. Billy, in front of his dad, asks if he can play first base. So far Billy's face has caught almost as many balls as his glove. I say I'll think about it as I'm not sure that's safe, but he's asking in front of his silent dad, so something's up. I'm pitching to the boys on my team while the other coach is pitching to his boys. Players on both teams routinely getting tips hollered in from parents; reminds me of the portrayal of adult voices in the Charlie Brown movies. If they're not looking at you, there's about a 5 percent chance they'll change their behavior; if they're looking, the chance is about 10 percent. Parents also shouting lots of praise: praise because kid did well, praise because kid didn't do well, and praise as a period on a criticism.

My team is up by six runs by the fifth inning. Love it when the boys support each other and have fun. Don't mind them winning either. One parent hollers over to me, "What inning is it?" I say, "Thirtieth," and they chuckle and nod. I call one of my boys safe at second as I got a clear look from the pitcher's mound. Other coach comes trotting out to the mound. I remind him that I don't believe in arguing calls in front of the boys (part of our pre-game chat); I tell him I thought my boy was safe, but if he thinks it's important enough to have him be called out I'll do it. He backs down and jogs back. I've been pitching underhanded to little Sammy to try to build his confidence (his bat swing couldn't kill a sleeping, anemic flea). It's been working too, but now his dad hollers that I should toss it overhand. I ask Sammy if this is how he wants it and he sheepishly nods yes. One-two-three—he's out, head down, slinking back to the dugout. What good was that? Hear a mom holler that I should pitch it faster to her son. Lady, you're talking to a guy who tripped walking onto the field; if I can get that ball within their bat range, without throwing my shoulder out, that's a W.

Last Inning: The other coach has his son batting as a switch hitter. Yells at him for how he's holding the bat in relation to his body. Kid grounds out. Dad yells, "See, Jack!" I feel like hollering, "See, Coach!" My boys turn a double play! Where'd that come from? Turn to my parents and quip, "It's the power of coaching." More chuckles. Wish I had that play on video camera, as my son was in the middle of it. Wife offering a standing "O" as boys come off the field.

After Game: Line my boys up for the handshake as they cheer about the score. Remind them about good sportsmanship. They line up to shake the hands of the other team and say "good game" through the lineup. Other coach's assistants offer cheerful handshakes and looks that say, "Can you save me, please?" Other coach is polite and gracious at the end. We do our post-game ritual of running through a parent-made tunnel and huddling up.

Ask boys, one at a time, if they complied with our three team rules: Have fun, Try your hardest, and Be a good sport. They yell a loud "Yes!" in response to each question. (Would love to give kids a multiple choice test on most coaches' postgame speeches. Imagining how most kids would score keeps me from going over ninety seconds.) We break. Coaches help me double-check equipment bag. Somehow we're missing a helmet and two batting gloves; acceptable losses this late in the season, certainly less expensive than the speeding ticket. Son hugs me tight as we're walking out and says, "You're the best coach and dad a kid could ever want." Can heaven compete?

Self-Esteem versus Self-Entitlement

We value self-esteem and try to instill it in our children. However, we're often confused about how to differentiate between self-esteem and self-entitlement. The child with sound self-esteem feels her inherent value and knows her skills. Such a child can cope with adversity and her own failings; she also can use pain to become a better person. She doesn't unduly draw attention to herself, but she is able to enjoy it when it comes her way.

On the other hand, the child who is self-entitled has a distorted sense of competence, struggles to own responsibility for his failings, and copes poorly when things don't go his way. Such a child also struggles to connect with others, as these tendencies are unattractive.

We parents commonly (and inadvertently) interfere with the formation of a solid self-esteem in four ways:

- We give kids confusing messages about what constitutes success and failure.
- We promote self-entitlement.
- We overtax our child and ourselves.
- We don't discover our child's competencies.

Balance Success and Failure

Would you like me to give you a formula for success? It's quite simple, really. Double your rate of failure. You are thinking of failure as the enemy of success. But it isn't at all. You can be discouraged by failure or you can learn from it. So go ahead and make mistakes. Make all you can. Because, remember, that's where you will find success.
Thomas J. Watson, former president of IBM

We can't promote our children's self-esteem unless we're willing to accept the premise that they stink at some things. Our shrinking time for family life has made us more intense when we come together. We need to ensure that our children like themselves, and we want to try to keep them from being burdened by insecurities, but we need to accomplish this in concentrated bursts. We become like a contractor who is behind schedule in building a house. He hopes that all of his materials are sound, as he doesn't have time to cope with problems. Should he discover that some of the piping is ill-suited, it's easy for him to sell himself on the notion that it's not true. So it can be with parents. I may try to convince myself that my child has skills that she doesn't or that he has done well when he hasn't, because to consider the alternative is too difficult. This can morph into a pattern of behavior that can confuse my child.

> The recreational baseball team I coached a few years ago progressed to a playoff game. In that game one of the kids from the other team, Jim, came up to bat in the second inning. The bases were loaded, there were two outs, and my team was up by one run; should Jim get a hit, his team would go up in the score. However, he grounded out.
>
> As Jim ran past first base his shoulders sagged, probably because he felt badly for grounding out at a key point in the game. As he crossed the infield an adult cheerfully shouted from the stands, "Good hit, Jim!" I saw a confused look flash across Jim's face. I imagined he asked himself, *What was good about that hit?* He was young enough that this adult's opinion was a primary source of information. But, it was also as if the adult had shouted, "One plus one equals three!" What was obvious to Jim—that he had not had a good at bat—was not consistent with the statement being offered by this adult.
>
> If Jim continues to have experiences like this, one of two things is likely to happen. First, he might start ignoring that adult's input: "Mom thinks one plus one equals three, so how can I go to her for math help?" So, he learns to dismiss his mom's praise. Or, Jim might learn to blame others for what goes wrong in his life. "Hey, that was a good hit. Someone cheated!"

Besides learning what constitutes success, our kids need to learn to deal with failure and pain. Is pain not woven into the fabric of our lives? If we cannot share in experiences of failure with our children, we may be doing three things. First, we may be creating confusion regarding the nature of success. A child might come to wonder, "Is it only others who fail, but not me?" and "When I don't do well, is it someone else's fault?" Second, we may be depriving our children of the invaluable learning and growth that failure offers. Third, we may be diluting the intensity of the joy that can come from true successes that follow failure, learning, and persistence (see Chapter 6).

The problem is not just with us parent-lunatics. We seem to have a cultural problem with suffering. Even when we acknowledge that something bad has happened, we too often try to rush past or ignore the suffering.

Robin was a pretty, intelligent, athletically gifted, and vivacious sixteen-year-old girl. She was also dying from leukemia. She had a large family, lots of friends, and her battle with cancer was well known in the community. Robin had been in remission from her cancer for several years before the last and deadly relapse occurred. By the time it became clear that she was going to die, she was very weak. However, she was also interested in pondering both the meaning of her life and what happens after death. Because she was so weak and pensive, she asked for her visitors to be restricted to a very small number of people. Perplexed by this, her parents, who were equally but differently devastated, asked Robin for her reasoning. (From their vantage point, the more Robin received love and support from people, the better.)

Robin explained that most of the people who visited her felt the need to cheer her up and to embrace the possibility that she would recover. So, being the giver that she was, she would pretend to feel better, even though she was feeling lousy and didn't believe she was going to recover. Robin explained to her parents that she no longer had the energy to pretend to feel good in order to make her visitors feel better and that she just wanted to say good-bye to them, and this life, in peace.

Promote Coping Skills

Andy Bernard doesn't lose contests.
He wins them or he quits them because they're unfair.
Andy Bernard, *The Office*

We parents sometimes inadvertently promote self-entitlement when we intend to promote self-esteem, and a child who is self-entitled often copes poorly when things don't go his way. We love our child so much. He's so special to us, and we want him to do well so badly. These natural feelings can cause us to expect that he's entitled to the best efforts and judgments of others. If he doesn't get an A, we may wonder what kind of teacher ineffectiveness or unfair grading standards have been employed. If she doesn't make the all-star team, we wonder what personal agenda caused the coach to favor another child. If another kid wins the award, we obsess over the relationship between the judge and the winner's parents.

I'm sure most of us parent-lunatics fall prey to this way of thinking some of the time (I know I do). But, if such reactions become my typical response to my child's failings, I may be encouraging him to think that he is inherently entitled to be Number One. Not only does this promote self-entitlement, but it deprives my child of the opportunities offered by not being Number One. Even in instances when my child has not been treated with justice, there is the opportunity for her to learn to cope with situations in which people with power over her treat her unfairly.

> Brandon, age ten, was an above-average athlete, as was his father, Ben. Dan was Brandon's baseball coach, and Ben was Dan's assistant. Recognizing Brandon's skills, Coach Dan often used him as a pitcher. But, Dan made sure to rotate him evenly with boys who were likewise skilled. Early in the season, Ben complained whenever Dan didn't include Brandon in the group of boys to receive pitch coaching (Dan rotated this training). He once yanked Brandon out of the middle of a game when he was assigned to play a position that Ben objected to. By the end of the season, Brandon displayed some of the same attitudes, sulking whenever Dan assigned him to the outfield or took him off the mound.
>
> By the time he reached eleventh grade, Brandon was selected to be a starting player on the school baseball team; however, he was later suspended from the team because he threw equipment in anger. In response to this, Ben enrolled Brandon in a private school.

None of the feelings Ben had were freakish. But, Ben let his sense that his son was being treated unfairly overwhelm him. This caused him to miss the opportunities that were present to teach and model effective coping.

A related notion is that a child's intentions and circumstances, rather than her choices and actions, ought to govern how adults respond.

Claire was a fifteen-year-old, achievement-oriented, straight-A, ninth grader with two younger siblings. Her father was raising the children by himself, as their mother had died in an accident four years earlier. On Friday Claire had a major exam in history. In a week that was jammed with activities, she had designated Thursday night to study. However, Claire got a call Thursday night from her best friend, Haley. Haley was hysterical because her boyfriend had broken up with her. Very worried about her friend, Claire spent several hours trying to support her. She knew that Haley had recently thought about cutting herself, and she was concerned she might do so if she didn't get the support. As she was listening to Haley, Claire realized that she was probably compromising her ability to prepare for her exam, but she held out hope that the teacher might let her take it another time.

On Friday Claire explained to the teacher, Mr. Calvert, what had happened and made her request. Mr. Calvert saluted Claire for her selflessness but said that he still required her to take the exam. That night Claire explained what happened to her father, Mike, who became irate. However, he suggested that they wait to see what grade came back. When the grade came back as a 78 percent, Mike's fury erupted.

The next morning he arranged to have a meeting with the principal and Mr. Calvert, at which point he accused Mr. Calvert of being inflexible and harsh. Mr. Calvert, who knew about the family's circumstance, was not defensive. On the contrary, he expressed admiration for both Claire and Mike. However, he also explained that it's his teaching philosophy to not block students from experiencing the consequences of their decisions; he shared his view that this approach, while sometimes painful in the short run, promotes maturity, responsibility, and good decision making.

Mike was not moved by Mr. Calvert's arguments. The principal noted that while he could empathize with Mike's concerns, it was his policy to not overrule teachers on their grading unless there is evidence of a process violation or unfairness. Mike left the meeting threatening to hire a lawyer.

I don't believe Mr. Calvert would have been wrong to allow Claire to take the test a week later. But, I also believe his approach was sound. This is a trend I routinely see as a professor: students believing that they should be protected from the consequences of their choices as long as they're a good person with good intentions.

Trying to shift the world around so that it accommodates our needs is understandable. However, raging at the world when it will not comply suggests self-entitlement and compromised coping skills.

If my daughter doesn't get a good grade, it makes sense to feel bad. However, if my general reaction is to conclude that someone has let her down, then I do her a disservice. If my son comes home with a report that his behavior was inappropriate, it makes sense to be upset. However, if my primary response is to conclude that others are responsible for how he acted, then I let him down. Alternatively, if I try to help my child figure out how he contributed to the poor outcome, no matter to what small degree, I open a door to significant learning and growth.

Avoid Overtaxing Your Child (and Yourself!)

A man's got to know his limitations.
Dirty Harry, *Magnum Force*

There are at least two ways we parent-lunatics can overdo it when it comes to promoting our child's competencies. First, we may invest too many resources. Second, we might conceive the idea that the primary purpose of our child's sporting life is to land a college scholarship or a career in professional sports.

Of course, most ends of a continuum are not good, whether it's the continuum of assertiveness, how much we socialize, or how much we exercise. So it is with extracurricular involvements. Because we want our children to be happy, it's easy to overdo it. For instance, according to a 2006 survey conducted by the KidsHealth KidsPoll, 77 percent of the kids reported that they wished they had more free time, while 41 percent indicated that they felt stressed most of the time because they had too much to do.

Becky was a cute but anxious seven-year-old with two siblings. Becky's parents, Bill and Rose, were both highly devoted to their children and very busy. Becky and her older brother had nine extracurricular contacts each week. To pull this off, Bill and Rose relied heavily on family and friends.

Getting homework done each night was exceptionally difficult. Suffering from a learning disability, Becky was unable to successfully complete her academic work within the short bursts of available time, even though her older brother could. The mounting pressures were causing Becky to suffer impairing anxiety.

Bill and Rose actually felt relieved when I asked if there could be value in limiting each child's extracurricular involvements to two per week.

There is no magic number for extracurricular involvements. Capping Becky's family at two was based on their unique circumstances. Just ask yourself, *Has the amount of extracurricular involvements become toxic for us?*

To begin discussing youth sports, I'd like to quote Randel Hanson and Kathryn Milun from www.onthecommons.org: "A sea-change in the world of youth sports has been underway over the past decade, in which a 'professionalization' and 'privatization' has transformed the experience of these activities for parents and players . . . For youth baseball, this professionalization often means playing yearround on hypercompetitive and exclusive club teams for as many as 120-plus games annually, regularly traveling to interstate and even international tournaments, teaching kids to throw curve balls at ever younger ages, and demanding time commitments which rival that of Major League Baseball participants. This development reflects a broader trend of adults pushing an increasingly pressurized atmosphere on kids to get the jump on competing in an insecure world. As one observer acidly put it, 'We fought and won the Cold War only to get the East German model of youth sports?'"

Our intensity with sports can cause troubling outcomes. For instance, a 2005 study published in *Journal of Research in Character Education*, found that one out of ten kids reported that they had cheated during a game, while 13 percent had tried to hurt an opponent, with 8 percent and 7 percent of their coaches, respectively, encouraging such behavior; moreover, 20 percent of coaches reportedly had made fun of a kid on the team.

This brings me to a less intense, but perhaps more pervasive, problem. I've shared that I coached youth baseball for years. At the start of each season, coaches gather with a commissioner and the same ideals are endorsed. What matters is that each child has fun, increases his or her skills in playing the game, and learns to play well with others. It's all wonderfully conceived, and 100 percent of the coaches nod that this is the right way to proceed.

However, once the season begins, a consistent minority of coaches *behaviorally* make the win most important. Kids who play well get more playing time while less skilled kids play less. Remember, I'm talking about recreation sports with kids who are ten and younger.

Why does this happen? What unresolved childhood issues do we bring to our games with our children?

To those coaches who feel challenged to stay on the high path, I would offer a question to reflect upon when the heat of the moment pressures you to deviate from your ideals. Ask yourself, *"When I'm on my deathbed, looking back at this moment, how will I wish I had behaved?"* The answer may help you to chart a true course in the midst of a storm.

Shepherd toward Competence

Because of time pressures, I may find it excruciatingly difficult to allow more than one or two extracurricular activities for my child. If fortune has smiled on me, my child is good at school and at one or more of those extracurricular activities. Otherwise, I have a challenge on my hands. If my child is not experiencing successful outcomes, his emerging self-esteem may be fragile. Moreover, if my child is not succeeding, I'm at risk to start engaging in any number of unhelpful strategies: telling my child he's good at something that he's bad at or insisting that my child stick with something that he hates. The more my child doesn't experience success for his efforts, the more he's at risk to reach negative conclusions about himself, despite what I might say.

Developmental psychologist Dr. Emmy Werner, in a 2006 research review in *Handbook of Resilience in Children,* noted that possessing a "talent or special skill" in childhood was one of the key variables that both protected children from the adverse impacts of stress and predicted good midlife adjustment. In a similar vein, psychologists Drs. Robert Brooks and Sam Goldstein wrote, "To be resilient, children need to feel they're skilled in at least one or two areas that are esteemed by others."

Alternatively, children with low self-esteem are at an increased risk for a wide assortment of maladies: depression, anxiety, substance abuse, eating disorders, and delinquent behavior. What does a person do when he can't accomplish admission to club competence? He worries about it; he gets sad about it; he self-medicates his feelings; he forms or joins club counterculture; or he engages in some combination of the above. As just one elaboration, depressed kids view themselves as incompetent across all or most important areas. And, when their parents try to dispute their negative statements, such children often respond by declaring them in even more negative terms.

> Sam was a ten-year-old boy who was depressed. His parents believed he was sweet and intelligent. Thus, when he'd make comments like, "I'm weird," his parents would try to reassure him. However, the more they reassured him, the more irritable and depressed he got and the more adamant he became about his weirdness. Because Sam's parents were so unsuccessful in their efforts to help Sam, they were starting to feel hopeless and were beginning to distance themselves.

A review of his history indicated that Sam had previously failed at a number of sports, much to his father's disappointment. They also tried 4-H; however, the other boys mocked him for his eccentricities. So, Sam spent his free time in his room engaged in imaginary play. Sam was depressed, in part, because he judged himself to be incompetent.

The treatment included multiple components, but the most important thing we did was to discover and support two of Sam's competencies: drawing and writing science-fiction stories. His parents decided to enroll him in art lessons and to enter some of his writing and art products in contests. Shortly afterward, his depression lifted.

THE STRATEGY

Self-esteem has two interrelated aspects: It entails a sense of personal efficacy and a sense of worth. It is the integrated sum of self-confidence and self-respect. It is the conviction that one is competent to live and worthy of living.
Nathaniel Brandon, as quoted by Chris Mruk,
Self-esteem Research, Theory, and Practice, Third Edition

Psychology professor Dr. Chris Mruk argues that self-esteem has two core components: worthiness and competence. I would suggest that this happens by having experiences of unconditional positive regard and conditional positive regard. First, a child must feel inherently worthy and valuable. Second, a child must see himself being successful and to have that success mirrored in the eyes of people who are important to him. If a child feels worthy but doesn't have legitimate experiences of competence, she may become self-entitled and falter in relationships. Likewise, if a child feels competent but not worthy, his sense of self may be fragile and vacillate widely depending on recent feedback.

To have a solid self-esteem, a child needs experiences of unconditional love (to create a sense of worthiness) and experiences of success in important endeavors (to create a sense of competence). Chapter 1 deals with the former while this chapter deals with the latter.

Assumptions about Competence

This is the true joy in life, the being used for a purpose recognized
by yourself as a mighty one; the being thoroughly worn out before
you are thrown on the scrap heap; the being a force of Nature instead
of a feverish selfish little clod of ailments and grievances complaining
that the world will not devote itself to making you happy.
George Bernard Shaw, *The True Joy in Life*

Experts use a number of terms when discussing competence. For instance, Dr. Martin Seligman describes how we all possess *signature strengths*. Dr. Mihaly Csikszentmihalyi talks about how, when we execute our competencies, we enter a state of *flow*. Drs. Sam Goldstein and Robert Brooks describe *islands of competence*. And when I was a theology student at the Gregorian University in Rome, we were taught that all people are gifted with *charisms*. These concepts all assume two things: We all possess special aptitudes that, with sufficient attention and focus, can grow into valuable skills and that executing these skills in ways that matter produces meaning.

In collecting data for an experiment, researchers talk about "outliers." If a research study includes multiple measures, across multiple subjects, invariably there are data points that are extremely low or extremely high relative to most others. Your child has thousands of variables in her (e.g., coordination, speed, intelligence, strength, sense of humor, patience, and many, many others). With this huge number of variables it is a near certainty that some of them are at the bottom of the bell curve (she stinks at them) and some of them are at the top of the bell curve (she excels at them).

My kids laugh at me when we're at the local mall: Left unchecked, I go *exactly* opposite of where I'm supposed to go. I'm at the bottom of the bell curve when it comes to spatial orientation. I also have almost no ability to sink a basketball, fix a machine, or draw. On the other hand, I'm at the top of the bell curve in my ability to teach, to understand others, and to heal people who are in psychological pain. In having things that I both excel at and stink at, I'm typically human.

Help Your Child Discover Her Competencies

I have found the best way to give advice to your children is to
find out what they want and then advise them to do it.
Harry Truman, Interview with Edward R. Murrow
on CBS Television (May 27, 1955)

How can you discover your child's competencies? You can observe him, you can sample the world together, you can find out which activities cause time to speed by for her, and you can survey his personality strengths.

Observe Your Child

The world is mud-luscious . . . [and] puddle-wonderful.
e.e. cummings, *In Just*

In the DVD *Positive Psychology*, Dr. Martin Seligman tells how one company hired its janitorial staff. They'd set up an interview time but would not show up at the designated location. Instead, they would go to the parking lot and peer inside the applicant's car. Their thinking was that people whose competency is cleaning do not have to be forced to clean as it is in their nature to do so.

Watch your child. What does she choose to do when not sleeping or sedated by electronic pleasures? The answers offer clues regarding her aptitudes. She might draw, sing, toss a ball, dance, run, swim, put on shows, write stories, build things, climb, wrestle, perform gymnastics, or read fishing catalogs. The range of activities kids elect to do, when unfettered and unsedated, is wondrous. And just as a healthy tree grows its branches around obstacles and toward light, a child is drawn toward his competencies.

> My son Gannon is right handed. A few times each year, for years, he has asked to bat lefty. I discouraged it because I wanted him to develop his skills batting righty. His Little League coach recently brought a retired high school baseball coach, with a positive local reputation, to one of our Little League practices. After watching Gannon hit multiple home runs, and having had no conversations with either Gannon or anyone else about him, he pulled me over and said, "You really should teach him to bat lefty." My jaw dropped.
>
> In Gannon's two subsequent one-on-one batting practices that week, he tried batting lefty and hit four home runs. Trying to keep him grounded, I said, "Okay, those are good, but they're essentially long fly balls. You'll really have taken the next step when I fear pitching to you from the mound." A few swings later he hit one off my left arm that left a pronounced bruise that started two inches above my wrist and extended to the midpoint of my bicep.

I think this was God's way of helping me to realize how easy it is to miss clues about my own kids' competencies. (I actually was disappointed when the bruise went away, as it was a great show-and-tell tool in my lectures about competence. I hope I will be allowed to have it back in heaven.)

Sample the World Together

Come to the edge, He said. We are afraid. Come to the edge,
He said. They came. He pushed them and they flew.
Guillaume Apollinaire, *Come to the Edge*

*Twenty years from now you will be more disappointed by the
things you didn't do than by the ones you did do. So throw off the
bowlines. Sail away from the safe harbor. Catch the trade winds
in your sails. Explore. Dream. Discover.*
Unknown, though often attributed to Mark Twain

What a glorious world we live in. What an adventure it can be to discover our child's competencies. Walk through a sporting-goods store and see what strikes her interest; go on the Internet and ask him what he's curious about; go to libraries, museums, parks, and zoos; go to unusual events; break some molds; breathe some air; experience the grandeur. I hate to sound like I'm recommending that you climb the Swiss Alps and twirl around like Maria in the *Sound of Music* (do you really need to Google that one?). But, then again, why not? Maybe part of discovering our children's competencies involves us getting out of our own ruts, too.

Let's brainstorm. Here are some activities to explore:

bowling	ice hockey	golfing
martial arts	swimming	tennis
basketball	running	debate
baseball	gymnastics	archery
soccer	writing stories	writing poems
fishing	wrestling	horseback riding
skiing	dancing	photography
snowboarding	painting	gardening
ice skating	drawing	woodworking
fixing cars	playing a musical	needlework
Ping-Pong	instrument	lacrosse
roller skating	singing	bicycling
videography	acting	racquetball
billiards	performing comedy	waterskiing

I bet if you invest twenty minutes you can double this list.

Find Out What Causes Time to Stop

Dr. Mihaly Csikszentmihalyi, in his book *Flow: The Psychology of Optimal Experience*, describes eight characteristics of peak experiences. "First, the experience usually occurs when we confront tasks we have a chance of completing. Second, we must be able to concentrate on what we're doing. Third and fourth, the concentration is usually possible because the task undertaken has clear goals and provides immediate feedback. Fifth, one acts with a deep but effortless involvement that removes from awareness the worries and frustrations of everyday life. Sixth, enjoyable experiences allow people to exercise a sense of control over their actions. Seventh, concern for the self disappears, yet paradoxically the sense of self emerges stronger after the flow experience is over. Finally, the sense of the duration of time is altered; hours pass by in minutes . . ."

So, what does your child do *that has value* that makes time speed by for him? Your child says things like, "I can't believe an hour went by already," "Is it the fourth quarter already?" or "Is it really time to go?" You'll hear yourself say things like, "She'd sleep in the outfit if I'd let her," or "If he asked me once he asked me a thousand times how long it was until we leave for the game," or "The only way I can get her to do her homework is by telling her we're not going to art class until her work is completed."

Survey Personality Strengths

You can have your child complete a survey designed to assess her personality strengths. For instance, the University of Pennsylvania's Positive Psychology Center, under the direction of Dr. Martin Seligman, has published the *VIA Signature Strength Survey for Children* on its Internet site www.authentichappiness.com. This survey can assist you in developing theories regarding your child's top character strengths. The printout will suggest five strengths, which are called signature strengths. While this printout cannot be equated with the tablets coming down the mountain, it can be helpful for generating theories about your child's personality strengths. An alternative assessment tool can be found at www.strengthsexplorer.com.

Tyler was a twelve-year-old boy with problems controlling his anger. After helping his parents put a behavioral plan in place, Tyler was much improved. However, he was still erupting more than seemed healthy. So,

Tyler and I started meeting one-on-one.

One of the things we learned was that Tyler did not think of himself as having any talents other than playing video games. He also thought that his only personality strength was his loyalty to his friends. I asked Tyler to complete one of the surveys I mentioned above to help us get a better sense of his personality strengths.

Much to his surprise, he came out high on Bravery, Kindness, Fairness, Forgiveness and Mercy, and Humor. After a brainstorming session, Tyler thought that he might be good at helping younger kids. Hence, we arranged for him to volunteer at a local children's hospital, joining a team that was assigned to lift children's spirits. Tyler loved this work and felt very proud of it, as did his parents. A few months later his anger outbursts dropped to normal levels.

Grow Social Competence

While your child's social competence has a significant impact on her self-esteem, we know that her skills in this area are highly affected by her temperament (biologically based personality characteristics). We know that genetic endowment has a major impact on the personality that we have. Yes, environment plays a significant role. However, parenting and environment only place a child within boundaries heavily influenced by genetics. A parent is more like Bo Peep (a shepherd) than Michelangelo (a sculptor).

Some kids have an easy time engaging effectively with others. These children are naturally sociable and cheerful. In these situations, all you need to do is to not get in their way and support it. Other children may be withdrawn, moody, find it difficult to relinquish control, or find it challenging to make friends. If this sounds like your child, you will probably need to be proactive to increase his odds of being socially effective.

For children who need extra help, a good place to start is to arrange for play dates in your home. As your child is interacting with a friend, you may observe (from a distance) how well she is playing with the other child. If your child makes substantive social mistakes you can arrange to create a break, take your child aside, and offer instruction.

Later, you could increase the number of kids who come over. If your child is unclear about whom she wants to invite, her teacher may be willing to make suggestions. You can also try to bring about social contact through structured activities offered through private, civic, and religious organizations; for instance, one girl I treated experienced an interpersonal oasis whenever she attended her church's youth group.

Also, arranging for your child to engage with other children in structured activities can provide him with a less stressful venue for learning how to relate well, especially if the leader is skilled with children and willing to partner with you in this cause. If these less formal interventions don't work, you may need to get outside help (see Chapter 10).

Also keep in mind that promoting competence in one domain can promote the discovery of a competence in another.

> An insecure boy with few friends, Noah was an intermittent victim of bullying. While he earned decent grades, he was not involved in any sports (mostly due to his parents not thinking to sign him up for them) and thought of himself as being weak and uncoordinated.
>
> In the sixth grade, another boy took and stomped on his lunch bag, and Noah cowered. Learning about this, his parents decided to enroll him in karate. Within six months Noah no longer experienced any bullying, even though he never used his martial arts skills outside of class. His growing sense of competence in his body caused him to send out signals that he was no longer a weak member of the herd feeding on the edges. Moreover, he made new friends through karate, and by the time he was a senior in high school he was teaching martial arts classes and had landed a lead in the school play.

Promote Academic Competence

Getting good grades opens doors. That said, kids obviously have differing aptitudes when it comes to academics. As a parent I want to strike a middle ground. At one end of the continuum lies the laissez-faire approach. If I start to parent in this way, I succumb to fatigue and am not active unless a teacher or school administrator lights a match. At the other end of the continuum lies the overly intense approach. If I parent in this way, I tolerate nothing less than an A, without considering other important factors. As a fellow parent-lunatic I can empathize with folks in both camps; I'm capable of becoming tired and letting the report card be mystery theatre. I'm also capable of getting my sphincter in a bunch and riding my kids too hard.

So, what's the middle ground? It starts with a clear sense of my child's academic potential, the majority of which appears to be influenced by genetic endowment. Do I want his mental health sacrificed on the altar of good grades? Absolutely not. Do I want her to learn to apply effort when she doesn't feel like it and to gradually increase in her ability along these lines every year? Absolutely yes. I increase the odds of finding the middle ground if I do the following four things:

1. Monitor my child's homework compliance and effort. In the earlier grades, this includes checking homework and quizzing my child before tests. I might continue to need to do this in the latter grades as well, depending on how independent my child is able to be. When do you take the training wheels off a bicycle? The same principle applies here. If I find that I cannot provide this structure on my own, I would do well to ask for help.

2. Consult with your child's teacher(s) regarding how long homework is taking each night. No one wants a child's mental health to be sacrificed on the altar of homework. Moreover, research suggests that too much homework serves no good purpose. Quoting University of Missouri–St. Louis education professor Dr. Cathy Vatterott, in her excellent book *Rethinking Homework: Best Practices that Support Diverse Needs*: "Both the National Education Association (NEA) and the Parent Teacher Association (PTA) have long endorsed what is called 'the 10-minute rule' (origin unknown). The 10-minute rule states that the maximum amount of nightly homework should not exceed 10 minutes per grade level per night, all subjects combined. In other words, a first grader should have no more than 10 minutes of homework per night, a sixth grader no more than 60 minutes per night . . . when the amount of time spent exceeds the 10-minute rule, that is the point at which a leveling out or decline in achievement is observed." This point is also well made in a recent documentary titled *The Race to Nowhere*, which is listed in the Further Reading and Viewing section of this chapter. (Also see Chapter 9 for guidelines on how to communicate with teachers during a school conference.)

3. Using school testing data, my knowledge of my child, and feedback from teachers, I realistically appraise the kind of academic performance

my child should accomplish if he works at it. This can be difficult to do and is almost impossible for me, as a parent-lunatic, to accomplish on my own. I need good testing data, good independent consultation, and a sincere willingness to rise above my subjectivity.

4. I try to instill a sense of joy for learning as early as possible. Most kids are born with an innate curiosity about everything.

Creating a culture of curiosity and learning supports good attitudes about school. Here are some ideas:

1. Read stories to your prereaders that are interesting and fun. Even twenty minutes each week can add up over time.

2. Provide your readers with stories that are interesting to them. It's a big universe out there. There are pirates, whales, spaceships, romance, and adventures galore. Go to some bookstores, your local library, or garage sales and see what strikes your child's interest.

3. Don't shy away from using larger words with your child (just ask him if he knows what it means, define it, and ask him to use it in a sentence).

4. Model reading. This might mean rediscovering how much fun reading can be.

5. When your child comes to you with a question, congratulate her for her curiosity and suggest how you can discover the answer together (e.g., going on the Internet, grabbing a book in your home, going to the public library).

6. Look for (and watch together) TV programs or movies on topics of interest to your child.

7. Sign your child up for science fairs, spelling bees, and math bowls and then partner with her in preparing for the event.

8. Provide your child with access to tools for self-discovery and partner with him as he learns how to use them (e.g., microscopes, telescopes, calculators, computers).

9. Subscribe to kid publications that promote curiosity and discovery and encourage frequent visits to their Web sites.

10. Do everything in your power to associate school with positive emotions and thoughts.

Carter was a five-year-old kindergarten student. He had an older sister (a straight-A student) and a younger brother. Halfway through the year, Carter's teacher recommended that he not go into first grade the following year but instead go into a transition classroom (indicated by the school to be a grade in between kindergarten and first grade for kids who could use an extra year to mature socially or academically). The teacher explained that Carter was very bright but behind the other children socially and that this lag was interfering with him actualizing his intellectual ability.

Carter's parents were both professional and achievement-oriented people. This recommendation surprised and shocked them. But, they tried to stay open-minded to what the teacher was suggesting and researched the issues. After about three weeks of investigation, they spoke with an education professor who suggested that they make their decision based on which choice they thought would most likely help Carter to enjoy learning. They answered that they thought it would probably be the transition classroom, but they were concerned about Carter suffering self-esteem damage and having to wait one more year to start college.

The professor countered by pointing out that the transition classroom was not the same thing as being held back a grade, that Carter would probably take his cues about how to think about this mostly from them, and that being one year older when starting college was probably a good thing (plus, she said he could always choose to accelerate his studies by taking summer classes in college). Her positioning the decision around this fundamental question of joy for learning sold the parents on the decision to follow the kindergarten teacher's recommendation. Three years later, Carter was one of the more popular kids in his class, a straight-A student, and a devout reader.

If your child doesn't appear to be enjoying learning, think of that as a symptom worthy of attention. Assessing and intervening around this issue as soon as possible is one of the most valuable gifts you can give your kid. Partner with other parents, key school personnel, and mental health experts. The goal is to craft an empathic model for what has gone awry and a reasonable intervention plan. The stakes are too high to not do this.

Help Your Child Cope with Pain

Our deepest fears are like dragons guarding our deepest treasure.
Rainer Maria Rilke

Everything that irritates us about others can lead
us to an understanding of ourselves.
Carl Gustav Jung, *Memories, Dreams and Reflections*

Maintaining credibility with our kids requires that we accurately discriminate between praising them and allowing them to feel real pain. "That really hurts, doesn't it?" (No "buts." Just, "That really hurts, doesn't it?"), "I understand. What happened is painful," or "I'm sorry. It stinks that that happened." Such comments typically generate more opening up. After all, empathy is to a child what the sun is to a spring tulip bulb. I continue to provide empathy, without reassurances, until my child is finished venting. I might provide examples of my own related failings (being careful not to make the conversation about me) or simply offer a hug or caress her back.

Katie was an eleven-year-old girl who very much wanted to make the all-star basketball team. She had tried out the year before and didn't make it. However, she and her parents, Marge and Jack, concluded that this might have been because she was less prepared and experienced than the girls who made the team. Hence, they arranged for Katie to attend several basketball camps, installed a small basketball court in the front of their home, and routinely coached her. Throughout the year both Katie and her parents enjoyed her growing skills, with Jack particularly enjoying the fact that he could no longer beat her in games of HORSE.

Then came the big day of the tryout. Katie fared well, but, as is often the case in these situations, she did not perform to her maximum ability. The call came during the following week that she did not make the team. As Jack broke the news to her, Katie put her face in her hands and started crying. Jack had urges to say several things that were running through his mind: "I'm sorry, baby. I found out who made the team, and it's really a lot about who you know," "Listen honey, I know this hurts, but think about how much better you've gotten. If you continue at this pace you're bound to make the team next year," and "This stinks, but it would have been tough to fit all-stars in with your dance lessons, homework, and social life. So, maybe this is for the best after all."

Jack believed each of those thoughts, but he suppressed them. Instead, he put his arms around her and said, "This really hurts, doesn't it?" To which Katie responded with torrents of tears. This was very difficult for Jack, as he felt miserable that his baby was hurting like this. But, all he did was whisper things like, "I'm sorry, honey" and "It really stinks when things like this happen." Then, a few minutes later—which felt like a week to Jack—she was finished crying and went to her room to do her homework.

Later that evening Katie came to Jack, put his face in both of her hands, drew close, and with both intensity and softness said, "Thanks for being the world's greatest dad." Then it was Jack's turn to cry.

Jack decided that he could share opportunities for perspective and growth later with Katie and that validating her pain was important unto itself, as difficult as it was for him to experience. His insight allowed him to give Katie a present that she clearly appreciated.

Coping with pain can also mean helping our child to see the opportunity imbued within all crises.

Zack was an eleven-year-old gifted athlete. His father, Rick, had been his basketball coach for several years. Rick took a great deal of care to not favor Zack over the other boys on the team. Even in instances when Rick believed that Zack would have performed better than another boy, he kept playing time even, as they were playing in a recreational league.

For one basketball season, however, Rick was unable to coach. Thus, Zack was assigned to Coach Travis, whose eleven-year-old son, Charles, was also on the team. Rick attended most of the practices and games early in the season. As best as he could tell, Charles and Zack had comparable skills. However, Coach Travis sat Zack for two quarters of every game and never had his own son out of the game for more than a couple of minutes. Coach Travis frequently designed plays for Charles to be given the ball, and if Charles failed, Coach Travis faulted the play of the boys around him. Also, plays were rarely called for Zack to take the shot.

Rick gradually became incensed, especially when Zack started playing below his skill level and saying that he wanted to quit, even though basketball had been his favorite sport for years. Rick took several approaches: He endorsed that it made sense for Zack to feel frustrated and gave him time and space to express that. Next, he challenged Zack to think of this as an opportunity to learn from, to rise above adversity, and to consider how he might be making it easier for Coach Travis to bench him. Finally, he asked his wife, Susan, to get in touch with Coach Travis about his coaching philosophy (Rick was concerned that he would "tear the coach's head off" if he called him).

Susan's question raised Coach Travis's awareness, and he played Zack more. Rick's support and challenges to Zack led to improved performance (he led the team in rebounds and assists). Zack also pointed out at the end of the season that the experience taught him a lot about how to deal with people who are unfair.

Celebrate Successes

Once your child is doing well, you can give yourself a great parenting experience by enjoying it together. You can create ceremonies, take pictures, tell others (within moderation), create videos, and post symbols of success around your home. Certainly you want to keep perspective (e.g., a city doesn't usually host a ticker-tape parade after the first victory in the season, but I believe it's better to risk going a little overboard than to underappreciate how your child has performed).

What about Time?

One premise of this book is that time matters a great deal to us parent-lunatics. In this chapter it may seem as if I've forgotten about time constraints, but let me offer three qualifying thoughts:

First, I'm only suggesting that you help your child find two competencies.

Second, think of the time it takes to deal with low self-esteem, depression, anxiety, substance abuse, eating disorders, and harmful acting out. The research makes it clear: Kids who view themselves as lacking competence often do poorly in key areas and vice versa. This is not to say that children who do not view themselves as being competent are destined for poor outcomes, and vice versa. However, we're talking odds here.

Third, we're sometimes a little too inclined to follow the parent herd when it comes to our children's extracurricular life. As a coach, I routinely work with kids who have near-zero ability to participate in a given sport. As their coach, I see my job as helping them to be successful, and I do all that I can to facilitate that. However, it's easy to see that such kids are not engaging in a self-esteem-enhancing activity, even though they continue to play it for years.

What might it be like if we parents stopped unsuccessful herd activity and substituted something that our child is good at—to take energy that is not producing success and to redirect it toward activities that allow our child to experience competence? I'm not decrying herd life on all counts. I like it in the herd but not if conformity doesn't produce a return that is commensurate with the investment.

Tom Rath, in his book *Strengths Finder 2.0,* makes this point in reference to the movie *Rudy* (save the Google: It's a movie about a young man who devotes years of effort to a sport that he was not good at): "While Rudy's perseverance is admirable, in the end, he played a few seconds of college football and made a single tackle . . . after thousands of hours of practicing . . . Unfortunately, this is taking the path of *most* resistance." Mr. Rath wonders what greater accomplishments the character could have realized if he had taken that same energy and applied it toward a strength.

Caveats

I have six caveats on this topic:

First, it can take well into adolescence and beyond to find your child's competencies. This is a journey. If you are diligent and fortunate, the discoveries may come early. But, you can be diligent and it can still take years. Plus, for some talents, it might take years of effort to determine whether your child is truly good at it (e.g., playing the violin).

Second, bountiful coin is not required to do this kind of parenting. When money is tight, creativity, persistence, and humility can overcome most obstacles. I've known parents who have asked for reduced fees, approached parents of older children for used equipment, scoured eBay and the Salvation Army for deals, offered to trade labor for their child's access, and asked clergy and friends for help. The capacity of the persistent, creative, and humble parent-lunatic to overcome large obstacles continues to delight and amaze me.

Third, I would not recommend investing a lot of money before discovering if an activity represents a competency. Buying a piano in the hope that Billy will tickle the ivories is risky. Should Billy not possess aptitude in this area the expenditure could cause me to feel resentment and create unnecessary pressure on Billy.

Fourth, we all must be prepared to set aside biases when questing for competencies. For instance, if I'm an athletically gifted dad and my child is not, I have to be careful to keep the focus on what really matters in order to develop his self-esteem and to minimize tension between us. Likewise, if I'm a mom who detests cheerleading *only* because I believe it runs counter to a feminist agenda, but I have a daughter who very much wishes to try it, and I forbid it, I risk alienating her and dampening her capacity for independent decision making.

Fifth, we parent-lunatics have to admit to ourselves that we are highly biased when it comes to judging our children's competencies. Many of us have experienced moments like this:

> Mary is a cherubic eight-year-old girl. Her parents pay for her to take singing lessons. Her teacher notes that she is "making progress every month." Mary's parents, at the next social gathering at their home, arrange for Mary to sing three songs. After a few moments it's clear that the only thing unusual about Mary's singing is its potential to threaten the integrity of fragile objects and inner ear canals. While guests squirm, Mary's parents beam with joy. After each of the three songs, guests cheer nervously and make comments like, "Isn't she just so cute?" and "It's great to see how much you guys love Mary."

If my child is enjoying an activity, and participating in it is not unduly stressful, there is no harm—and often there's an upside—in her continuing. After all, I'm not suggesting that a child's extracurricular life be limited only to those things she excels at. But, this is not the same thing as giving a child exposure to her core competencies.

Sixth, it's usually a mistake to make a child do an extracurricular activity, year in and year out, that he is begging to quit. Such insistence can be either a mutation of the persistence lesson or an example of our unwillingness to let go of *our* dream for our child.

If I signed my child up for basketball and she told me she wanted to quit after the third practice, I would probably insist, barring unusual circumstances, that she continue through the season and then reevaluate. Meanwhile, I would be trying to collaborate with her and the coach on facilitating higher doses of joy and success. However, if she indicated she did not want to play the next season, I would not make her play unless I had strong and verifiable reasons to believe that playing was in her best interest.

Supportive Strategy

Develop a Vocational Mission Statement

What are your top strengths? If you don't know them, start by taking one or both of the assessment surveys mentioned for your child.

Once you have a reasonable sense of your top strengths, ask yourself how you can use them to serve others. Show me a person who, in her vocational life, uses her top strengths in service to others, and I will show you someone who feels excited and engaged. If you're not sure how to serve others, tune in to your agitations, as what bothers you can often serve as a guide.

Use this information to write a mission statement for your vocational life, whether that be inside the home, outside the home, or both. Doing so will help you to make decisions. Try to say an enthusiastic "yes" to requests that are consistent with your mission and a polite "no" to those that are not. Living this formula will not only help you to experience deeper meaning in your life but will also probably give you more energy for your family.

Later, once you're experienced in this, invite your family to join you in writing a family mission statement. What a gift that would be!

Strategy Summary

Believe that your child possesses competencies that put her at the top of the bell curve and that part of your charge as a parent is to discover two of them.

Try to avoid crippling other important family goals by overinvesting in your child's extracurricular life.

Avoid denying the fact that your child experiences failure and allow him to experience the learning that comes from it while you provide empathy (see Chapter 6).

Be open to trying activities that are outside of the norm. It can be exhilarating to find success on the path less traveled.

Remember that an absence of money to spend on activities creates opportunities for you to be more creative, assertive, and persistent. Such parenting is living art.

The Skeptical Parent's Challenge

Parent: Wait a second. On the one hand you say that parents should not overemphasize winning over other important goals. But then you go on to say that parents do well to ensure that their kids have experiences of success. Aren't you talking out of both sides of your mouth?

Author: Winning is sweet. I love it when my kids win. It is just that I don't believe it is a psychological win if it comes at the cost of damaging kids in other ways. I also believe that children may secure victories even when the score suggests a loss. Has my child performed well? Have she and I realized an important set of goals? If the answer is yes and overlaps with a winning score, great. If the answer is yes and overlaps with a losing score, that's still great.

Parent: Horseback riding?! Waterskiing?! Why don't you just recommend that I purchase an airplane so my kid can try skydiving?! Give me a break.

Author: I hear you. There are more than a few days that I come home and want to kick the dog too (maybe that's why he's neurotic). Also, I'm not suggesting that you try even a fraction of the ideas I brainstormed earlier. Remember, brainstorming is like casting a line when fishing. Most of the casts yield nothing. But, if you keep trying, you're bound to get lucky. (By the way, it was Thomas Jefferson who said, "I find that the harder I work, the more luck I seem to have.") Also, if you believe that the effects of stress often leave you unable to parent with intention, you may be experiencing an invitation to take better care of yourself (see Chapter 7).

Parent: If my child is hurting, shouldn't I try to make her feel better? Why should I allow her to feel bad when I have the power to lift her spirits right away?

Author: I was a fan of the TV program *Lost*. In one of the episodes, character Charlie Pace petitioned character John Locke to lighten a burden he was feeling. Locke's response was to offer a metaphor. He took out his knife and pointed to a cocoon that was hanging from a tree. He noted that if he gently cut the outside of the cocoon he would make it easier for the butterfly to escape. But, he said doing this would cripple the butterfly, as the process of struggling to break the cocoon provided it with the strength it needed to be healthy. So too it is with the pain our children experience. If we try to take it all away, we risk crippling them. Part of finding the middle ground is to let my child experience doses of pain that she can handle, even though that's grueling for me to endure. There will be plenty of opportunities to offer encouraging words later. Finding this middle ground increases the odds that she will learn to fly right and well.

Strategy Three

Monitor Your Child

One thing they never tell you about child raising is that
for the rest of your life, at the drop of a hat, you are
expected to know your child's name and how old he or she is.
Erma Bombeck, *Forever, Erma:*
Best-Loved Writing from America's Favorite Humorist

Effective monitoring promotes wellness in your child. However, this raises an important general issue: Most of the suggestions in this book require adjustments as a function of your child's age (i.e., effective shepherding of a six-year-old look quite different from that of a twelve-year-old). If you have more than one child, and vary things such as privileges and monitoring among them, you will find yourself confronted with sibling rivalry.

Ten Tips for Dealing with Sibling Rivalry

How many parents has the sibling-rivalry beast gored? To help deal with it, here are ten guidelines:

1. Avoid wasting energy. Don't intervene in sibling disputes unless not doing so would cost you money (e.g., to fix property, to pay for an ER visit) or *significant* psychological damage is occurring. There is no getting to the bottom of that which you have not observed.

2. Be insightful. Realize that birds fly south in the winter, flowers bud in the spring, and siblings argue, *nearly* 24/7.

3. Try to see it coming. Do not be surprised—even if you split a sandwich at the atomic level, using an electronic microscope—that one child will be absolutely convinced that he got the smaller half, while the other child gloats.

4. Be wise. Realize that when you say, "Because she is older" to justify giving a sibling a later bedtime, it's more likely that the younger child will understand the calculus behind a lunar landing.

5. Be psychologically minded. Appreciate that a child who is raging about a sibling's behavior is operating at the same intellectual level as a frat boy who has just chugged a six-pack.

6. Know yourself. Understand that if you try to resolve the age-old who-touched-whom-first argument, you will quickly regress to the intellectual functioning of a frat boy who has just chugged a six-pack.

7. Avoid fretting needlessly. Appreciate that when your children play competitive games, the loser is almost always convinced that the winner cheated.

8. Be observant. Know that when siblings are arguing, and each is trying to get the last word in, the sun's fusion reactions will cease prior to a natural ending of that back-and-forth.

9. Know your children. Do not suspect that an alien has taken over your older child's body when she stoutly defends a sibling who is in a conflict with a child *outside* of the family.

10. Be patient. Know that if you love your children, and if you do somewhere near a reasonably good job of raising them (the best any of us can hope for), they'll end up being close . . . probably not until after you're dead, but at some point.

If you can figure out a way to consistently remember and apply these ten guidelines, would you please share that methodology with me? Such information will help to retard the ever-gradual thinning of the blood vessels in my prefrontal cortex that occurs whenever sound waves from my children's arguing traverse my inner ear.

The Herd Mentality

*Whenever you find yourself on the side of the
majority, it's time to pause and reflect.*
Mark Twain

With a dizzying array of new cultural forces coming at us, we can feel confused about how to parent. What movies should I let him watch? Can I let her go on the Internet when I'm not around? What should I say about the "erectile dysfunction" commercial that came on at halftime? Should I let him get the hot new M-rated video game? Should I let her download songs unsupervised? Is a sixth-grade coed sleepover okay? My kid told me that a fifth grader was caught taking pictures of overweight girls in the locker room with her cell phone; what should I do?

In our fatigue and confusion, it is easy to adopt a parenting approach suggesting that there is no objective standard of wellness. All I need to do is determine what a sizable group of parents are allowing their kids to do and then let my kid do those things. All of my son's friends have that video game, and none of them seem to be getting into trouble, so I guess it's okay. All of my daughter's friends are going to that movie, so I guess it's okay. I don't know of any other parents who check their kids' iPods for content, so I guess I don't need to.

In my confusion, it is all too easy to look to my local parenting herd's behavior. But, this is a risky way to parent. Let me fast forward to adolescence and then rewind to make my point.

Surveys of teen behavior conducted by the Centers for Disease Control and Prevention, the National Longitudinal Study of Adolescent Health, and the National Institute of Drug Abuse indicate that just about half of teens, at least by the time they're seniors in high school, have had sex or drink alcohol.

As a confused and fatigued parent, it can be easy to say things like, "Teenagers drink. You can't stop it," and "Teenagers are going to have sex. You can't stop it." These statements are then accompanied by a passive (and sometimes active) participation in giving teens access to circumstances that facilitate these behaviors (a recent survey from the CDC indicates that the majority of sex that teens have is in one of their parents' homes between the hours of 7 p.m. and midnight). I can even start to salute the flag of disengagement: "Hey, I drank as a kid and I turned out okay. It won't kill my kid to do the same," or "I had sex when I was a teenager and it didn't damage me." Imagine a combat troop, having just crossed a minefield, hollering back to his buddies: "Hey, it's okay. I made it across just fine! Don't worry!"

Teenagers are typically not developmentally ready for the weighty burdens and consequences that are often attached to intoxication and sex. A full-grown donkey can handle giving a 250-pound man a ride, but one would not place the same burden upon a foal.

> Hannah was a wonderful sixteen-year-old girl. She was attractive, loving, sensitive, intelligent, articulate, and skilled at debate. Hannah's single mother brought her in for counseling because she recently started suffering from a suicidal depression. The precipitating cause was her becoming pregnant with her boyfriend's child. As debates between the two families ensued about what to do, Hannah suffered a miscarriage. These experiences threw her into a crippling depression; previous to this she had been free of any significant psychiatric problems. As talented as she was, her personality was fractured by this excessive burden.

> Ray was an exceptional fifteen-year-old. He was attractive, popular, an honor student, and star athlete. He had a gentle and charming personality that caused others, including me, to like him instantly. His parents brought him in for counseling because he was suffering from post-traumatic stress disorder (PTSD). His teammates, after defeating their chief rival in a championship game, decided to have a keg party in the woods. On the way home the driver took a turn too fast and flipped the car into a ravine. Ray's girlfriend, who was sitting next to him in the car, died in the accident. Ray watched her die during the time it took for the paramedics to cut the teens out of the wreckage. Before this event, Ray had been free from any significant psychiatric disturbance. But, this was too much weight for him to bear.

It has become common for marriages to end in divorce and for Americans to engage in poor health habits. However, no one argues that these behaviors should be strived for, as necessary as divorce may sometimes be. But, we're overwhelmed and confused as parents, and so we look to herd behavior to guide us. If I consistently succumb to it, then, at best,

I'm setting the stage for a risky adolescence. At worst, I may be setting my kid up to develop psychiatric symptoms. And, it is much easier to start an effective monitoring protocol in childhood than in adolescence.

Avoid Overstimulating Children

To overstimulate a child means to expose him to material that he's not prepared to handle. Sometimes a child shows distress when overexposed, while at other times she may be fascinated. The former situation is easier to deal with, as we can see that the child is hurting. For example, if my child starts to cry and cover her ears as her mother and I argue, it's easy for us to figure out that we need to establish better boundaries. On the other hand, if my ten-year-old son acts like I'm the world's greatest dad if I buy him the latest and hottest M-rated video game, it's easier to not see the damage.

Kids can become overstimulated by hearing adult conversations about adult topics (e.g., marital problems, financial pressures, anger at key adult figures in the child's life), hearing or seeing adult sexual activity (e.g., because of thin walls, open doors), and viewing or hearing inappropriate material in various media.

In past generations, parents could trust that certain inappropriate material would not appear on television during daytime hours. Today, we can assume nothing. (A few years ago, my last remnants of trust in this regard were wiped out: During a baseball game that my then eight-year-old son and I were watching on a Sunday afternoon, a commercial came on depicting two invisible characters taking off their clothes and jumping into bed together.) Moreover, a number of the video games marketed to kids seem to be intentionally over the top in their celebration of violence and soft porn, as that is what sells.

Of course, there are also plenty of ways for kids to gain easy access to material not marketed to them. Show me a family that has no active media controls in place, and I'll show you children who are at risk of becoming overstimulated. For instance, in a 2005 study published in *Pediatrics*, researchers surveyed 1,422 kids on their Internet usage. Forty-two percent of the kids said that they had witnessed pornography, with two-thirds indicating that it was unwanted (this represented a 68 percent increase from the 1999 to 2000 edition of the survey).

Kids vary greatly in their responses to overstimulation. Some key factors include the age of the child, the psychological wellness of the child and the family, and the severity and chronicity of the exposure. It's really not possible to say what the outcome will be if a six-year-old boy is consistently exposed to an M-rated video game. There are just too many other variables to consider.

Some kids remain unscathed after enduring horrible traumas while others become symptomatic when exposed to ordinary stress. When kids are overstimulated they often demonstrate particular signs and symptoms such as insomnia, nightmares, attention problems, becoming withdrawn or aggressive, the undoing of a previously mastered developmental outcome (e.g., staying dry through the night), poor appetite, a drop in grades, headaches and stomachaches, and becoming more fearful, sad, or defiant. Fortunately, attentive parents can often tell if their child's behavior is worsening.

Alex was a kindergarten student who lived for his video games. His parents, Ellen and Richard, believed that too much of this activity was not healthy, so they limited it to one hour per day. They also were strict about only letting him play E-rated games. One of his favorite games involved using a lightsaber to vanquish foes. Alex loved playing this game and acting it out whenever he could find anything that could imitate a lightsaber. This all seemed fine to Ellen and Richard. However, reports started coming home that Alex was becoming rough with other children.

At first, Ellen and Richard tried talking to Alex about it. After this strategy failed, and after considering all possible causes, they decided to suspend the video game, arranging for him to play a sports game instead. Within a week all reports of rough behavior stopped. Six months later they tried letting Alex play the game again; this time, there were no reports of aggressive behavior.

Why did Alex's behavior improve in six months? I don't believe anyone can know for sure. Kids develop rapidly at that age, so the passage of time was probably a factor. But, also probably in the mix were the facts that adults praised his emerging controls, he started enjoying the self-respect that comes with increased interpersonal success, and his parents made it clear that lightsaber activity was only being reintroduced because they guessed he could now handle it better. He probably knew that if experience proved them wrong he could count on being banished from the Jedi Academy for an even longer period of time.

Consequences of Poor Monitoring

In my professional life I often present material on developments in the child psychopathology literature (one teaches what one most needs to know). Years ago I noticed the verb "monitoring" used often in this scientific literature. For example, youth who are not monitored are at increased risk to abuse substances, break the law, have suicidal thoughts, have lower self-esteem, attempt suicide, have sex, and engage in an assortment of risky behaviors. It is not necessarily that being unmonitored, by itself, is a direct cause of these problems; but, being unmonitored is often a necessary ingredient for a wide assortment of poor outcomes and risky behaviors.

To illustrate these issues I encourage my graduate students to spend some time in a juvenile court. Juvenile court personnel can speak chapter and verse on the importance of monitoring.

Mike and Sharon Smith appeared before Judge Taylor with their son, Jacob. Jacob was charged with stealing audio equipment out of cars. It was immediately clear that there were several things that were different about this case in relation to most of the cases that had appeared that morning. First of all, both of Jacob's parents were present. Also, Mike and Sharon, as well as Jacob, were groomed and dressed as if they were in an important place. Finally, they were respectful and clearly ashamed to be there.

Sharon declared: "Your Honor, we don't know what happened. We've always given Jacob everything. He was in Boy Scouts and baseball for years. Up until recently he always got good grades. We provide a good home for him. We have a good marriage and good jobs. We all get along as a family. No one abuses alcohol, uses drugs, hits each other, or even argues excessively. No one on either side of our families has ever been arrested."

Mike declared, both palms upturned and with a very painful look on his face, "We don't know *what* happened!" At this point Sharon put her face in her hands and started sobbing.

During all of this Jacob kept his head down and acted ashamed. When the judge asked him for input he cried a little, said he was very, very sorry, and promised he would never do anything like that again.

The therapist assigned to this case later discovered that the root cause was that Mike and Sharon were not monitoring Jacob. Though they loved Jacob more than their lives, they were too heavily engaged in maintaining their standard of living. So, they often had little idea where Jacob was, who he was with, or what he was doing. They said that they "trusted him" (a side effect of which was that they were required to invest less energy in monitoring). The therapist discovered that Jacob's social network was comprised of kids from similar homes, who were also monitored poorly. Thus, when these kids got together they created a synergy that went in a thrill-seeking and dysfunctional direction.

Without appropriate monitoring, our kids can be excessively exposed to material that teaches deeply flawed philosophies. A well-grounded adult can watch a movie with a ridiculous interpersonal premise without suffering any perceivable damage. It is, however, unclear how much an impressionable child can be unduly influenced. My experience with college students and young adults suggests that many of them are confused about how to invest their energy. How many young people have as a primary life goal to make money and to acquire possessions? How many believe that a way to be satisfied in romance is to make yourself sexually alluring and to have intercourse with people you barely know? How many believe that the way to deal with conflict is to dominate or destroy the other person? Or that it is possible to be happy by lying, cheating, or stealing, as long as it produces profitable outcomes?

THE STRATEGY

Most children threaten, at times, to run away from home.
This is the only thing that keeps some parents going.
Phyllis Diller

To monitor our children well we need three things. First, we need to take a deep breath and adapt a mindset for doing this work. Second, we need some technical knowledge. Third, we need partners.

Adopt a "Battleship" Attitude

The first strategy in monitoring is to adopt a certain attitude. A good friend gave me a metaphor that well defines what I mean.

One day I was unwinding with my friend Bill after we had both had a long and challenging week. Bill was reviewing some recent interactions between him and his two sons, ages eleven and twelve. These were mostly organized around his boys asking to do things with their friends that Bill judged to be unhealthy (e.g., jumping on a trampoline with no protective fencing around it). Bill reviewed his annoyance that so many of his sons' friends were allowed to do these things and reviewed how his sons pounded him with that fact. I asked him, as we both sat there feeling weary, "Bill, how do you stand the barrage week in and week out?" He chuckled softly, and with a twinkle in his eyes said, "Spitballs off a battleship. Dave. Spitballs off a battleship."

We all need to steel ourselves to stick to our principles in the face of the sometimes nonstop barrage that comes from our children, their friends, the surrounding culture, and, yes, even other parents. For instance, the term "helicopter parents" is used sometimes to refer to parents who over-monitor. But, in my experience, this judgment is sometimes rendered toward parents who have found the correct middle ground. For instance, the 2008 National Survey of Student Engagement indicated that college students whose parents actively partnered with them in decision making reported more satisfaction from their college experience, and better learning outcomes, than students whose parents were less involved.

Stick to the Ratings

The rating systems on movies and video games can be very helpful. My wife and I adhere to them rather strictly with our kids, unless one of us has sufficiently sampled the video game or movie first and judged it to be okay. Sticking to the ratings can cause a number of challenging situations.

My son was eight years old, and he adored the *Star Wars* movies. He had seen the first five multiple times, owned about twelve lightsabers, had his entire room decorated in a *Star Wars* motif, and played several like-themed video games. So, when *Star Wars: Episode III - Revenge of the Sith* came out with a PG-13 rating, I was crushed. In reading the reviews I could tell that the rating was warranted. I told my son that seeing the movie was not an option. He proceeded to offer several well-constructed appeals to the court. But, when these failed he accepted that he would not be allowed to see the movie.

I continued to feel crushed for him (and, it did not help that several of his friends reported seeing the movie). So I went to see the movie with my wife, with an eye toward cataloguing the objectionable scenes. Then, I offered Gannon a choice. He could wait until he was older to see the movie, or he could go with me to see it now, but put on headsets and lower his head so he could not see the screen whenever I prompted him (there was a potential embarrassment factor for him involved). He jumped at the deal and complied with my instructions (I had established that we would immediately leave the movie if he resisted).

Of course, a couple of years later I had to hear from him how the scenes that I judged to be objectionable were, in his well-traveled opinion, not cause for concern. To which I responded, "Gannon, I'm comfortable with the reality that you are uncomfortable with the fact that I'm comfortable with my previous decision." (It drives my kids nuts when I deliberately talk like the caricature of a psychologist. You should try it.)

Remember, the rating guides are only that, "guides." Your eleven-year-old may be able to view a number of PG-13 movies without it being a problem; indeed, such movies can serve as a helpful prompt for discussions about relationships, substance abuse, and human sexuality, but I would not let her view one unless I had learned what the movie was about and what the potentially objectionable content entailed. I've played all levels of the M-rated Halo games with my son and, *for him*, I do not see the harm in us destroying aliens together. On the other hand, I could see that the PG-rated ghost movie that we had rented to watch as a family was overwhelming my then-nine-year-old daughter, so we turned it off.

There are a number of allies on the Internet willing to partner with you in your cause of not wanting your child to view inappropriate content. Look around these and similar sites to find reviewers that fit your values. Then, if your child wants to see a movie that you're not sure about (i.e., the rating is okay but you're not sure if you're okay with the content) you can look it up on one of these sites.

As a final word, and this may be obvious to many, the fact that a program is a cartoon, on a major network, at a time that your children are awake, doesn't mean that it is suitable for them, even though they may love it and laugh heartily. Check the rating and your partner Web sites, or watch a few episodes yourself.

Restrict Inappropriate Media

An advisable strategy is to lock out media that you do not believe is appropriate for your child. Without such protections in place your kids are at high risk to consume, either accidently or deliberately (despite their angelic denials), content that is potentially harmful. Here are some recommendations:

1. Lock out programs or stations containing material that is potentially objectionable. Most satellite and cable providers allow you to do this by rating, time of day, or station. (It can be very helpful to call the provider for help.) And, lock up movies and adult materials that you don't want your children to view.

2. Use DVR or VCR machines to record programs and then fast-forward through the commercials.

3. Control your child's access to material on the Internet by only allowing him to use browsers that include comprehensive parent controls.

These programs typically come with a database of Web sites that are rated for a variety of content (e.g., profanity, violence toward animals). If your child wants access to a Web site not in the database, he must come to you to enter a password (I use something like "dadiscoolandgoodlooking").

4. Do not allow your child the capacity to install applications on any computer without your approval. This can keep your child from creating workarounds for your security measures. The system preferences on your computer let you decide who is allowed to install applications. A how-to book on your system software can help or ask a computer-literate friend.

5. If you've any doubts about what your child is accessing on the Internet, you could install spy software. I would not use this software to unduly violate your child's privacy (e.g., to find out what he is saying about you to his friends—assume you are intermittently made to sound like a harsh prison warden or a nerdy dork) but only to confirm that he is not viewing objectionable material or engaging in risky behavior.

6. If you discover that your child is violating your rules, and you are unsure if the safeguards you have in place are working, I would not allow computer usage unless you are in the vicinity and can monitor it. You can set up passwords on the computer or lock your child out using devices that lock onto the end of power cords (see the Further Reading & Viewing section of this chapter).

7. Inspect the music on your child's electronic music player. Most of these devices hold songs that your child has downloaded from an Internet site by way of her computer. The software on the computer usually has controls that restrict downloads of explicit content; iTunes, for instance, lists the word "explicit" in a red font, in a square box, right next to the name of the song. Most of the songs with explicit ratings have a nonexplicit version. (Expect your child to render passionate protestations that listening to the nonexplicit version instead of the explicit one is like listening to "Amazing Grace" played on a church organ by the Pope when you really want to hear "Freebird" played on an electric guitar by Slash. This is why I include Web site information on how to acquire a quality set of noise-canceling headphones in Further Reading and Viewing.)

8. Be sure that your child's portable game player or cell phone doesn't have Internet access. (I cannot tell you the number of times a parent has told me that their child's device had no Wi-Fi access but it really did.) If

it does, make sure that you can put controls on it; if you cannot, call your provider to disable the Internet access.

9. Keep in mind that if your child has online access through his gaming equipment he may be playing games with much older people who are free to use whatever language they like. I think it's a good policy to not allow this sort of access unless you can hear what's going on or can be reassured that it's not happening.

10. If your child possesses a cell phone with a camera, make sure you explain to him that the storage of nude pictures of kids on the phone is against the law and could get *you* arrested.

11. Make sure that your child understands that you maintain the right to inspect any hard drive in your house, and any cell phone that you pay for, whenever you want and without notice—and that you will intermittently exercise that right. If your child has cause to believe you, he will think three times before storing objectionable material or engaging in risky behavior. Of course, you can keep to yourself the fact that you plan to do this sparingly, checking only enough to ensure that your child is well tolerating the access you've allowed. When you do check, make sure to check all the relevant places (e.g., picture mail on a cell phone), and, if you're not sure where to look, ask for help from a trusted friend.

12. From a parent's perspective, Facebook.com and similar sites are like dust mites. It would be great to live in an environment without them, but that's not practical, at least once your child reaches an age when her friends are on social networking sites. But, make it clear that a condition of your child joining is that they "friend" you (i.e., give you access to their site) and that you will exercise your monitoring rights whenever you want (once again, you are only doing this as much as seems necessary). Also, you want to be sure that your child does not have two Facebook sites: the one that friends you and the one that goes rogue. Other strategies in this chapter can help you to ascertain this (e.g., cautious and intermittent use of spyware).

13. Offer a technologically savvy twenty-something person a gift card to hack around your controls. Tell him you'll double the value of the gift card if he is successful, can show you how he did it, and teach you how to increase your security.

14. When I'm working with families on these sorts of protocols, kids who have previously been unmonitored howl like wolves at the moon!

"Why don't you trust me?!" or "How can we be close if you think I lie to you?!" or "You're treating me like I'm a baby!" or "You must think I'm a horrible liar!" I suggest to parents that it is their child's job to seek independence, and that such howling is a sign of health, but it is their job to monitor. If they need it, I sometimes share stories like Jenny's:

Jenny was a thirty-year-old first-time mother who was coming to me to treat anxiety. I learned that Jenny's parents, Dennis and Marie, had divorced when she was five. During her childhood she lived with Marie and visited Dennis two weekends each month. Marie remarried while Dennis floated in and out of relationships. Dennis was a surgeon who maintained a significantly higher standard of living than Marie and her husband. While she was growing up, and especially during her teen years, Jenny much preferred staying with her father. Dennis's residence was filled with toys that she and her friends could enjoy, and he did not monitor her. When challenged by Marie, he would say things like, "I think it is important for kids to believe that their parents trust them," and "Teens have to learn to make their own decisions while they're living with their parents so that they don't crash and burn later."

Jenny shared that they would have drinking parties at her dad's place, always being careful to clean up afterward, and that she would take her boyfriends there to have sex. She also indicated that her mother, except when she was at her father's residence, always knew where she was, what she was doing, who she was doing it with, and what adult was responsible for monitoring her, if only from a distance. Jenny noted that she hated her mother for this and that they fought often. In contrast, she was very affectionate with her father and they rarely argued.

By the time she entered her midtwenties, however, the relationships had reversed. Jenny had come to appreciate that it was her mother, out of love and devotion, who did the tough work during those years. For the past six years she and Marie spoke daily, and she often took her mother's counsel regarding relationships and parenting. Alternatively, she and her dad only spoke on holidays, or when she made special efforts to be in touch with him. As he continued to be unwilling or unable to exert effort in her direction, they had grown apart and she concluded that she was not a priority in his life.

The strategies reviewed in this book depend on and strengthen each other. For instance, in the case I just reviewed, the fact that Dennis and Marie did not partner more in Jenny's childhood promoted some of the acting out that Jenny did at her father's residence (see Chapter 9). Moreover, Marie and Jenny could have probably averted some of their wars if Marie had consistently employed a strategy such as special time (see Chapter 1).

How do you know if a young child needs training wheels on his bicycle? Easy, right? Likewise, when is it time to try taking the training wheels off? Again, the answer is obvious. Neither of the following is advisable: to not use needed training wheels and to use unneeded training wheels. Effective monitoring operates according to this same principle.

As a loving parent, you only allow your child access to the materials and experiences that he can handle. Upon evidence of being able to handle the materials or the freedoms in question, you *very gradually and with dispassionate reasoning* allow a wider array of exposures and freedoms. Upon evidence that your child is not handling an exposure or freedom, you reintroduce the necessary structures.

Assess Visits to Another Child's Home

A key starting point is to make an assessment of the household that your child is going to. Can you trust the judgment and monitoring standards of the other parent(s)? Some good signs are when

- the other child is at your house, the media he reports consuming are in a range that is acceptable to you;
- the other parents are organized, fair, and polite when arranging for pickups and drop-offs (parents who are routinely late or disorganized in their approach to such matters are at high risk of being similarly organized at home);
- the parents call to check up on their child, at least if your child is young and until you and they get to know each other;
- the parents ask you questions regarding any activities outside the home that you plan to do with their child (e.g., What movie will they be seeing?);

- you have the occasion to go inside the other family's residence, and you see no signs of significant problems (e.g., people screaming, anyone appearing intoxicated);
- you show diligence (e.g., calling when your kid is at their house), they welcome it and let you know that they understand and agree with your concerns.

When first starting these arrangements, it's a good idea to let the other child's parents know about the rating system you subscribe to: "Janet, my wife and I prefer for Lauren to not see any programming above a PG rating and to not play any video games above an E rating. Does that inconvenience you at all?" I find most parents don't have a problem with that, and those who do may not be creating an environment that I want my child in anyway. If I subsequently hear that one of the parents embarrassed my daughter by pointing out that the kids were forbidden to do something because of our standards, or otherwise did not adhere to our preferences, I would limit my child's access to that residence.

Some other tips for promoting monitoring outside the home are as follows:

1. Socialize with the parents of the kids with whom your child associates. I once knew a single inner-city mom who scheduled a monthly breakfast with the moms of her son's friends. This was extremely helpful to her in establishing effective monitoring and for better understanding her son's social landscape. You could invite them over for a barbeque, situate yourself next to them on the soccer field, or sit next to them at the school play.

2. If your child has a cell phone, consider adding a GPS function.

3. If your child is not socializing much, ask teachers to suggest children with whom you might encourage contact.

4. As deftly and as kindly as you can, try to direct the majority of your child's social contact toward those children who seem to be doing well and who seem to have psychologically healthy families. I also think we do well to encourage engagement with kids from different cultures.

5. My wife and I have been prepping our kids for years that they're going to find, especially as they get older, that they'll not be allowed to do things that other kids are allowed to do. (My teen children now

roll their eyes and mockingly finish the standard sentence I've rendered on this point over the years—isn't it nice when your children demonstrate that their brains have developed to the point that they actually understand where you're coming from?) As long as my child is not acting disrespectfully I explain my reasoning. I don't do this because I'm trying to get her to say, "Gee, Dad, you're right. Thanks for being such a good dad." (Actually, I might fear the presence of a serious neurological disorder if I heard such commentary.) No, I do so because I'm trying to be respectful.

To get your point across it can be helpful to use analogies that your child can relate to. For instance, our neurotic Portuguese water dog is named Dakota. So, I ask things such as, "How do you think Dakota would feel if we let him eat nothing but ice cream for his meals? Right, he'd probably like that, but what do you think would happen to him over time if we did that?" or "Dakota would also be very happy if we would let him go outside even though we can't watch him. But, what do you think could happen to him if we did that?"

Sometimes one of my kids will act grouchy and say things like, "He'd be okay outside! It's a safe neighborhood!" or "Maybe he wouldn't be afraid of water if we let him eat ice cream more."

In which case I say something like, "Maybe you're right. Let's just say that your mother and I are dorky control freaks with arbitrary and capricious standards and motives." (I enjoy using large words during these little moments, as they tend to encourage the child to exit my eye line while simultaneously prepping for SATs.)

Monitor Yourself

Please keep in mind that you could choose to ignore any number of the recommendations in this book and find that your child ends up doing just fine, thank you very much. As I said earlier, you are one of the world's leading experts on your child. Thus everything that I offer has to be examined through the lens of your unique intuition and knowledge. For instance, cultural factors may suggest modification to some of the recommendations in this book, including what I am about to counsel. All this notwithstanding, I wish to offer a few guidelines for how we might avoid overstimulating our children (i.e., show me a child who has unfettered access to his parents' lives and agenda, and I'll show you a child who is at risk for becoming overwhelmed).

Although challenging, it's advisable to not have any major arguments with your significant other in front of your children, especially younger ones. Younger kids think in magical and egocentric terms: Everything that happens is for them, caused by them, or intimately connected to them. They're like the excessively self-involved adult: "Enough about me. What are *your* thoughts about me?"

For example, younger children often think their parents' problems are their fault. I can't tell you the number of times separated or divorced parents have been surprised to learn from me—and with their child's permission—that their child feels either partially or totally responsible for their split-up. A good policy to *strive for* is to wait until your child is out of the home, asleep, or out of earshot, to let your partner know about the many opportunities he has to improve upon in his performance. I stress "strive for" because few of us are able to pull this off all of the time (I know I don't); it is just something to aspire to. Here are some additional suggestions:

1. Test the soundproofing between rooms in your residence. Some parents end up being surprised that their kids can hear them having sex. If you find out that sounds are capable of bleeding between rooms, you can add sound suppression (TV, music, etc.) to their room, your room, or both during your amorous encounters.

2. Change clothes and use the toilet behind closed doors. Sometimes we don't realize our children's needs for privacy as they grow. Also, because we feel so close to them, we may not realize the effect that seeing our bodies can have on our opposite-sex children as they age. Of course, I'm not suggesting we should act as if anyone's body is something to be ashamed of. (It's curious how privacy can be equated with shame. Sure, if we are ashamed of something, we strive for privacy. But, there are plenty of private things that are not shameful.)

3. We all lose IQ points when we're angry and become less than we would wish to be. Hence, *strive* to accomplish separation from the moment and the person when angry, at least if you don't risk harm by

pausing. Simply vowing not to discuss nonemergencies when you're very angry is a start. Then use strategies that calm you down. Not once in my life have I regretted waiting to deal with a problem until I calmed down, especially when it involved those I love.

Consider Child Privacy

I've worked with parents who have thought it best to violate their child's privacy. They read their diaries, rifle through their book bags and drawers, read their email, check their voicemail. I can understand what motivates this. We're lunatics, after all. We want to know what important things are going on in our child's life. We also don't want our child to make decisions, maintain relationships, or say things or hear things that are ill advised. However, it's critical to draw a line between that which is truly damaging and that which we do not care for.

For instance, when my son was ten he started locking his bedroom door. Initially, I forbade it. However, and upon reflection, I had to admit that my son demonstrated no evidence of not being able to handle this degree of privacy, and his primary motivation was to impede enemy encroachments by his sisters. So, I needed to relax that rule. Now, if my son were to later indicate that he was likely to engage in harmful behaviors in his room, I'd have to go back to forbidding a locked door.

Our kids need to learn the same way we did: through trial and error. They need to make their own mistakes within the confines of our monitoring. If we try to eliminate their privacy, or overmonitor them, just to keep them from making mistakes, we risk both depriving them of learning opportunities and damaging our relationship needlessly.

Letting go in ways that benefit our kids takes some getting used to. But, once we find that middle ground, we may discover that it feels very right to be there, both for our kids and ourselves.

Supportive Strategy

Give Thanks

There are a number of ways to do this. But, here I will cover two: Make a commitment to be thankful on either a daily or weekly basis and keep either a weekly or a daily gratitude journal.

If you go for the once-a-week approach, try putting this activity in your schedule until you get in the habit. Here are ten weeks' worth of activity:

1. Make a list of the top ten people you are grateful for and indicate what they've done for you.

2. Make a list of the top ten events in your life that you are thankful for and indicate why.

3. Write a handwritten thank-you card and mail it.

4. Let God (or the Universe or your Higher Power) know what you are most thankful for.

5. Go out of your way to let at least one person in your life know why you appreciate him or her.

6. Give a token gift of thanks to someone who did something nice.

7. Make a list of the ten things you have done to make the world a better place and give thanks for those (e.g., in prayer, in a discussion with a loved one, in meditation).

8. Write a letter of thanks to a service provider who did well by you or someone you care for (e.g., an auto-repair shop, a landscaper, an accountant) and mail it to the person and to his or her boss.

9. Make a special meal for your significant other and let him or her know what he or she does that you appreciate.

10. Stop a cleaning staff person, whose work you benefit from, and thank him or her for his or her service.

A gratitude journal is simply a list (either weekly or daily) of the things you are grateful for. These can be simple things like the birds singing, a good meal, or good service at a restaurant. Or, they can be more elaborate like earning a raise, focusing on the blessing of having a child, or winning an award. The significance of what you are grateful for doesn't appear to be as important as taking the time to focus your mind on objective blessings. The research suggests that a consistent gratitude practice promotes happiness. Moreover, surprising blessings can come back at you. I recently learned that a former intern laminated a praising sticky note I once attached to a report he wrote, and a professional baseball scout (who coaches my son in the off-season) told me that he keeps a thank-you note I wrote to him in his traveling bag.

Strategy Summary

Remember that children who are not monitored are at increased risk for developing an assortment of psychiatric symptoms.

Steel yourself to stand against the inevitable currents in our culture that wish to overstimulate your child, your child's passionate protestations for you to stop monitoring, and the influence of other parents who are less on-the-job than you.

Realize that there is always a way to effectively restrict your child's access to harmful content, though you may need help to pull it off.

Ensure that when your child is outside your home that you know where she is, what she is doing, and what responsible adult is in charge of monitoring.

Accept that it can be tough to find the balance between adaptive (wellness-promoting) monitoring and the promotion of your child's independence. Effective parents routinely assess whether they need to make adjustments to find the middle ground.

Keep your child from hearing the conversation when you are heatedly pointing out your significant other's opportunities for growth or when you are having sexual encounters.

The Skeptical Parent's Challenge

Parent: It sounds like you want me to take on a part-time job with all of this monitoring stuff.

Author: While it may sound like an effective monitoring protocol takes a lot of time, it's mostly front-loaded. That is, once you've installed the software, programmed the units, established the rules, and approved of playmates, it all takes little more than enforcement. Plus—and at the risk of over emphasizing this point—pay me a little with time now or pay me a lot with time later. That is, the time it takes to do a little prophylactic work up front is much less than the time it takes to cope with and respond to the symptoms and problems that are at risk to emerge if your child is not monitored well.

Parent: Hey, you act like we have tons of money to be buying cell phones, computers, and gaming systems. Not all of us are Donald Trump!

Author: I hear you. I realize that not every child has a computer with Internet access, an iPod, and an Xbox. I just need to review these gadgets for parents whose kids do have them. (By the way, not having these things, as best as I can determine when examining the scientific evidence, will not cause a child to have a transient ischemic attack, contrary to what kids assert. Actually, the fewer things that your child has to plug in, the fewer things there are for you to have to monitor.)

Parent: Don't kids have to learn to make their own decisions, too? I mean, I don't need to act like a warden and make my house like a prison!

Author: You're absolutely correct. It can be hard to find the balance between effective monitoring and the promotion of child independence and decision making. The art is to find the middle ground in which your child can thrive. For this reason, think of Chapter 6 as a companion chapter to this one.

Strategy Four

Establish Enjoyable Family Rituals

In truth a family is what you make it. It is made strong, not by number of heads counted at the dinner table, but by the rituals you help family members create, by the memories you share, by the commitment of time, caring, and love you show to one another, and by the hopes for the future you have as individuals and as a unit.
Marge Kennedy, *The Single-Parent Family*

Life happens pretty fast. If you don't stop and look around once in awhile you could miss it.
Ferris Bueller, *Ferris Bueller's Day Off*

This chapter reviews the power of healthy family rituals. I say "healthy," as families can have unhealthy rituals, too (e.g., Dad comes home, drinks some beers, and starts yelling). Rituals need to account for a chorus of competing family agendas, the complexity of which appears to rise exponentially with each additional child. Chart 4.1 is a tongue-in-cheek illustration of how our parenting rituals can change across children, partially because our experience grows and partially because we have more to do as the tally of our children rises.

If you have 3.0 children or more, you will most likely identify with the changing priorities outlined in the chart. If you have one or two children, you may end up laughing or climbing a tower with a high-powered rifle; as the former is cheaper, I'd try to lean that way.

Chart 4.1

	1st Child	2nd Child	3rd Child
During Pregnancy	Each month Mom and Dad check software tracking for what is going on with the baby's development.	Share moments when the baby is kicking.	Mom: "The baby is kicking." Dad (while watching ESPN): "That's great, hon." Mom: Takes a silent vow of celibacy.
Changing the Baby	Don't touch the baby's bottom with a wipe unless it has been warmed with a wipe warmer.	Use unwarmed wipes.	Use dampened paper towel.
Mom's Feeding Strategy at Night	Wakes up and feeds the baby whenever she needs and lets Dad sleep.	Pumps milk every third night and asks Dad to take over.	Insisting on a 50-50 split, pumps enough milk for Dad and uses noise-canceling ear plugs on off nights.
Transporting the Baby	In a snuggle pouch.	In a stroller.	By the ankle.
Defensive plan	Double coverage.	Man-to-man.	Zone.
Strategy to Help the Baby Fall Asleep	Rock the baby until she falls asleep.	Gently shake the crib, while sitting next to it in a chair, until the baby falls asleep.	Attach a vibrating massager, on a timer, to the crib.
Most Common Method to Stimulate the Baby	Scientifically engineered mobile, classical music, and cranial massages.	Read a magazine to the baby.	Put the baby in front of the TV during *Blues Clues*.
Method to Get Baby to Laugh the Most	As the parachute goes up and down over the baby in weekly Gymboree class.	As Dad tosses the baby up and down during commercials.	As the dog licks the baby's toes.

Family Rituals and Stress

Adults with matured brains, relevant experiences to draw upon, and independence have more resources when coping with stress. However, children are much more vulnerable by virtue of having fewer coping skills, fewer experiences to draw upon, less freedom, and less developed brains.

Studies indicate that adaptive rituals help to protect kids against the toxic effects of common stressors (e.g., alcoholism in the family, divorce, medical conditions, pain, and disability). Moreover, infusing adaptive rituals into the home life of children living in harsh urban environments helps to protect them from becoming symptomatic. Before elaborating on the power of rituals, let's review some common stressors kids (up to age eighteen) endure in the United States:

1. Most kids will not reach the age of eighteen living with both birth parents, and about 40 percent of all children do not live with their birth father.

2. About 19 percent of U.S. kids suffer from chronic illness or disability.

3. About 28 million children have lived with a parent who abused alcohol for some period during childhood; children who live with a parent who is alcohol dependent are three times more likely to be abused and four times more likely to be neglected.

4. Approximately 16 percent of kids have been bullied.

5. Averaged across the year, on each day in America
    1,186 teens give birth;
    4,440 youths are arrested (366 of these arrests pertain to drug abuse);
    1,887 children in public schools receive corporal punishment;
    17,072 students are suspended from public schools.

6. Between 25 and 68 percent of children and adolescents experience a very traumatic event by age sixteen, with 6 percent of kids experiencing one in the past three months.

7. Being a minority (e.g., African American, Hispanic, Native American) often adds an assortment of additional stressors. Such children are more likely to be in foster care, to have a parent incarcerated, to experience indicators of low socioeconomic status (e.g., fewer clothes, less food to

eat, more subsidized lunches), to have their mothers enter the workforce when they are younger, to have a parent die, and to not receive needed mental health care.

8. About 75 percent of U.S. children live in an urban setting. Living in such a setting is associated with higher rates of exposure to trauma (e.g., seeing someone shot) and stressful events (e.g., divorce, substance abuse). Moreover, almost one in four kids live in poverty, which is associated with another set of toxic stressors.

9. Learning about national and international traumas in the news (e.g., school shootings, 9/11, wars, tsunamis, hurricanes, devastating oil spills) can also cause significant stress, especially for younger or vulnerable children.

While stressful events can be very difficult for our children to handle, we parent-lunatics, perhaps because we can't bear the thought that our kid is hurting, often underestimate the impact. For instance, the 2010 edition of the American Psychological Association's *Stress in America* survey found that only 7 percent of parents rate their kids stress at an eight or higher on a ten-point scale, but nearly one in five children state that they worry a lot or a great deal.

About 30 percent of children exposed to a nonviolent serious trauma develop PTSD. The number jumps to 70 percent if the trauma is violent. The primary symptoms of PTSD include painful thoughts about the trauma that a child cannot control, bad dreams, reenacting the painful event(s) (including in play), significant distress when reminded about the trauma (e.g., seeing TV shows on related themes, hearing music associated with what happened), and efforts to avoid people, places, and things that remind a child about the painful event(s). The child suffering from PTSD also often displays an assortment of anxiety and mood-based symptoms.

If a child suffers from PTSD, his basic assumptions about the safety and stability of his world have been severely compromised. (Keep in mind that this is the exact opposite message generated when adaptive rituals are consistently present). The world used to feel safe and predictable, but not now. Now significant aspects of the world feel dangerous and unpredictable. With core assumptions about safety and security threatened, if not shattered, a child experiences significant symptoms of anxiety.

Josh was a twelve-year-old boy brought in for treatment of PTSD. He was living with his birth mother, Alicia, and his stepfather, Todd (he never met his birth father). His stepfather entered his life at age eleven.

Six months before seeing me, Josh had suddenly reported to his mother that Todd had been sexually assaulting him for the past year. Immediately Alicia called the police and told Todd that she wanted him out. Todd, while denying Josh's claims, went to the garage and said that he was going to asphyxiate himself by running the car in the closed garage. The police got there in time to save Todd (some questioned whether Todd had actually intended to hurt himself).

Seeing how upset his mother was, Josh changed his story and said that Todd had not assaulted him. Josh said that someone else had sexually assaulted him; he added that he was unwilling to state who it was. In subsequent months both the police and welfare personnel tried to get Josh to say who had assaulted him. Whenever their questioning became heated, he would experience an unwanted psychological penetration, regress, and need to be hospitalized.

The therapist's review of Josh's history indicated that until age eleven he was cheerful, academically accomplished, and popular. However, following the entrance of his stepfather into his life, he became depressed, anxious, highly inattentive, reclusive, and a poor student. The stress of being sexually assaulted fractured this boy's personality, view of himself, and view of the world. A couple of years later Josh was doing better in treatment, but his therapist thought that he would likely need care well into his thirties.

Josh's story illustrates a severe case of PTSD, but in any case a fracturing of the psyche occurs to some degree. A number of studies have tried to identify what differentiates—among those children exposed to severe stressors—those who become impaired and those who don't. Among the identified factors is the presence of rituals in the family.

Think about it from a child's perspective. Planes may be crashing into buildings, but we still have family pizza night. Children may be shooting up schools, but we still go to temple each weekend. I was just in a serious car accident, but we still rent movies on Sundays. Mom and Dad just got divorced, but I still do the same sports, go to the same church, and attend the same school. Rituals support a child's basic assumptions about personal safety and predictability. If your parenting facilitates such assumptions, you are providing your child with an effective defensive layer against stress, across many levels of severity.

Rituals serve other important functions as well. Quoting psychologist Dr. Froma Walsh: "Family rituals store and convey each family's identity and beliefs in the celebration of holidays, rites of passage . . . and family traditions . . . as well as routine family interactions . . . Rituals also facilitate life cycle transitions and transformations of beliefs. Rituals are encouraged in family therapy to mark important milestones, restore continuities with a family's heritage, create new patterns, and foster healing from trauma . . . ."

The Value of Rituals

Enjoy the little things, for one day you may look back
and realize they were the big things.
Robert Brault

A growing body of evidence suggests that the presence of rituals in family life lowers the risk of developing common mind-body psychological problems. For example, the Add Health study, published in the *Journal of the American Medical Association* in 1997, surveyed 12,118 high school students and found that the collaborative practice of daily routines was associated with a wide array of lower health risks. Other findings in the literature indicate that the presence of rituals differentiates families in need of psychiatric care from those that seemed to be doing better.

Moreover, when specific kinds of rituals are researched, benefits are usually found. One example is the practice of spirituality. In 2003, Drs. Peter Hill and Kenneth Pargament did a comprehensive review of the scientific literature on the associations between religion and spirituality and physical and mental health; this review appeared in the flagship journal of the American Psychological Association, *American Psychologist*. They reported that the practice of some sort of spirituality or religion was associated with a longer life, better health-related outcomes (e.g., lower cholesterol, less hypertension, and lower rates of heart disease and cancer), less depression, higher self-esteem, higher interpersonal connectedness, higher maturity, and better coping after a variety of significant stressors (e.g., surgeries, illnesses, and natural disasters).

Similarly, in 2000, Drs. Linda Barnes, Gregory Plotnikoff, Kenneth Fox, and Sara Pendleton reviewed this literature in regard to youths; their review appeared in the flagship journal of the American Academy of Pediatrics, *Pediatrics.* Spirituality and religiousness in kids has been associated with less depression, less substance abuse, an improved sense of well-being, better immune functioning, and better coping in response to a wide array of stressors (e.g., heart disease, racism, sexual abuse, hospitalization, cancer, disability, and terminal illness). They also indicated, "Low religiousness also tends to be related to higher rates of smoking, drinking, drug use, and adolescent pregnancy."

Many of us know of instances when religion promoted pain and alienation more than wellness and love. However, the research indicates that rituals associated with religion or spirituality are generally both adaptive and protective. Moreover, Dr. Walsh quotes a recent Gallup survey that indicates that nearly 75 percent of Americans report that their family relationships have been strengthened by religion in the home and that the top factors thought to strengthen the family are, first, "family ties, loyalty, and traditions"; and, second, "moral and spiritual values."

Practices surrounding religion or spirituality are just one type of adaptive ritual. Another ritual that has been found to be potent in its protective function is sharing a family meal. For instance, a 2004 study published in *Archives of Pediatric and Adolescent Medicine,* reporting on a large survey of more than 4,700 teens, found that the frequency of eating a family meal together was associated with lower substance abuse and a better diet in both sexes as well as better grades and less depression in girls. Other studies have likewise found an association with reduced rates of obesity and better health habits.

When I do an assessment on a family, I almost always ask about their rituals. I've noticed that families that cannot easily tell me about their rituals seem to be much more overwhelmed than those that can. Also, show me a family that is starting to surrender its rituals secondary to stress and I'll show you a family that is on the ropes trying to avoid a knockout blow: "We used to go to the mall together as a family on Saturdays, but *it's just gotten to be too much* to do that lately," or "We always used to take our kids to Chuck E. Cheese's for their birthdays, but *there's just too much going on* to do that now."

The Jacksons were a middle-class family comprised of Dad (Robert), Mom (Leslie), and three kids, Abby (age fifteen), Paul (age eleven), and Susan (age nine). Both Robert and Leslie worked outside the home in satisfying careers. They were also content in their marriage. Each of the children did well academically, participated in at least two extracurricular activities, and was socially effective. The Jacksons highly valued family life and had an active schedule of rituals that they did on a weekly, holiday, and seasonal basis.

However, the family was thrown into upheaval when Leslie's father died and her mother, Ester, became very depressed. As Leslie became concerned about her mother living alone, she and Robert invited Ester to live in their home.

Many changes came with this move for the family. Susan moved into Abby's room to create a bedroom for Ester. Leslie and Robert told the kids that, for at least the next year or so, they would need to limit themselves to one extracurricular activity. The family also eliminated their weekly rituals (i.e., playing sports at a YMCA and visiting a local mall on Sunday mornings).

The family came to me to treat a mood disorder in Paul. Paul had always seemed like a moody child, but never to the point of becoming depressed. I did a course of cognitive-behavioral therapy with Paul, but also arranged for the family to do two things. First, they established new weekly rituals that fit better with Ester's presence. Second, they asked for support from other family members so that the kids could continue with their extracurricular involvements. Five months later Paul's depression was healed, and it remained so one year later at a booster session.

Another thing I do when getting to know families in my practice is to ask children, in an individual interview, to tell me their best and their worst memories. I'd estimate that 75–80 percent of the best memories that kids report are attached to a family ritual.

Jackie's single dad, Gus, brought her in for an assessment because she had attempted suicide. I learned that Jackie had two younger sisters and that Gus worked about seventy hours per week as a surgeon. Gus indicated that he very much wanted to work fewer hours, but he believed he didn't have the freedom to do so.

When I asked Jackie, in an individual interview, what her favorite memory was, she said that it was a vacation that she and her sisters took with Gus to the shore several years earlier. This had also been their last family vacation, given the collective demands on their time.

Jackie gave me permission to review this memory with her father. When I did, he expressed surprise. In his mind, that vacation was lackluster as his kids complained about being bored and they had a difficult time agreeing on activities. It was important for Gus to hear what this ritual meant for his daughter; he was able to use this information to make changes in how he spent his time.

THE STRATEGY

Enjoyable rituals are islands of respite and rejuvenation in the strong currents of our culture. I propose that a healthy family have at least two weekly rituals and consistently engage in seasonal rituals and rituals for special events. The following are examples of rituals:

Daily Rituals
- morning routines
- sharing meals
- saying hellos and good-byes
- bedtime routines
- bathing routines
- activities involved with relaxing
- saying prayers
- caring for pets

Weekly Rituals
- having pizza night
- having game night
- going out to eat
- playing a sport together
- attending religious services
- going to a local Y

Weekly Rituals (continued)
- sharing meals
- movie night
- going to a local mall or park
- reading with discussion
- going to the library
- going for a walk
- watching a TV program with discussion
- bicycling
- going to a local museum
- fishing
- going to bingo night at the local church
- playing a role-play video game
- having special time
- watching old family videos

Seasonal Rituals

- going to sports games that your child is playing in
- following a college or pro sports team together (e.g., checking out daily news stories, watching the games, texting each other about developments and opinions)
- taking a summer vacation or inexpensive staycation
- putting up seasonal household decorations
- taking part in academic fairs at school (e.g., the annual science fair)
- going to dance recitals
- going to school plays and performances
- going to school-sponsored annual events (e.g., the annual father-daughter dance)
- going to a local farm in the fall to pick out pumpkins for the home
- having an annual mother-son day: You spend a day together doing mutually planned activities in a city, maybe including a sleepover
- going to the first game of a favorite sports team each year
- sharing meals with extended family on holidays
- taking part in church-sponsored service activities
- going to the annual church bazaar, picnic, or carnival
- going to an annual parade
- creating an annual family newsletter
- creating a family Web site

Rituals for Special Events

- birthdays: having a cake, singing happy birthday, sharing a breakfast, going out to dinner, having family over, taking a trip
- your child brings home a pleasing report card: going out to dinner, acquiring a new fun toy or gadget for the family, taking a weekend day-trip to a favored place (e.g., the zoo that's ninety minutes away), putting the report card on display
- your child gets special recognition or wins an award (in addition to the ideas above): submitting it to a local paper, giving it to the principal's office for possible announcement, including it in an annual family newsletter events that can be ritualized
- your child brings home pleasing state-achievement testing results

Other Events That Can Be Ritualized
- Mom or Dad gets a promotion, is recognized for excellence at work, or otherwise accomplishes something professionally
- a wedding anniversary

We want to create in our child's mind the statement, "We always do (some adaptive ritual) on (some time frame or event)." If children have these "We alwayses" in place, they are less vulnerable to the toxic effects of stress because their world seems more predictable, safe, and under control.

Give Yourself Credit

While creating lists of potential rituals, I've had pangs of guilt, thinking *I should really do this or that more often.* But we all need to think of such lists as being like a menu at a good restaurant: You can't eat/do it all, and it would be unhealthy to try. Moreover, we may already be doing more than we realize. For instance, I recently read an account of the value of rituals written by Dr. Robert Brooks, who shared that his father used to keep folders of his children's mementos and accomplishments. He elaborated that seeing his father engage in this ritual made him feel special. I have been doing this for each of my kids since the day they were born, and they know about it. However, it took reading Dr. Brooks's account for me to connect the dots. You also may be managing adaptive rituals for your family for which you have not been giving yourself credit.

Changing Rituals

As our children become more engaged with friends, it's common to find them lobbying us to surrender certain rituals. However, as these rituals are enjoyable, it may not take much to solve these challenges. At least one parent needs to be firm: "No, we're not having a sleepover tonight because it's movie night and that's the one time that we have together as a family each week." Encouraging children to plan their weekend activities earlier, rather than later, can also help reduce these competing concerns (says a man who is unable to escape the annual ritual of helping my children with their science projects *the night before they're due*).

However, as your family and kids develop, it's important to evolve the rituals. Were amendments to the U.S. Constitution made quickly, in the heat of some temporary cultural stress, our laws would be too fluid and would lose credibility. Likewise, if amendments were not possible, our laws would become archaic and insensitive to important cultural shifts. A middle ground is dispassionately and thoroughly reasoned change. So too it should be with our rituals.

> Edward and Mary Robinson had two children. Melissa was twelve and Cody was ten. The Robinsons had a weekly ritual of ordering pizza and playing board games on Friday nights. At the point of this story, this ritual was five years old, and they pulled it off 85 percent of the time.
>
> Melissa was entering seventh grade, a grade level at which her school sponsored biweekly chaperoned dances. Melissa very much wished to attend these dances, even if it meant not taking part in the family ritual. Recognizing that this was not a symptom of a problem in the family, Edward and Mary reluctantly agreed to let Melissa go. However, they still ordered pizza and played a game with Cody on Fridays.
>
> They also adopted a new ritual for the four of them—having popcorn and watching a movie together on Sunday nights. This included sharing reviews midway through the movie and at the end.

One of the saddest things to me about being a parent is the fact that my kids are growing up. Don't get me wrong; I enjoy the new opportunities as the wheel turns. But, I often wonder if I've gotten the most out of each phase. This is best illustrated by the passing of a ritual with my eldest child, Morgan.

> One of the rituals my three kids and I did every Christmas Eve was to track Santa's progress around the globe on www.noradsanta.org. We sometimes travel for Christmas. But, no matter where we were, my kids and I found a private spot and huddled around a computer monitor for hourly updates. The kids would then enthusiastically share the updates with everyone else in the residence. At a certain point in the nightly journey, the narrator declares: "Santa is over the Atlantic. Children on the East

Coast of the United States should now get to bed!" This was pretty funny, because the command to get to bed had the same effect as giving them a shot of espresso (i.e., my kids would get wide eyed and *rush* to bed). It was one of our favorite rituals, seasonal or otherwise.

As Morgan got older, she became more and more elaborate in the way she interacted with this ritual; for instance, she would imagine she saw a particular present she asked for in the QuickTime video of Santa's sleigh. However, by age ten, she had figured out that what she had been told about Santa defied the laws of physics. She was slow to let on about her insight because she didn't want to give up on this and the other Santa-based rituals that we had (writing him a letter, getting a letter back, going for a *Polar Express* ride on a local train). But, eventually she confessed what she knew.

Shortly thereafter, my son went through the same transition, leaving only one of my kids believing in Santa. Heaven would do well to allow me to go back and experience rituals like these whenever I wish.

There is no getting around it: Becoming a parent opens wounds. We hurt over the passage of time. We hurt with concern and worry. And, we hurt with overwhelming love.

Would any of us have it any other way?

Supportive Strategy

Call an Old Friend

Because of our hectic lives, it's easy for our social circle to shrink to co-workers, family, and the parents of our kids' friends. Many of us have deep connections from the past that have fallen by the wayside. It can be rejuvenating and life-giving to call up an old friend with whom you've lost touch. I did this recently with a friend who was the best man at our wedding; my wife was out of town, the kids were in bed, and my thoughts turned to Bob.

With such friends, you need not have an excuse. They get why you're calling after the first sentence or two, and this was the case with

Bob. After he playfully mocked me for asking if it was an okay time to talk, we spent about two hours catching up, sharing our joys and sorrows, and reconnecting. The conversation put air under my wings for the next couple of days.

Next time you're tired, but still want to do something useful, why not give it a shot?

Strategy Summary

The presence of adaptive rituals in a family serves a protective function against the toxic effects of stress and trauma.

If you have not already done so, try establishing two weekly family-level rituals.

Try to establish pleasurable routines and rituals for each season and in response to special occasions.

Try to find the middle ground between clinging to your rituals with white knuckles and releasing them with every little wind gust that comes along. The middle ground is marked by dispassionate and well-reasoned change.

As with the other strategies in this book, a parent need not spend a lot of money to engage in rituals. It is the interpersonal shared experience of fun and meaning that matters. Show me parents who lack for discretionary funds, and I will show you parents who have the opportunity to model creativity and persistence and to demonstrate that wealth doesn't cause happiness.

The Skeptical Parent's Challenge

Parent: I thought this book was about strategies for *busy, working* parents. How do you account for all the time these rituals take?

Author: I know. I know. I worry about that too. But, these strategies are not independent from each other. For instance, a parent who is doing weekly special time is doing a weekly ritual. A child who has discovered a competency playing basketball, and whose family supports that with their attendance at games, is benefiting from a consistent seasonal ritual.

Strategies overlap. The time it takes to do the interventions in each chapter independently is much greater than the time it takes a parent to employ all of the strategies. Plus, a huge amount of time is freed up when a parent doesn't have to deal with psychological illnesses and symptoms. (I lean towards over making key points. It comes from having no real authority at home.) So, yes, this is a strategy that improves parenting efficiency.

Parent: My kid acts like he doesn't want anything to do with me, so what's the point in setting up rituals?

Author: I would think of this as a symptom. As a starting point, invite your child into deciding what the new ritual could be. If he declines, make your best effort and kindly insist on his participation. If that fails, try the interventions in the next chapter or consider securing the services of a good child mental health professional (see Chapter 10).

Strategy Five

Practice Sound Discipline

The gem cannot be polished without friction,
nor man perfected without trials.
Chinese Proverb

The word discipline comes from the Latin word *disciplina*, which means "instruction given to a disciple." As we parents wish to teach our children to be successful, we are required to be disciplinarians. This doesn't mean being punitive or harsh. And it doesn't allow us to be aloof. Being a disciplinarian means to lovingly teach our child critical lessons, even when they'd just as soon not have them. Show me a parent-child relationship that doesn't involve skirmishes, at least some of the time, and I'll show you a symptom.

In contemporary family life, we parent-lunatics are often so overextended by life's obligations that discipline is done on the fly. We let our children go on autopilot when they're behaving. If they act up, then we decide what to do—often on the spot and when we're upset.

Vexing Prosecutorial Invectives

Children who get into skirmishes with their parents often try to cast themselves in the role of district attorney and their parent in the role of defendant. When railing on like a DA, a child is not attempting to garner insight regarding the reasoning behind the parent's decision. No, these are efforts to get the parent to plead guilty and to make reparation. To that end, I recommend the following responses to common prosecutorial invectives:

Chart 5.1

Child Indictment	Parent Quasher
But all of my friends are allowed to do it!	Do you think their parents would consider adopting you?
But, you let (name of a sibling) do that.	I love her more than you.
Can I (do something you've already indicated the child is not allowed to do)?	If your father divorces me maybe your next mother will let you do that.
I can't believe how unfair you are!	You have no idea. I can be *way* more unfair than this. Just ask your mom.
You don't trust me!	Don't you just love it when we understand each other?!
You treat me like a baby!	No I don't! Oh, by the way, I'm going to the grocery store later. I forget if you prefer the strained peas or the strained carrots.
The fact that you didn't do it as a kid doesn't mean that I can't!	Grandma and Grandpa would have let me if they could have, but we lived in a hut and had no money.
I haven't gotten a new pair of Nikes in over a year!!	You should call child welfare. Their number is on the fridge.
Why are you so out of it?!	Multiple head injuries over the years.
You're so embarrassing!	Yes, but I don't pee myself in public. You have to give me that!

I'm all for teaching our children the reasoning behind our discipline. But, if I try to teach when my child is trying to prosecute, I act like a defendant. So, try the above retorts, as they've been baptized by fire in the Palmiter household.

Effective discipline requires a plan. How many important tasks are done well without some planning? In the discipline arena, a lack of planning can make us reactive, punitive, and ineffective. Planning, on the other hand, facilitates compliance, wellness, and harmony.

Let's begin by reviewing four basic parenting styles the research suggests we have when we discipline, and then review specific strategies that either generally fail or generally work.

Four Parenting Styles

An infallible way to make your child miserable is to satisfy all his demands.
Henry Home, *Introduction to the Art of Thinking*

My clinical experience and the scientific literature suggest that parenting styles can be grouped into four categories. Parenting that falls in one of the quadrants in Chart 5.2 is associated with much better outcomes for children. (I bet you can guess, by just glancing at the chart, which is the successful quadrant)

Style #1: Warm and Permissive

Kids may act as if this is their preferred parent style. This parent is affectionate, engaged with her child, and emphasizes closeness. Moreover, she often doesn't make her child do things he doesn't want to do, nor does she tend to forbid him from doing things that he wants to do. In the short run, the kid acts like he has been set free in a candy factory. However, in the long run, this child is less likely to learn the skill of doing things when he doesn't feel like it; he can also become mighty self-entitled. Show me an adult who only does things when he feels like it, and who believes that others owe him, and I'll show you an adult whose life is in shambles.

In my clinical experience, one common reason a parent parents in this way is that he is experiencing significant unmet needs for intimacy. Of course, there is nothing wrong with such needs. We all need love, affection, attention, and closeness. However, if my adult relationships chronically do not satisfy these needs, I can (albeit unintentionally) look to meet

Chart 5.2

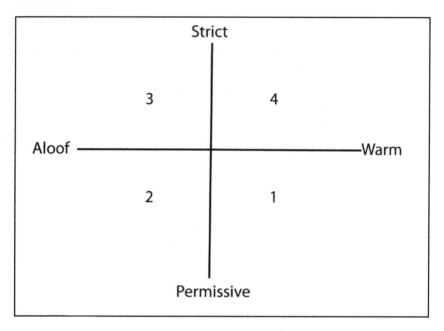

my nonsexual needs for intimacy through my relationship with my child. This leaves me dependent on my child's good will. In this regard, I feel like I dare not displease her, as it could leave me feeling even more isolated. So, I appease and please. Of course, this usually won't work, as our children are ill equipped to meet our needs.

Style #2: Permissive and Aloof

This parent tends to treat his child like a roommate. He often justifies his disengagement by noting that it's important for kids to learn to be independent. "You can't grow up well if your parents are always hovering over you," or "Kids have to learn for themselves what behaviors work and what behaviors don't work." In my clinical experience, parents who parent in this way are overwhelmed by the demands of life. Hence, they often don't invest, or can't find, the energy to parent well. So, they're either trying to reduce stress' lashes by knocking off to-dos and/or they're trying to numb themselves from their pain. Children raised in this way may end up feeling unworthy and diminished in their capacity to do things when they don't feel like it.

Style #3: Aloof and Strict

This parent often considers herself to be a disciplinarian. She emphasizes respect and duty. "Too many kids are not held accountable for their misbehavior," "Children who are not punished sufficiently end up spoiled," and "You have to let kids know that they can't act like savages." When a parent emphasizes this perspective, without also providing significant doses of warmth, then control and adherence are emphasized at the cost of closeness and dialogue. In the short run, these children may be good little soldiers. In the long run, they may be lacking a sense of worthiness. I also find that they tend to become harsh with themselves and others and/ or become rebels without a cause.

Parents falling in this quadrant often had emotionally harsh or restrictive childhoods with parents who did not know how to discipline well. Moreover, they tend to impose their harsh standards on others. Since most people don't like to feel like they're not measuring up, these folks often find themselves lacking in opportunities for affection and closeness. They're "right," and they're alone.

Style #4: Strict and Warm

This is the style we should all strive for. Some research calls this style "authoritative" and makes it crystal clear that children experiencing this sort of parenting have the best outcomes. These children see themselves as worthy and they have internalized values that promote self-discipline and success across a variety of vocational and interpersonal areas. They engage in fewer risky behaviors and are mostly well. Parents who consistently practice the ten strategies in this book are more likely to be falling squarely in this quadrant.

By the way, I find that parents who adopt styles #1, #2, and #3 love their kids no less than parents whose style is #4, nor are they typically aware of the damage that their children may be experiencing. I also often find that their self-care is often poor; indeed, it is much easier to parent effectively if you are well, and vice versa. This is why parental self-care is such an important theme in this book (see the Supportive Strategy at the end of each chapter, as well as Chapter 7).

Ineffective Strategies

*Well meaning parents have been known to apply the same
approach with their children for weeks, months, or years
even when the approach has proven ineffective.*
Dr. Robert B. Brooks, *Handbook of Resilience in Children*

*Insanity: doing the same thing over and over again
and expecting different results.*
Albert Einstein

Want to save yourself a lot of time? Ask yourself if a parenting strategy you're considering would work if your boss applied it toward you. For instance, how would it work if your boss hit you, even if he was 100 percent in the right? What about if she screamed at you? Right. Same thing from you to your child. Ask yourself what it would be like to receive the intervention.

Even a broken clock is right twice a day. So, just about any parenting strategy works some of the time. Imagine you had some man bellow at you as he's waiving a wrench around: "Don't tell me you can't use a wrench to change a light bulb, 'cause I just did 'er that way!" In all of this, I'm talking about the odds of success.

Following are some common ineffective disciplinary strategies:

- Rewarding your child for disruptive behavior
- Administering corporal punishment
- Lecturing
- Setting impulsive monetary fines
- Shielding from negative consequences
- Allowing fear to reign

Rewarding Disruptive Behavior

If you filled an auditorium with parents who have a defiant child and asked, "How many of you reward your child for his or her defiant behavior?" hardly anyone would raise a hand, and just about everybody would be responding honestly. It's not obvious how this happens. We reward our children by yelling at them, bribing them, and letting them off the hook. I covered yelling in Chapter 1 and will review the other two points here.

Bribery. If I'm parenting reactively, and my intervention spins toward anger, I'm more likely to yell or hit. However, if I'm parenting reactively, but I wish to remain kind, I may end up bribing.

> Jesse was an active five-year-old who was not particularly engaged by the religious services his parents took him to. Thus, Jesse would seek out his own entertainment, including kicking the pew in front of him and making a loud thunking noise.
>
> Because this sound was much more interesting than the sounds coming from the minister, and because making it earned him the cheerful attention of other children, Jesse thunked away. While his dad seemed unhappy with the thunking, Jesse imagined that his father must not have thought this through, as he could see no downside.
>
> As the thunking continued, and because some adults were starting to cast an evil eye, Jesse's father's embarrassment grew. Sensing that saying, "Stop that" and showing his displeasure were not working, he whispered this to his son: "Jesse, if you stop kicking the pew, we'll rent a new video game right after church is over." Since Jesse *lived* for his video games, it became in his best interest, as he perceived it, to stop; so he stopped. And, his father kept his word regarding the rental.
>
> Now, come the following Sunday, Jesse really loves thunking! Not only does it create an interesting sound and the admiration of friends, but it also leads to his dad renting him a video game! Wow, what a no-brainer!

There is a huge difference between a reactive and bribe-based intervention (what Jesse received) and a proactive and reward-based intervention (what I am reviewing in this chapter). With the former, the offer of the reward is given after the onset of the undesirable behavior. With the latter, a parent would establish with Jesse, prior to going to church, that proper behavior (e.g., including not kicking the pew) would be rewarded by the video game rental and that kicking the pew would lead to nothing, or a punishment.

Off the Hook. The following vignette illustrates how letting a kid "off the hook" can reward negative behavior:

Nine-year-old Grace despises cleaning her room. From her perspective, her room need not be tidy in order to be satisfying. Plus, cleaning her room is boring, and, as far as she can tell, devoid of upside.

So, when her single, working mother, Jen, tells her to tidy it up each morning before school, she's nonplused. In these moments Grace tends to whine an assortment of entreaties: "I'm tired!" or "Why?!" or "What does it matter?!" or "I'll do it when I get home!" or "No one will see it today!" and so forth. As Jen is generally tired and rushed in the morning, her defenses can only tolerate a couple of these volleys. So, she either starts screaming at Grace (which generally results in Grace cleaning her room and Jen later feeling badly for having lost her composure) or she lets Grace off the hook and walks away in frustration.

Thus, Grace's whining is often rewarded by either increased attention (albeit a raw radish) or the avoidance of having to do an unpleasant task.

This is called negative reinforcement: A behavior (whining) is encouraged when it leads to escaping a perceived negative outcome (cleaning the room). Taking the above example, let's imagine two households: the Smiths and the Joneses. In both households a mother tells her child to make her bed for ninety straight days, and in both households the child resists every day. However, Mom Smith caves every day and lets her child off the hook while Mom Jones sticks to her guns every third or fourth day and makes her child make the bed no matter what. Now, let's say on the ninety-first day both moms have a change in heart: Neither is going to let her child off the hook after giving a command. Mom Smith (who had caved all preceding ninety days) will have an easier time of it than Mom Jones.

Think of it from the kid's perspective. Kid Jones has seen her mom insist before. She has also seen her mom cave in after insisting; it takes her longer to accept that there's a new sheriff in town. However, Kid Smith has never witnessed her mom acting this way before so she more quickly accepts the change. (This is why gamblers go back to the roulette wheel even though they lose most of the time. If they won every time, and then lost a few, they'd give up more quickly.)

In most households where kids are let off the hook for acting poorly it happens intermittently—not every time. Hence, not only are such training programs common but they are actually well "designed" for promoting defiance.

Corporal Punishment: Undisciplined Discipline

Never raise your hand to your kids. It leaves your groin unprotected.

Red Buttons

Corporal punishment is undisciplined discipline. How often do we hit our children when we're calm? To parent when I'm enraged is akin to parenting when I'm intoxicated; both states involve transient brain dysfunction. Saying to my child "control yourself" while I've lost my composure is like a customer relations manager screaming at his subordinates, "Treat our customers with kindness and respect!"

Hitting also reinforces a number of unsavory notions: "The person who is physically stronger wins conflicts," "When you're mad at someone, you should hit her," or "People should use hitting as a method of solving problems." The scientific evidence concerning corporal punishment indicates that it varies from having a neutral impact to being quite harmful. In my clinical experience, if you slap your kid for picking his nose you'll usually succeed in getting him to not pick his nose when he's around you. However, once he's not around you, he may dig away, and/or become preoccupied with nose picking, and/or resent you.

In making these comments about corporal punishment, I'm not trying to shame you for any occasional performance lapses you've shown (I've had a few of those myself). Instead, I'm challenging the perspective that would fly corporal punishment up the flag pole and salute it. Please also know that I'm not coming at this from a moral perspective. I'm coming at this as a behavioral scientist. Moreover, I'm not saying that effective parenting doesn't involve punishment—far from it. What I'm lobbying for is to drop corporal punishment as a choice and to substitute it with more effective interventions.

Lecturing

This is one of the most overused and ineffective strategies known to parenthood. According to parenting expert Barbara Coloroso, for a lecture to change behavior two conditions must be met: The person doesn't have information, and the person wants the information. If your boss wants to scold you about performing better, do you want her to use more or fewer words? If you've already understood how she wants you to change, how does her lecture go over?

If, by lecturing my child about an undesirable behavior, my goal is simply to blow off steam and I'm willing to deal with the side effects, I have the right tool for the job. But, if my goal is to change my child's behavior, lecturing is like trying to drive a nail in the wall with the handle of a screwdriver—it might work, but there's a much better tool available.

Reactively Inflicting a Monetary Fine

Imagine that a boss grew weary of an employee wearing scruffy shoes to work because she believed it was unprofessional. She tells the employee about it, but doesn't mention potential consequences. When she then sees the employee wearing the scruffy shoes again, she responds by telling him that she is docking fifty dollars from his pay. Can you imagine the employee's rage?

> Ben was a feisty five-year-old boy who, by his parents' estimation, had an unlimited capacity to find new ways to mix things together that nature never intended to be joined (e.g., a piece of bologna in the DVD player, a matchbox car in the toaster). Frustrated by his seemingly unending cascade of rogue science experiments, his parents put getting permission for such activities within the behavioral program they set up for Ben (i.e., not using something like it was not designed to be used, unless permission was granted, yielded fifty cents per day); no take-away of money was indicated for infractions. But when Ben appeared proudly displaying a jar that mixed his father's hair coloring product with ketchup, declaring that it doesn't work as well on ketchup as it does on Dad's hair, his father told him that he was taking one dollar away from him. Ben then threw down the jar—initiating the unintended experiment of discerning whether the mixture could change the color of the rug—and stormed off to his room. Later Ben's dad agreed with his wife that his decision to do the deduction needed to be retracted, as he had provided no warning for such up front.

Protecting a Child from Consequences

We parent-lunatics hate to see our child suffer and wish to eliminate it. However, trying to eliminate all suffering, without regard to whether it serves an important function, can have the opposite effect of what we intend.

Nick, age ten, was caught shoplifting a pack of baseball cards. In the prior month he'd been caught stealing a toy from the same store but was let off with a warning. On this second occasion, the manager called the parents in.

The manager asked the parents what they thought should be done. They said that Nick should apologize. The manager asked that he put the apology in writing and that the town sheriff be alerted. Nick's parents, in front of Nick, said they thought that was overkill. The manager, surprised by their reaction, indicated that perhaps it would be better to call the police to the store and have them weigh in.

Nick's father excused himself and called the store's owner (they were friends). The owner called the store manager and told her to allow Nick to issue an oral apology and to then consider the matter closed.

During the car ride home, more time was spent reviewing the manager's behavior than Nick's behavior.

Nick's parents were being protective. Any parent can empathize with that. However, they were losing sight of the value Nick could have gained from experiencing the consequences of his behavior. It would have been excessive if the manager had asked for Nick to be arrested. But, the manager looked to be pursuing both Nick's and the community's welfare. By their response, the parents did not promote Nick's sense of responsibility nor did they do anything to associate shoplifting (which already had its thrill for Nick) with a significant negative consequence.

Allowing Fear to Reign

Children with anxious temperaments can act defiantly out of fear. In a typical scenario they resist being exposed to a situation that is developmentally appropriate (e.g., sleeping alone, going to soccer practice, getting on the school bus). It would be an understandable knee-jerk reaction for me to allow my child to avoid such situations in order to reduce her anxiety. Such a coping style of avoidance, however, can become easily ingrained and may hamper a child's capacity for overcoming fears.

When my child expresses a desire to avoid something out of fear, I should ask myself, "Is (the feared experience) developmentally appropriate for her?" If the answer is yes, then it would often be a mistake for me to let my child use an avoidance coping response; in these situations we do well to "avoid avoidance."

Jim's four-year-old daughter Ashley had always shown a shy and anxious temperament. Hence, he knew that attending daycare was going to be a challenge. Jack did the necessary groundwork (e.g., taking a few trips to the daycare with his daughter so she could meet the people there, talking with her about the experience, and sharing his confidence that she was ready).

On the first day, Jack knew that Ashley would likely cry when it came time for him to leave, and she did. He also knew that it was not likely that he would be able to calm her. So, he just left and asked the staff to call him if she did not calm down in fifteen to twenty minutes. Ten minutes later a staff person called and said that Ashley was playing with another group of girls. As Jack had been leaving, he noticed that a woman was trying to reassure her son into a calm state. Jack asked if she was still there comforting her son. The daycare staff responded affirmatively, and noted that she usually stayed for thirty minutes before giving up and going to work.

Some children suffer from an anxiety disorder. For them, exposure strategies done on your own (i.e., avoiding avoidance) may fail. For such children, consulting with a mental health professional is usually advisable (see Chapter 10).

THE STRATEGY

It is amazing how quickly the kids learn to drive a car, yet are unable to understand the lawn mower, snow blower, or vacuum cleaner.
Ben Bergor

Three key strategies of an effective discipline plan are to *be clear about your expectations,* to *emphasize rewards* to motivate changes in behavior, and to *use well-reasoned punishments.*

Be Clear about Expectations

A proactive parent asks herself, *"What is it that I expect from my child?"* Typically there are four categories of expectations: grooming, chores, academic work, and behaving well toward others, which includes managing frustrations.

Good Grooming

My favorite undergraduate professor was Edward Gannon, s.j. (my son is named after him). Wrapped in a gruff and Irish temperament, Father Gannon was exceptionally witty, insightful, and loving. I remember when he would jokingly talk about young children. With a twinkle in his eye, and begging for a debate, he would say things like, "I have no idea why people call toddlers cute. As best as I can tell they're savages: pooping and peeing themselves, thinking only of their own needs, and tolerating others only when they can offer them something. They're completely uncivilized, and I can't fathom why anyone would ever want one." How right he was.

Chart 5.3 is a rough timeline for civilizing your child's grooming.

Parental teaching, monitoring, encouraging, and admonishing are typically all that is required for promoting these skills. In some instances, a contract or a token system may also be helpful (see page 119 for more information). However, if your child is demonstrating a significant developmental lag in one of these areas, and the strategies in this book don't help enough, a consultation with a mental health professional would be in order (see Chapter 10).

Doing Chores

Ready for my next obvious statement? It's good for your child to do chores. The primary motivation is not to make your life easier (not that

Chart 5.3

Age	Task
2–4	Has accomplished daytime (first) and nighttime (second) continence; helps wash body, brush teeth, dress, and brush hair
5–6	Washes body, brushes teeth (electric brushes with timers are useful), dresses, and brushes hair; then parent adjusts
7–8	Less parent adjusting
9–10	Visual inspection by parent with occasional adjustments; add application of underarm deodorant
11–12	Intermittent adjustments by parent

there is anything wrong with that!), but to promote your child's character development. Even very young children, assuming an absence of disabilities and developmental delays, can do chores. Then, as the child gets older, more elaborate tasks can be added. Chart 5.4 serves as a rough guide (some may vary depending on the safety of your neighborhood).

Keep in mind that older children ought to be able to do the tasks indicated in the younger children's brackets. Of course, I'm not looking to turn my daughter into Cinderella, as tempting as that may be following the twelfth eye roll of the day. Nor is it good for her to be a spoiled princess. I've worked with affluent families who've agreed to un-hire help so that their child could make these contributions. Doing chores not only facilitates a child's capacity to do things when he doesn't feel like it, but it also promotes a community mindset. Sometimes we parents can miss the benefits that accrue to our children when we're consistent along these lines.

When my son was ten, he and I volunteered to staff a Little League spaghetti dinner. The boys who volunteered served as waiters for each table. However, he noted that one, then two, other tables were not staffed. Gannon took it upon himself to manage three tables. As I would pass by, I noted that he was using very polite speech, such as, "Would you like more coffee, sir?" and "Would you like to hear the dessert choices, ma'am?"

Chart 5.4

Age	Chore
2–4	Help to make the bed, pick up dirty clothes, carry things back and forth from the kitchen to the table, put away toys
5–6	Do her best making her bed, put her things where they belong, help with pet care
7–8	Help with trash, help parent shovel snow or grocery shop, set and clear the table, load the dishwasher, help with vacuuming and mopping
9–10	Make his own lunch on school nights, take out the trash, fold and put away laundry, help pull weeds and clean up the yard, walk the dog
11–12	Help prepare meals and grocery lists, vacuum, do laundry, do simple paint jobs, shovel snow, clean cars

Several adults went out of their way to tell me how attentive he was as a waiter. I'm telling you, if a squirrel had walked into the hall and started speaking to me, I would have been less shocked. Even Dr. Parenting Expert is capable of not fully appreciating that this stuff actually works!

Academic Responsibilities

What constitutes academic responsibilities varies, depending on your child's age and the level of challenge in her school's curriculum. However, setting a routine for homework on school days is usually advisable. (Keep in mind that many education experts subscribe to the 10-minute rule for homework. Reviewing, this rule suggests restricting the amount of time for homework to your child's grade multiplied by 10 minutes–see Chapter 2.) Assuming your child has regular homework, it's good to do the following (some of these tasks may also be done by tutors or other people caring for your child after school):

1. Set aside a regular place for homework to be done that is outside of the flow of significant distracters. (Some kids do best with music on, so their study place need not necessarily be quiet.) It is also a good idea to set a regular time for homework to be done, and to have clear rules regarding how it will be done when there are competing activities.

2. Review with your child each day what homework is due that day, when the next test for each class will be given, and what long-term projects are due when. This routine only takes a few minutes and affords you the chance to be proactive (more and more schools put this information online, often on a daily basis).

3. For children in younger grades, check all homework for accuracy and quiz for test readiness. In correcting homework, instead of providing the answers, encourage your child to fix incorrect answers; this can be aided by your questions (e.g., Have you considered looking it up in the dictionary? or Where in the book can you find that answer?). As your child grows older, begin to intermittently decrease this, using your child's academic outcomes as your guide.

4. Attend school conferences. This lets the teacher(s) know that you are engaged and often provides helpful information. I recommend doing these even if your child is successful. You can also use these conferences to compare notes about homework (e.g., how long it is taking your child

to complete it on average) and get a sense of your child's general effort, behavior toward the teacher, and social skills. Finally, it is advisable to set up a regular communication system from school to home when your child is faltering (see Chapter 9).

Behaving Well toward Others

This goal is difficult to describe because children struggle in this area in a great number of ways. It's good to begin by stating the specific and alternative positive behavior you desire. "John, I want you to learn to express your anger with words and without yelling or cursing," "Sally, I want you to learn to let your friends take their turn first when they're your guest in our house," or "Peter, I expect you to treat your dog well and to not flip his ears back and tuck them under his collar." (Okay, I confess that this is what I used to do to my best friend's dog in graduate school.) The next step is to establish what reward your child would earn by complying and what punishments she would experience by disobeying.

Emphasize Rewards

There are three levels of interventions for when your child acts defiantly, and each of them link desired behaviors with rewards. The first characterizes an initial response (the starting point). The second is for when your child is displaying a consistent, but narrow, number of problems that are mild to moderate in severity (the contract method). The third is for when your child is displaying consistent and wide-ranging behavioral problems in a mild to moderate range (the token economy).

The Starting Point

Instead of telling your child what bad thing will happen if she messes up, it's more effective to let her know what good things will happen when she acts well. I consider there to be five categories of rewards: praise and attention, access to privileges, cash, special experiences, and purchases.

Praise and Attention. The most common reward in effective child rearing is proportionate, intermittent, and positive parental attention and praise. Obviously, an effective parent doesn't throw a parade just because a child has cleaned his room or praise her every single time she does it well; nor does she consistently ignore those events. If we're crazy busy, we may remain silently grateful for compliance and wait for foul-ups to express our thoughts. Such an approach sets the stage for noncompliance.

Access to Privileges. Privileges can be a powerful incentive. But, it is very important to not use the language of punishment: "Jimmy, clean your room or I'm going to take your TV away!" In the language of punishment, you have all the power, so it's easy for your child to conclude that he's a passive victim. In the language of reward a parent says to her child: "Jimmy from now on you will earn your TV privilege by cleaning your room." In using such language you're establishing yourself as an empathic bystander who hopes your child will make good decisions.

Let's imagine a mom who told her child that he was to earn access to TV by cleaning his room and then let's say he asked to watch TV without having cleaned the room. The conversation might go as follows:

Jimmy: Can I watch TV?
Mom: Did you clean your room?
Jimmy: No, but I will later.
Mom: Then I guess you haven't earned your TV.
Jimmy: Why won't you let me watch it?!
Mom: I'm sorry. Was I not clear? I don't decide if you earn TV; you do. If you clean your room without a hassle, then you earn TV. If you do not, then you don't. I know you like TV, so I hope you'll make a good decision for yourself. I'm rooting for you!
Jimmy: But none of my friends have to earn their TV!
Mom: Their parents probably love them more.

Additional privileges include access to electronic gear, to special toys, phone use, going outside to play, and so forth. You could also use an earlier-versus-later bedtime as an incentive. For instance, if you judge that a good bedtime for your child is 8:30 p.m., but she is noncompliant in the morning, you could say the following: "Since you've been acting up in the morning, you're telling me that you need more sleep. So, from now on your bedtime is 7:30. However, if you do what you're supposed to do in the morning (and this would need to be spelled out) you will earn an 8:30 bedtime."

Cash. In many instances, it's desirable to tie an allowance to responsibilities. Not only can this be a powerful reward, but there are additional skills that your child can learn (e.g., saving, giving to charity, budgeting, banking). The amount of an appropriate allowance varies greatly among families. But, you can begin with half of your child's age for a weekly allowance and then adjust up or down as seems advisable.

It's important for you to determine what expenses your child is then responsible for. In my household I consider my children responsible for elective purchases that neither my wife nor I had already intended to acquire. (In fairness, I confess that I'm not above being manipulated. For instance, Lauren, my youngest, uses her dimples like a ninja uses throwing stars; recognizing this, I call out for my wife's help. Of course, now Lauren has been conditioned to wait until my rescuer is out of range.)

Special Experiences. These are things such as going out to eat, arranging for a sleepover, going to an amusement park, and staying up late. A child might earn staying up late on a Friday night by having effectively completed the morning routine four out of five school days, or earn a fishing trip by having done his homework for two weeks. The bigger the behavioral expectation, the bigger the reward.

Purchases. Within moderation, using experiences or desired purchases as rewards can be quite effective. This can range from simple things like earning a game rental to more elaborate rewards like purchasing a video game system. However, please remember that a reward need not be large to be motivating. According to one of the fathers of behaviorism, Dr. B. F. Skinner: "The way positive reinforcement is carried out is more important than the amount."

In a resilient household, a parent has proactively established clear expectations for her child each day and week. You are on your parenting game when you then meet your child's success with a combination of intermittent praise and attention, access to privileges, cash, special experiences, and purchases. In such a household children are more often caught being good than caught being bad, and a feeling of joy often permeates the air.

Parents in my practice frequently ask: "But shouldn't he do some things without a reward?!" The answer is yes. A generally compliant child may clean his room and do his homework on any given day, or even many days, without an external reward. But, it is advisable to reward (at least intermittently), and especially if your child is struggling in a particular area. Decisions regarding how much to reward are similar to decisions regarding how much to monitor: The degree and organizational level of the dosing increases and decreases depending on how successful your child is. Please also remember that praise and positive attention count as rewards.

We parents sometimes underestimate the power of incentives in our own lives. Even when I give to charity, I'm rewarded with self-respect and a sense of meaning. But, children living in a run-and-gun household can believe, or intuit, that no desirable outcome is attached to a given responsibility.

Despite their parents' best efforts and intentions, some kids get into a pattern of defiant or disruptive behavior. The next level of intervention, a contract system, may solve the problem(s).

The Contract Method

Whenever your child is misbehaving, it's desirable to articulate what specific positive behavior is expected (instead of emphasizing what is not expected) and to attach a specific reward to that behavior. If your child has mild, but consistent, problems with compliance, there can be value in writing up a formal contract that articulates which privileges are tied to which responsibilities. Here are the steps:

1. Draw a vertical line in the middle of a sheet of paper. On the left side list the responsibilities. On the right side list the reward that is earned by fulfilling each responsibility. The contract should be written and posted where your child can see it.

2. Be as specific as possible in defining responsibilities and rewards. "Clean your room" is not specific. "Make your bed, put your dirty clothes in the clothes hamper, and put your clean clothes where they belong (folded in a drawer or hung up in the closet) by 8:30 each evening" is specific. Any limitations to rewards should also be spelled out (e.g., if an allowance is once a week and on a certain day, if a certain reward can only be done on certain days or during certain blocks of time, if TV or other

rewards can only be enjoyed for a certain length of time). Err on the side of being compulsive.

3. Include bonuses in your contract. Bonuses are extra rewards that are earned by performing all tasks in the contract for a designated period of time. For instance, you may want to administer a bonus if your child fulfills all of his responsibilities for some block of time: five days straight, three out of five days, seven days straight, or three out of four weeks. You can also use an allowance as a bonus (e.g., your child earns one dollar for every day that she completes every responsibility, payable once a week).

4. Chart your child's progress. Consider a grid, using columns for the days of the month and the rows for the responsibilities. Block out any days on which a given chore is not required. If your child completes a responsibility, he gets a check mark; if he doesn't, he gets a zero. The chart informs you if your child did the responsibility the night before, all week, three out of four weeks, or whatever the contract calls for. Not charting, and relying on memory, is not advisable—nor is allowing your child independent access to the chart.

5. Reward your child as soon as possible. Some responsibilities last all day or are done late in the day. In these cases the reward may come the next day. Bonuses—rewards based on appropriate performance over the course of several days or longer—may also need to wait.

6. If a reward has been earned, it is allowed. If a reward has not been earned, it is not allowed. (The only exception would be if your child is in the middle of a tantrum. She must be calm in order to be given access to what she has earned.)

7. Once you have to tell your child to do something three times, she loses the opportunity to earn the reward, even though she must still do the task. If you're a ten-year-old, would you rather do the task and get your reward or do the task without your reward? Right. And, your child will quickly figure this out without you ever having to explain it.

By the way, I've seen behavioral programs that suggest using two strikes and you're out. But, just as I would not want to get into trouble with my wife if she has "asked" me to do something twice, I have a hard time expecting this of my kids. Of course, you can always use an annoyed tone at the second command.

8. It's ultimately your child's responsibility to make sure you've charted completed chores. If you happen to see that your child finished a

task and you chart it, that's fine. But, if you did not chart the completed task, and your child did not point it out to you, and you are no longer able to verify that the task was completed in the required fashion, then your child doesn't get credit for that work. The alternative is to encourage lying. Plus, you're teaching your child that it's her responsibility to let you know that she completed a task.

Sticking to the terms of the contract can avert many common problems. First, you may become annoyed with your child for an unrelated matter and attempt to withhold an earned reward. (This would be akin to your boss withholding your earned pay for something annoying you did.) Such behaviors threaten the integrity of the contract. Likewise, your child may have pleased you in some unrelated fashion and so you might be inclined to offer a reward articulated in the contract without the attached duty having been completed. Remember, if your child is not eligible for a reward in the contract, he hasn't completed a reasonable expectation. Allowing the reward anyway reinforces non-compliance. Pick some other way to reward your child for the unrelated matter.

The following story typifies the potential for contracts to correct mild problems:

> Joseph was an intelligent five-year-old enrolled in a half-day pre-school, who was not controlling himself well when frustrated. These behaviors were starting to overwhelm the preschool teacher, who had begun asking the parents if another preschool might be a better fit.
>
> In response, Joseph's dad constructed a reward program. The first part of this program was a daily report card that articulated three responsibilities. The first three lines read "behavior toward teacher," "behavior toward other kids," and "work behavior." Across from each behavior was a sad face, a neutral face, and a happy face. Joseph was told that the teacher would circle one face for each of the three behaviors each day. He was told that he gets two points for a happy face, no points for a neutral face, and one point would be taken away for a sad face. He was told that three happy faces would give him two extra points that day (i.e., so the most he could earn each day was eight points). Joseph was told that once he collected one hundred points his father would buy him a video game that he had been longing for.

Each morning Joseph's dad reviewed with him what each responsibility entailed and made encouraging remarks about Joseph's capacity to pull it off. After Dad and Joseph were both home, they went over the day's sheet with either appropriate praise or problem solving, depending on the result.

It took three weeks for Joseph to earn the new game, at which point the sheets were consistently coming home with all happy faces. Joseph's father then indicated that the reward of playing the game system each day (for a maximum of one hour) was earned by bringing home a sheet with three happy faces on it. Three weeks after that, the preschool teacher said she believed the sheets were no longer needed.

In this example, Joseph's dad was one of the world's leading experts on his son, so he had a good intuition for how long it would take Joseph to earn the video game. If Joseph had a more severe problem, his father could have established a weekly or a daily reward for the happy faces. And, if such a program didn't work, a consultation with a mental health professional would have been advisable (see Chapter 10).

The Token System Method

If your child is acting defiantly much of the time, there can be value in developing a token system. There are many published accounts of how to do a token system, but the methods below are adapted from Dr. Russell Barkley's book *Defiant Children: A Clinician's Manual for Assessment and Parent Training*.

The steps are as follows:

Step One: Develop a list of responsibilities: chores, negative behaviors you want your child to stop (expressed in positive terms), and any inconsistent grooming. It is important to create an accompanying duty card for each responsibility (i.e., an index card that spells out what effective task completion is and how long it should take). For prereaders, duty cards can be portrayed pictorially.

Step Two: Develop a list of rewards. These should include daily pleasures (e.g., TV, video games), weekly pleasures (e.g., renting a video game, having a friend over), and long-term pleasures. Long term means something you allow your child to earn somewhere between every two weeks to two months. Long-term pleasures can be as simple as allowing a sleepover and as extravagant as your resources, and the stakes involved, allow. You want at least a dozen rewards on your token system, but you can have as many as you'd like, as these items compete with each other (e.g., if she is saving up for the trip to the amusement park, she is not spending her points on DVD rentals). You want your child's eyes to get big when he looks at what he can earn. For ideas, go to a toy or sporting goods store and ask your child what he'd like to earn or turn your child's long-standing petitions for this or that purchase into earning opportunities.

Step Three: Decide how many poker chips or points your child will earn. Use tangible chips for kids in lower grades (about third grade and younger) and points for older kids. If you use chips, assign the colors values of one, five, and ten, and set an approximate range of one to twenty for responsibilities. For points, assign an approximate range of twenty to two hundred for responsibilities. The more challenging a task is for your child to complete, the more chips or points you should assign to it.

Step Four: Add up how many points/chips your child would earn doing only those responsibilities that you require on a daily basis. Now take two-thirds of that number (approximately) and disperse it among those rewards that you allow your child to have access to on a daily basis (i.e., the daily pleasures referred to in Step Two). So, the total cost of all rewards allowed on a daily basis should approximately add up to two-thirds of the minimum number of chips/points your child is allowed to earn *every* day.

Step Five: Figure out the greatest number of chips/points your child will be banking each week if he's an angel. So, there is the one-third left over from the daily responsibilities, plus those he earns for those responsibilities that don't occur every day. With that number in mind, determine how much you want to charge for the weekly and long-term pleasures. There are two extremes to avoid: If you set the values too high, the rewards will seem unreachable and she won't be motivated. If the values are too low, you'll be spending too many resources on your token system and you'll start to resent it. Strive for that easy-to-find middle ground.

Step Six: For chips, establish a bank—an empty plastic milk container with the top cut off works fine. For points, get a tablet or checkbook register for recording deposits and withdrawals. Whenever your child completes a task he's responsible for, you make a deposit. Withdrawals occur whenever your child accesses a reward.

Step Seven: Work out a rough draft of the system, and then tell your child that you've decided that you want to give him more credit and recognition for his good behavior. Then explain how the system works, emphasizing that if you have to tell him to do something three times, he still has to do it but he will no longer get his chips/points. Then ask if there are other rewards he'd like to earn that you hadn't thought of. If yes, recalculate and finalize the system. (Visit www.resilientyouth.com, the Web site supporting this book, for sample contracts and token systems.)

Bonus Advantages of Behavioral Programs

Kids *love* well-constructed behavioral programs. While there might be some initial grousing to the court over having to earn things such as TV and admonishments and that no other child in the universe must endure such horrific burdens, this passes quickly. Your child knows that rules often vary based on your mood. But, a good behavioral program changes that. The program becomes your family's constitution. And, your child becomes a constitutional attorney, often referring to the terms of the program when making her arguments to the court. While having your child act like a constitutional attorney can be annoying, it's usually a big upgrade over his previous criminal status.

In cases of a token system, don't be surprised if your child asks if he might be allowed to do additional chores. (In these moments, it's important to not chuckle out loud.) It has now become in your child's best interest, as he perceives it, to do chores or other things that please you. It's good to offer such opportunities, trying to respect the economy of your system (i.e., that the number of chips/points you allow is proportionate to the amount of effort your child needs to invest).

Another advantage of token systems is your child learns to make decisions about how to spend his resources. Sometimes the initial decisions can be surprising. I once had parents very surprised that their "TV-addicted" daughter decided to go four weeks without watching TV. She didn't want to spend her points on it, preferring to get a new computer sooner. Also delightful to the parents was that once their daughter started watching TV again, she was no longer as enthralled with it, as she had found some other interesting activities during her TV break.

Use Well-Reasoned Punishments

Parents aren't interested in justice—they want QUIET!
Bill Cosby

When it comes to crafting punishments, your expert knowledge of your child is critically important. Alternatively, we parent-lunatics have an Achilles heel when it comes to punishing our children. When our kids hurt, we hurt—and often worse than they do. So, punishing our child, when we're acting with intention instead of with anger, can feel as if we're punishing ourselves. However, we must be willing to endure this pain for the sake of our child; if not, our child will need to learn critical life's lessons from others, often when he's older and the stakes are higher.

One of the trickiest parts of crafting punishments is to figure out if they're needed to begin with. Some punishments are imbued in the situation (e.g., teacher disapproval, feelings of guilt and remorse, social rejection) and so we may need to do very little. If we're tuned in to our child, we likely have a good feel for whether her suffering is commensurate with the transgression. (Also keep in mind that the reward strategies I reviewed above have an inherent punishment built in: When our child is noncompliant, she doesn't get access to a reward that she wants.)

Time-Out

The most helpful and effective punishment for younger children is time-out. Some of you may have tried this without success. Time-out usually fails for one of two reasons. First, some methods of doing time-out are ineffective. Second, time-out doesn't tend to work as well if it's the primary intervention. On the other hand, if you use a conceived time-out in conjunction with the other techniques in this book, it is highly likely to work. Let me explain the two paths into time-out.

The first path into time-out is when your child defies you. It involves four steps:

Step One: Give an *effective* command (making eye contact, using as few words as possible, and making it clear that you're not making a request).

Step Two: If your child hasn't started moving in five seconds (count inside your head to avoid sounding like a drill instructor), reissue the command, but more sternly, adding the threat of time-out. "Sally, get moving on making your bed or it's going to be time-out!"

Step Three: Count five more seconds inside your head. If your child hasn't started moving, tell her to go to the time-out chair. (Notice, only about fifteen seconds has elapsed. So, assuming you were relatively composed to begin with, you're less likely to be suffering from transient brain dysfunction.) Your child should sit in the chair for a minimum sentence of one minute per year she has lived outside the womb. You should not tell your child the length of the minimum sentence, or set a timer for her, as it is more punishing for her to not know how long time-out will last. (Imagine the dentist is going to be twenty minutes late for your next appointment. Which is more painful? Someone telling you it will be twenty minutes, or no one saying a word.)

Step Four: After the minimum sentence has expired, check on your child. If she is fussing, then a new minimum sentence is applied (e.g., another eight minutes for an eight-year-old). Don't tell your child that you're adding to her time, as this could needlessly escalate her fussing. You then continue to add periods of minimum sentences until two conditions have been met: Your child is sitting quietly in the chair, and she agrees to comply with the command.

The second path into time-out is when your child does something objectionable. There are three steps:

Step One: Your child does something especially negative. Let's say your son gets mad at you and knocks his glass of milk over in protest. That's a straight shot to time-out.

Step Two: After the minimum sentence has passed, two conditions must be met for release: He is sitting there quietly, and he is remorseful. If both conditions are not satisfied, begin a new minimum sentence.

Step Three: If your child causes damage to another person, it is important to have him make reparation. It's not good for your child's character development to only apologize. He should try to make it right with the other person. I recommend waiting until your child and you have calmed down (that might be when time-out is over, or it might be the next day) and then do a psychological autopsy of what happened. Part of this review is to discuss how someone else was harmed and to ask your child what he might do to make the situation right. If he can't or won't come up with something, you can decide.

> Seven-year-old Joey got very angry with his eight-year-old sister for besting him in a game (he was convinced she cheated). So, he went to her room and tore the head off her favorite Barbie. When his sister told their parents what Joey had done, Joey was put in time-out. This was infuriating to him because he was being punished while his sister was not. Joey did the time-out and told his sister that he was sorry for destroying her doll, but he was still burning about the alleged cheating.
>
> The next day the matter seemed to be calmed down enough for his parents to discuss the incident further with him. By their questioning, they helped him to decide that it would have been more effective for him to walk away from the game. They questioned him further and got him to acknowledge that his sister had been harmed by what he did. He then decided that the best way to make it right was to replace the doll with his allowance. Joey's sister later thanked him for purchasing her a new doll.

Here are a few suggestions for time-out:

1. When you first start doing time-out, orient your child to the procedure. "Johnny, I really like all of the good things that you do around here. You've mostly been behaving very well. However, there are still a few days when you don't listen. I really hope that won't continue, but if it does, I'm going to tell you to go to time-out. When I do, come and sit in this chair until I say you can get out. The more you fuss, the longer it will last. Also, when you are in time-out, no one will speak to you. Again, let's hope that we won't have to use this that much." Then, for a few weeks, place the chair in a part of the house where it usually doesn't reside. Every time Johnny sees the chair he is reminded that there's a new sheriff in town.

2. Once you've told your child to go to time-out, nothing should keep her out of time-out. Keeping this principle in mind will help you know how to answer a variety of questions: "What should I do if the phone rings?" or "What should I do if my child starts to comply with the command?" or "What should I do if someone rings our doorbell?" or "What if he runs to go do the task?" or "What if he says he has to go to the bathroom?" Barring exotic circumstances, the answer to these are all the same: Nothing should allow your child to escape time-out once you've told him to go there. You want to avoid creating exceptions to your following through on the "go to time-out" command lest you condition those behaviors.

3. The time-out chair should be relatively uncomfortable and placed where you can monitor your child and where he cannot consume entertainment, kick walls, or grab objects.

4. Pretending that you cannot hear your child will answer several questions: "What do I do if my child says he has to go to the bathroom?" or "What should I do if my child says something disrespectful?" or "What should I do if my child says she is sick and is about to throw up?" Barring exotic circumstances, the answer to these questions is the same: There is nothing to do, as you cannot hear your child. To respond to any of these entreaties is to reward that behavior and to increase its frequency when you employ time-out.

5. Time-out needs to be practiced consistently. If your child gets the idea that time-out won't be practiced on Sunday nights, when company is present, or when Dad's watching football, then more unsavory behavior may occur during those times.

6. The real intervention becomes the threat of time-out, not time-out itself. If you're a nine-year-old girl, would you rather spend nine minutes in time-out and then have to make your bed, or just make your bed? This is a no-brainer that you won't have to point out. However, the results will depend on your delivering a time-out each time that you say you will.

7. Some children may need to be restrained. First, I would very clearly define "remaining in the chair," as no matter where you draw the line, your child will stick her toe over it. So, remaining in time-out means both butt cheeks on the chair and all four legs of the chair on the floor for the duration of the time-out. If your child violates this, and assuming you're physically able, the preferred method is to sit behind your child and to cross his arms across his chest as you grip his wrists. (Avoid doing this if

you're angry.) You would say to your child, "I'm doing this only as long as you need me to. Once you can sit here on your own I will let you go." Once you let go, the minimum sentence begins, without you pointing that out.

8. If physical restraint is not practical for you, an alternative method is to tell your child that every time he gets out of the time-out chair he will have to endure a fifteen-minute "no-spend zone." This means that he cannot spend his chips/points (or, if you don't have a token system, he cannot use any pleasures that plug in or run on a battery) and must stay in the house. So, if he gets out of time-out four times, he is on metaphorical bread and water for one hour afterward.

9. If you are in a two-parent household, and one of you is not physically up to doing physical restraint, wait until the other parent is at home when first instating time-out.

10. Once time-out is over, avoid acting apologetic or ingratiating. She committed a crime, served her time, and is now ready to return to polite society: No additional rituals, lamentations, or parades are advisable. As a fellow parent-lunatic, I know how tempting it can be to do otherwise.

11. Sometimes you can avoid time-out scenarios with warnings that commands will soon be forthcoming: "Billy, I'm giving you a head's up that I'm going to be asking you to clean your room in twenty minutes." A related method is to give your child choices in advance: "Susan, would you rather take out the trash before or after dinner?"

Show me a household where time-out doesn't work, and I'll show you a household where one or more of the following is probably true: The children are not being given adequate doses of quality or special time, the primary methods for getting children to behave are punishment-based, or the child or parent is overwhelmed by stress, psychiatric pain, or physical pain. Otherwise, time-out is usually pretty effective.

Token System Penalty

There is also a punishment option if you are using a token system. You can pick one to three responsibilities that your child does inconsistently and add a penalty (or "take-away") of the same number of points/chips that would have been earned had the task been done properly. So, if Jimmy earns ten chips by making his bed, a penalty of ten chips would be established if he doesn't make his bed. This is only done with advance notice and is limited to one deduction per infraction. (Remember, anarchy can result if your child's token system descends to zero.) If you're finding that you have cause to do a take-away for more than three responsibilities, something else is probably wrong (e.g., special time isn't being done consistently, the token system is not consistently applied, the token system is not designed well, your child has a psychiatric problem, or you are experiencing psychological or physical pain that is interfering with your capacity to parent with intention).

Caveats

I have five caveats on this topic:

First, try to avoid consistently using food as a reward. Doing so risks imbuing it with too much importance, which risks disordered eating patterns later.

Second, if you decide to target your child's physical health in your behavior program, don't set weight loss as a goal. Instead, target those behaviors that produce healthy habits. Setting weight or shape as a goal risks promoting an assortment of unhealthy behaviors.

Third, if you decide to target your child's academics in your behavioral program, don't set grades as a goal. Instead, target those behaviors that promote good outcomes. Then, your child will earn the grades that his potential, the appropriateness of the curriculum, and the effectiveness of the instruction allow (see Chapter 9).

Fourth, don't include special time as a reward in your behavioral program. However, don't let your child pull a fast one by trying to access an unearned reward during special time.

Fifth, avoid setting as a reward any activity that you believe is developmentally important for your child. I once worked with a mom whose daughter suffered from a reading disability. They had a weekly ritual of going to the library and reading together; they both enjoyed this and it was advancing the daughter's reading skills, so it was good to keep it out of a behavioral program.

Supportive Strategy

Commit Random Acts of Kindness

The Dalai Lama's . . . motto, "My religion is kindness,"
is one of the simplest, most efficacious statements I have ever
heard. It is like an E = mc² of the Spirit.
Piero Ferrucci, *The Power of Kindness*

Research indicates that the "helper's high" is real. So, pick a particular day in the week to do kind things. Consistent application of this technique could leave you walking through the world feeling as if you are a force for goodness, light, and love. Here are some ideas to get you started:

1. Make an anonymous donation to someone who could use it, telling him or her that you are making this gift in thanksgiving for what someone else did for you.

2. As you go through a drive-through, leave money for the car behind you.

3. As you pull out of the self-service gas station, tape an envelope labeled "for the next customer." Inside leave some money with a note that reads, "I'm cutting down on your cost for gas today. A friend."

4. Leave an outrageous tip the next time you get great service. Include a note on the bill that says, "I'm leaving extra for the pleasure of watching you do your job with excellence."

5. Buy a gift card at a bookstore. Write "You're not alone" in the card and stick it inside a book about a problem for which you have empathy (e.g., a book for parents who have a child with cancer).

6. Buy a gift certificate for a free car wash and stick it in a stranger's windshield wiper with a note: "From a stranger trying to put a little air under your wings."

7. Send a balloon bouquet of thanks to a secretary, nurse, or service provider who did a good job for you or someone you care about.

8. Buy a couple of movie passes, give them to a young couple with kids, and offer to babysit for them.

Strategy Summary

Try to routinely demonstrate your pleasure when your child behaves well.

When your child's behavior is faltering, let him know what *specific* positive behavior you expect from him and what reward he will experience if he follows through.

Make rewards proportionate to the responsibility and try to provide them as soon as possible after the responsibility has been met. Once a given behavior is well established, try rewarding more intermittently.

Avoid corporal punishment; instead, consider allowing your child to experience the natural consequences of his decisions. When those seem insufficient, use time-out.

When your child has damaged another person, arrange for her to make reparation.

When less formal strategies don't seem to be working, implement a contract or a token system. If these fail, or the problems are severe, seek the services of a child mental health professional (see Chapter 10).

Remember, if a behavioral plan is the engine, special time is the grease.

The Skeptical Parent's Challenge

Parent: I was spanked as a child and I turned out okay. What's wrong with giving a kid a whack, without abusing her, when it's called for?

Author: Yes, kids can be spanked and be fine, just as it's possible to drive a nail with a brick. But, many people driving nails with bricks run into problems that people using hammers don't run into. What if it had been possible for your parents to teach you the same lessons and reach the same good outcomes without hitting you? Would that not have been better?

Parent: Modern parents are too much about rewarding kids for doing what they're supposed to do. We're creating a generation of spoiled kids.

Author: Spoiling happens when a parent does not promote a child's capacity for doing things when she doesn't feel like it. Well-constructed behavioral programs not only do not do this, but they promote the development of this psychological muscle through gradated reward and punishment. Moreover, our rewards are often later replaced by self-satisfaction for a disciplined performance.

Parent: I've done time-out before, and in a very similar way to what you've described here, but it didn't work.

Author: I hear this a lot. But, I've never heard it from a parent who is both doing special time and consistently implementing an effective reward program. Should your child be an exception, I would advise securing the services of a child mental health professional.

Promote Healthy Decision Making, Independence and Adaptive Thinking

Illness is in part what the world has done to a victim, but
in a larger part it is what the victim has done with his world.
Karl Menninger, *The Vital Balance*

This chapter calls for some of the trickiest interventions in this book. Most important human endeavors encompass easy and difficult parts. In baseball, it is fairly easy to catch a baseball thrown at your chest as you stand still, and it's difficult to catch one over the shoulder on the run. In parenting, it's fairly easy to praise a child following success, and it's difficult to do the interventions in this chapter. However, before I delve into the subject at hand (and in cases you ever have the opportunity to travel back in time), here's a review of the top ten reasons to not have and to have a child.

Top 10 Reasons to Not Have a Child

10. You like wearing sexy swimwear.

9. You like coming home from work and unwinding without being confronted with questions like, "Why is it rude to fart?"

8. Too many mysteries at a time unseat you (e.g., How do Teletubbies reproduce? How's it possible for a baby to produce this much poop from breast milk? Why do we need three times more gear to travel on a vacation than we needed when it was just the two of us?).

7. You like having disposable income.

6. You were hoping to never have to sit in another one of those little hard chairs they made you sit in when you were in first grade.

5. You prefer to not make mindless statements like, "The next person who touches another person without that person having said that the person could do the touching or who touches with permission but in a different way than the person who gave permission intended, will be required to sit up on the roof rack of this minivan! So help me God!"

4. You never wanted to sound like your parents.

3. You prefer to keep your life between the lines and predictable.

2. You would rather avoid the pressure of having to videotape because you want to preserve every precious moment.

1. You never want to love another person so much that it sometimes interferes with your ability to draw breath.

Top 10 Reasons to Have a Child

10. You like giving the federal government less of your money.

9. You prefer to avoid the interpersonal conundrums affiliated with frequent sexual intercourse.

8. You like solving mundane mysteries like, "Who didn't flush their poopy down the toilet?"

7. You hate the time and expense required to wear the latest fashions.

6. You like sitting in the parents' room in church so you can talk through the homily.

5. You like being able to preboard airplanes without buying an expensive ticket.

4. You enjoy parting crowds at Disney World with your stroller.

3. You value meaning so much that you want it in doses you can't control.

2. You believe that one of the best ways to give back to the world is to give it a loving and talented person who will help to save it.

1. You enjoy an overabundance of hugs, laughter, song, dance, and adventure.

Value Independence

The greatest gifts you can give your children are the roots
of responsibility and the wings of independence.
Denis Waitley

The best-intentioned people are parents. Even when we err, it's with good intentions. In my years of asking parents their reasons for doing this or that ineffective strategy, I've never heard "I'm trying to block his success," "I want him to fail in his capacity to do things when he doesn't feel like it," or "I wish for her to remain dependent on me." No, when we act with intention we're usually trying to accomplish sound goals.

Most of us desperately want our kids to be successful. None of us engaged parents is happier than our least happy child. So, if an important decision needs to be made, or a significant problem needs to be solved, we take care of it. With only a here-and-now focus, this seems like a no-brainer. After all, a manager wouldn't appoint an immature and inexperienced employee to make a decision or to solve a problem when a mature and seasoned person is available; that would be stupid, wouldn't it? So, when our kid comes to us with a problem, question, or decision, we spring into action and secure the good outcome. But if our child becomes accustomed to others doing this for her, she may become hampered in her ability to make decisions and solve problems.

We parents are traveled and experienced people. We also realize that many of our best lessons were learned the hard way. We may have had someone telling us to do this or that to secure a good outcome, but we did it our way, got burned, and then learned that it would have been better to do it in the recommended fashion. It makes sense that we wish for our children's brains to be like hard drives onto which we can download the information stored on our wisdom flash drive. We know that as our children grow older they'll be asked to make more and more decisions, with greater and greater consequences, more and more out of our sight. This scares us. So, we tell them to "learn to think" and "learn to make good decisions." However, what we really mean is, "Read my mind and do that." If we condition our kids this way, they may be less accomplished in their capacity to think for themselves and to make important decisions effectively.

When Bad Things Happen

In Chapter 2, I review how *parents* typically react when a child experiences failure or when bad things happen. This chapter deals with *kids'* responses to painful or troubling events. Maladaptive reactions can include manifestations of self-entitlement, depression, and anxiety.

Self-Entitled Reaction

It's possible for us parent-lunatics to unintentionally condition our child to believe that others owe her a good outcome for her efforts. (See Chapter 2 to review how to avoid such conditioning.) Some kids, on the other hand, seem temperamentally disposed to believe that the world owes them. Such children are shocked when they don't win, when they're made to endure the consequences of their choices, or when something bad happens. They launch forth with tirades and fits. It's remarkable how ingrained this way of thinking can become, even among otherwise intelligent adults.

Depressive Reaction

The depressive reaction is another troubling response to poor outcomes. Unchecked, this can lead to a mood disorder and suicidal thinking. If we could do a psychological autopsy of the mind of a teenager who has committed suicide, we would likely find three predominating thoughts: life sucks, it's my fault, and it can't be changed. A mistake that we adults often make is to believe that we can determine our child's happiness by reviewing the circumstances of his life: being good in sports + earning good grades + being popular + coming from a good home = happiness. However, research suggests that only about ten percent of happiness is attributable to life's circumstances.

More predictive of mood is how a child *interprets* what happens in her life. Some kids think negatively. Thus, when something unfortunate happens, they blame themselves, use the event as proof that everything is fouled up, and conclude that this is just the way it is. Positive events are dismissed as temporary flukes; moreover, children who are depressed end up hearing "You're not really hurting" when their parents offer reassurances. Such children then escalate the behavior, as if to say to their parents, "Please recognize that I'm hurting and have cause!"

Anxious Reaction

The anxious reaction occurs when a child determines that a situation is dangerous, either physically or socially. Once anxious, the child lobbies to avoid the feared situation, person, or thing. As I covered in Chapter 5, enabling this style of coping often does little to promote wellness.

THE STRATEGY

> *Whether you think you can, or think you can't . . . you're right.*
> Henry Ford

Quoting developmental psychologist Dr. Emmy Werner's review of resilient children across studies and cultures: "They also drew on external resources in the family and community. Foremost were affectional ties that encouraged trust, *autonomy, and initiative (emphasis* added)." (Facilitating closeness is addressed in Chapter 1.) Or, consider the summary of happiness from researchers Drs. David Myers and Ed Diener: "In study after study, four inner traits mark happy people: self-esteem, *a sense of personal control (emphasis* added), optimism, and extraversion." (Self-esteem is addressed in Chapters 1 and 2, while optimism and extraversion are mostly a product of temperament, though some of the strategies in this chapter can promote optimistic thinking.)

The following section reviews a number of strategies for promoting decision making, independence, and adaptive thinking.

Promote Decision Making

Two strategies you can employ to promote your child's capacity to make decisions are 1) encourage your child to practice making decisions and 2) teach your child the method of problem solving.

Encourage Decision Making

The first strategy involves not jumping in with advice when your child asks you for help in making a decision, at least if an urgent response isn't needed. "Mom, I can't decide whether to go to Rachel's house to play her Wii or to go with Jennifer and her mom to the movies. What should I do?" Instead of first offering counsel, you might say, "Let's see if I can help you figure out what you want to do. What's good and what's not good about each choice?" After your child reviews her thinking, you can make your points by asking questions instead of by making statements.

Let's say Rachel has a brother who can be counted on to be intrusive, and you don't hear your child considering that point. You might ask, "Will Rachel's brother be there?" If the answer is yes, you can follow up with, "What do you think that would be like as you play her Wii?" Or, if you know the drive to the movie theatre is forty-five minutes but you don't hear that factor, you could ask, "What do you think it would be like to drive for forty-five minutes?" It usually doesn't take long for your child to make a decision. Then, and most importantly, if your child chooses a different choice from what you would have made, it's important to keep that between you and your guardian angel (unless the consequences would be unduly problematic). If she asks if you'd choose otherwise, you can say that what makes you most happy is that she figured this out for herself and feels good about her choice. Afterward, you can debrief her regarding how it went. If she wasn't pleased, you can go back and see if she could have thought about the problem differently at the onset.

To get more practice, look for opportunities to have your child make decisions. Parenting expert Barbara Coloroso would have us routinely give our children choices. She wants her child to wear pajamas. But, rather than just say, "Put on your white sneakers," she looks for an opportunity to have her child make a decision: "Do you want to wear the white sneakers, the black sneakers, or one of each?" Many daily activities can be turned into decision-making opportunities: "Do you want the beef or the chicken?" or

"Do you want to do your homework now or after supper?" or "Would you rather massage my head or my feet?" (Just kidding on that one . . . or am I?)

Teach Problem Solving

The second strategy for promoting decision-making skills is called problem solving, which is a lynchpin strategy. If you can teach your child to solve problems effectively, you will have given him a major gift. There are five steps to problem solving:

Step One: Write down the problem. I realize this might sound a little mechanistic. However, if you've ever had a "family meeting" to deal with a particular problem, you know that it doesn't take long for multiple problems to be on the table, including lamentations that seem to predate books in the Old Testament. Writing down the problem emphasizes that only one specific problem will be addressed at that time.

Step Two: Brainstorm. This is the most difficult step. All possible ideas for solving the problem are stated *without evaluation*. A light switch can't be on and off at the same time—one can't be effectively creative and evaluative at the same time. Say to your child, "Okay, now let's think of all possible solutions, without thinking about whether an idea is good or not. Let's try to get at least ten ideas." Don't stop until you have at least ten ideas followed by two minutes of silence. You want your child generating as many ideas as possible, so hold off with yours until you sense that your child is running out of ideas. When teaching brainstorming, I deliberately throw out impractical ideas. Sometimes the person will say, "But that won't really work," which gives me the opportunity to say, "Remember, we're not evaluating right now."

Step Three: Rate the ideas from one (poor idea) to ten (great idea). It's okay to give different ideas the same rating. At this point you can help your child consider the potential cost and benefit of ideas. Some ideas seem like they might solve the problem but would create new problems; you can help your child understand this by the questions you ask.

Step Four: Try it. This involves working out the particulars. Let's say your child decides the best way to approach not getting enough playing time on his soccer team is to ask the coach what he might do to improve. In this step your child could decide when he might approach the coach and what he might say. Role-playing can also be helpful.

Step Five: Evaluate it. After your child has tried the idea, you can consider whether the problem was solved. If yes, you can reinforce the power of problem solving and her emerging skills. If no, you can go back to the list you generated in Step Three and consider a fall-back option. The only thing you should avoid is deciding that the problem is unsolvable.

Tiffany was a level-headed, though anxious, ten-year-old. Her problem was that her best friend no longer sat with her at lunch. Tiffany generated several creative ideas. The one she settled on was that she'd ask her friend if she (Tiffany) had said or done anything to cause a problem in their relationship; Tiffany and I then role-played what she might say. Tiffany's friend ended up stating that her motivation for changing her lunchtime seat was to befriend another girl and that it had nothing to do with Tiffany (the friend shared that she was going to ask Tiffany to move too but was concerned that she'd be pressuring Tiffany unfairly). Tiffany ended up joining them and the problem was solved, much to Tiffany's relief.

You can also do problem solving as a family. Here's a form you could use:

Problem Solving Worksheet

Problem: _____

_____

_____

_____

_____

_____

_____

_____

_____

_____

_____

Proposed Solutions	Evaluations			
(Do NOT evaluate until you have	Mom	Dad	Billy	Suzie
generated at least 10 ideas.)	+ -	+ -	+ -	+ -
1. _____				
2. _____				
3. _____				
4. _____				
5. _____				
6. _____				
7. _____				
8. _____				
9. _____				
10. _____				
11. _____				
12. _____				

	Give a score from 1-10				
The numbers of ideas with all +s	Mom	Dad	Billy	Suzie	Sum
_____					
_____					
_____					
_____					
_____					

The entire family agrees on the wording of the problem, and each person gets a sheet to write down brainstorming ideas. After brainstorming, family members privately rate every idea by putting either a plus or a minus next to it on their sheet. When finished, everyone shares their ratings. It's typical to find that there are several ideas that everyone has given a plus.

Next, each person privately assigns a number, from one to ten, to each idea that had straight pluses. For each straight-plus idea, sum up the ratings. The idea with the highest total is the winning idea. If none of the ideas receives unanimous pluses (never had it happen), rank ideas that have a majority of pluses.

After you've come up with your number-one solution, try it and evaluate it. (Please see www.residentyouth.com for examples of completed problem-solving sheets.)

As parents, you'll need to declare up front whether you will be operating as a democracy (top score wins) or a benevolent dictatorship (parents decide after considering the scores).

Like special time, this strategy can seem mundane, but it proves to be surprisingly powerful. Psychologists Drs. Mary Firstad and Jill Goldberg Arnold, in reviewing research summaries of family psychotherapy, concluded as follows: "Any meta-analysis of marital or family therapy indicates that the key to [success] . . . involves improving two critical skills: communication and problem solving."

Practice it yourself before doing it with your child. Not only will this help to persuade you that problem solving is powerful, but it can help you understand the method before you try it with your child.

Promote Independence

The hardest part of raising a child is teaching them to ride bicycles. A shaky child on a bicycle for the first time needs both support and freedom. The realization that this is what the child will always need can hit hard.
Sloan Wilson, *What Shall We Wear to This Par ty?*

The guidelines I review in this section are designed to promote independence. The first suggestion, which I've adapted from counsel offered by parenting expert Barbara Coloroso, can be used when your child pushes for independence that you're inclined to forbid. In these moments, ask yourself three questions:

- Is the thing your child wants to do physically harmful?
- Is it psychologically harmful?
- Would it unduly tax your resources?

If the answer to one of these questions is "yes," then it makes sense to say no. However, if the answer to all three is "no," then it may be important to let your child exercise her independence, even though it might drive you nuts.

> Joel (age eleven) and his mother were in high conflict and in the process of getting an emotional "divorce." The top source of contention between them was how he wore his pants. Clothing was his Alamo. He decided that his mother should not have the authority to make him hike his pants up to a position that she deemed acceptable. Joel's mother thought that Joel looked like a gangster when he wore his pants around his hips. He wasn't tripping and suffering head injuries, nor was he violating any school dress codes. She just didn't like the way it looked.
>
> In a separate interview I encouraged Joel's mom to subject this issue to the three questions. Ultimately she decided to promote Joel's strivings toward independence. This decision also went a long way toward reducing the tension in their relationship.

I've also noted that if parents don't regularly use the questions above to help promote their child's independence, they can inadvertently start acting like prison wardens and their children like inmates.

> Nate was a twelve-year-old who was insecure about his appearance. Hence, he would spend twenty to thirty minutes in the morning trying to get the side of his hair to lay right. To do this he would employ a hand mirror so that he could see the side of his hair in the bathroom mirror. His father saw this and judged it to be ridiculous. When he could not get Nate to stop it, he confiscated all hand mirrors. So, Nate would lock himself in the bathroom and use the reflection he could collect in his mother's iron.

Jim was acting like a prisoner and his father a warden. The damage was occurring over a behavior that was not harmful or unduly taxing of the parents' resources.

I know how trying this can be. Two of our children have interests that my wife and I would rather they not have. We let them do these activities, but it's not easy for us.

As was similarly stated in Chapter 3 regarding monitoring, an effective parent loosens the reins a bit more every six or twelve months. The range of what could be physically or psychologically harmful for older kids is not as restrictive as it is for younger kids. You know you're erring too much toward the freedom side if your child is getting into trouble or not meeting her obligations. You know you're erring too much toward the restriction side if you and your child are too often in the roles of warden and inmate and your child is becoming socially isolated.

Promote Adaptive Thinking

The truth is that monsters are real, ghosts are real too.
They live inside us, and sometimes they win.
Stephen King, Introduction to *The Shining*

As I mentioned, less predictive of mood is what happens to a person. More predictive is how a person evaluates what has happened. Many children have temperaments disposed to think in depressive or anxious ways. Two methods that can successfully challenge depressive or anxious thoughts are *thought testing* and *happy thoughts*.

Tanner was a ten-year-old boy whose parents, Lynn and Dan, brought him in for counseling because he was depressed. Because he was not good in sports, had no discernable talents, and was quirky, his peers, especially boys, often rejected him. Testing suggested that Tanner's IQ was in a superior range, though his grades were up and down.

Tanner's parents were growing weary of his negative thinking. They were also feeling impotent in their ability to help him. They learned long ago that if they tried to reassure him following a negative thought (e.g.,

"I'm stupid!"), he would respond by declaring his position even more adamantly. The exchange would usually go like this:

Tanner (upon arriving home): I'm such an idiot!

Lynn: What happened?

Tanner: I got an eighty-five on math.

Lynn: Can I see your test? Well, I see you made some errors in calculation.

Tanner: Right! I'm such a moron!

Lynn: Tanner, you're not a moron. Morons don't make the honor roll like you did last quarter.

Tanner: I'm the biggest moron who ever made the honor roll! That was easy to do, but I'll never do it again because I'm such an idiot!

Lynn: No you're not an idiot. You're a very smart boy.

Tanner: No I'm not!! Everyone at school agrees that I'm a complete idiot!!

Lynn: Well, I disagree (then walks away in frustration).

Thought Testing

An alternative approach to the ineffective conversation above is to use the strategy of thought testing. This strategy is simple to execute but powerful in its impact. In the above example, Lynn might say: "Tanner, sometimes, like many of us, you get depressed. Just like a cold attacks your nose, depression attacks your thoughts. Depression makes you believe things that aren't true because it's a liar. There's a simple way for us to figure out if this thought you're having is true or depression's lie. Let's do an exercise together."

Step One: Write down the thought at the top of a piece of paper. In this case, the thought would be, "I'm an idiot."

Step Two: Draw a vertical line down the middle of the paper. On the left side write, "evidence the thought is true." On the right side write, "evidence the thought is false."

Step Three: Ask your child for all the objective facts that suggest the thought is true. Lynn might say to Tanner: "Okay, Tanner, let's write down all the facts that suggest your thought is true. When I say "facts," I mean things that a policeman could write down in his book and tell to a judge."

This surprises children. They're used to having their negative thoughts immediately argued against by adults.

If Tanner said things like, "I got a D in science last week," Lynn would write that fact down as evidence supporting the thought that he is stupid. However, if he said things like, "Everyone thinks I'm an idiot," she'd have to challenge by saying something like "Wait, Tanner. That is not a fact that a detective could know is true. He can look and see that you got a D in science. But he can't establish that everyone thinks you're an idiot."

If the thought is irrational, your child will have a difficult time coming up with more than a couple of facts that support it. But wait until he says he's done.

Step Four: Ask for all the objective evidence that suggests that the thought is not true. By now the child should understand what you're looking for. If he forgets an important piece of evidence, help him out.

Step Five: Review the sheet with your child. If the thought is irrational, there should be more evidence on the right side than on the left. This leads to the conclusion that the thought is not true. In this instance you can ask your child how he might remind himself that the thought is not true the next time it comes up or distract himself away from the thought (i.e., do something fun or use a happy thought—see below). If the thought happens to have more evidence suggesting it is true, use the problem-solving technique I reviewed earlier to solve it.

> *Change your thoughts and you will change your world.*
> Norman Vincent Peale, *A Guide to Confident Living*

Happy Thoughts

Happy thoughts (which can also be called "coping thoughts") can augment thought testing. Happy thoughts are true thoughts that make a child feel good. One type of happy thought is *something your child believes is true about her.* "I'm popular at school," "I'm a very good singer," or "I'm excellent at cheerleading." Another type of thought can be *something true about the circumstances of her life,* such as "I have a fantastic family," "We have an awesome pool," or "My dog isn't a crotch sniffer" (sorry, I'm just working out my pain). The third type of thought can be *something your child is looking forward to:* "Christmas this year is going to be awesome!"

or "I can't wait to go to the shore in June," or "Fishing on Saturday is going to be a lot of fun."

Thoughts are like jeans: Some are comfortable, while others are not. I often ask kids, "What do you do if you put on a pair of pants and they're so tight that it hurts to wear them?" After they respond with the obvious, I suggest that thoughts work the same way.

So, if your child decides the painful thought is not rational, suggest that she swap it out for a happy thought. Ask your child to make a list of all three categories of happy thought and encourage her to use them throughout the week when an irrational and painful thought attacks her.

Help Deal with Failure

Rule one: Never allow a crisis to go to waste.
They're opportunities to do big things.
Rahm Emanuel, President Obama's former Chief of Staff

Good judgment comes from experience and experience comes from bad
judgment. So, if things aren't going well it probably means you're learning a
lot and things will go better later.
Dr. Randy Pausch

Our children will fail. They will make poor decisions and have both life and others treat them poorly, both by accident and on purpose. What about when painful things happen? I want to share two quotes from scholars to illustrate where I'm going with this discussion. The first is from Dr. Robert Brooks: "Resilient children tend to perceive mistakes as opportunities for learning. In contrast, children who are not very hopeful often experience mistakes as an indication that they're failures." The second is from the psychologist Dr. Froma Walsh: "Studies of hardy individuals found three general characteristics: (1) the belief that they can control or influence events in their experience, (2) an ability to feel deeply involved in or committed to the activities in their lives, and (3) anticipation of change as an exciting challenge to further development . . . ."

In other words, crisis = pain + opportunity. It's the nature of crises to be both painful and to offer opportunities. We're not required to walk through the door of opportunity—and many don't—but it's always there.

Up front, let me caution that it's important to give the pain its due. We hate seeing our children in pain, so we're at risk of rushing to the learning when the pain has not been respected. Pain is the fertile soil out of which opportunity grows. If we rush past the pain, or try to ignore it, we may compromise our child's learning to cope with painful feelings. However, once the pain has been duly experienced, we can ask, What is the opportunity?

> Ryan was an athletically gifted eleven-year-old boy. His parents, Ron and Linda, were also athletically gifted. If there was an all-star team to go out for, Ryan would make it. He was also involved in martial arts and quickly rose through the ranks. Along the way to his black belt he won many tournaments, creating the pleasant problem of finding room for all his trophies.
>
> Because he excelled so, his parents decided to absorb the expense of sending Ryan to a national martial arts tournament a couple of states away. This took a lot of planning and a significant expenditure of resources. However, shortly after the tournament began, Ryan was eliminated from all three events. This was crushing to both him and his parents. In their despondency, they decided to fly home early.
>
> Three months later, the chief instructor at Ryan's karate club, Jerry, congratulated Ron and Linda for the instruction he imagined they'd been giving Ryan. Confused, Ron and Linda said that they didn't know what Jerry was talking about. Elaborating, Jerry said he noticed a new kindness in Ryan toward the less skilled children the club. He said he noticed Ryan giving them individual instruction and encouraging them when they failed. Jerry concluded by saying that Ryan was becoming a leader.
>
> When they got home, Ron and Linda asked Ryan about this. He noted that his failure at the tournament taught him what it is like to not do well at karate and that he didn't want other kids to have to go through that.

We all have many opportunities to model what it means to make lemonade out of lemons. On a recent family vacation to the Jersey shore, my family and I encountered rainy weather for most of the week. Knowing this was coming, I took my daughter Morgan aside and asked her to help me look for the opportunity that this bad luck was going to provide for us. This became our private game, and we discovered a number of opportunities: We got to see a movie in a boardwalk theatre with only our family in attendance (it was like our own private Hollywood screening), we very much enjoyed an afternoon at an arcade playing games, and we had awesome waves to play in when bursts of sun came out between the storms.

Sometimes it takes a while to learn what the opportunity is. Consider the following story:

> Michael was a university professor and father of two children. Both of Michael's children were scholastically accomplished. However, his eldest child, Sarah, who was in the sixth grade, earned a C on one of her report cards. This was the first time she had not had straight As. So, she felt dejected and was fearful that Michael would be upset. Michael realized that his daughter was motivated and that her C was probably due to some easily correctable problem. Seeing how badly she felt, Michael hugged her and told her that he understood that she felt badly. Sarah was grateful for the fact that he was being empathic, but his reaction did not relieve her sadness.
>
> Michael left for a few minutes and came back with a weathered document. He explained that it was his own sixth-grade report card. Sarah opened it and was surprised to read comments like "not a very good reader" and "doesn't seem to understand the material very well" and mostly C to B grades. Michael thought it a lucky break that he stumbled upon that report card (he wasn't looking for it and hadn't seen it in more than thirty years). Like Sarah, Michael had usually gotten sterling report cards, but that year the teacher and he did not connect.
>
> Michael remembered feeling very bothered by that report card. But, it took him more than thirty-five years to discover at least one opportunity that it provided. The fact that thirty-five years had passed provided an extra dose of meaning for both of them.
>
> Feeling extra delighted, Michael went on to joke, "And if that doesn't help you, let me share that once a chemistry teacher in high school, when I asked him what my grade on a midterm was, told me that I earned less than half of my age!" Sarah and Michael both belly laughed as she buried her head in Michael's chest.

Another opportunity imbued within painful events is represented by the formula comedy = pain + time. To illustrate, the following is a vignette from my personal life that I've used multiple times in my work with kids.

At this point I was around age twelve. Having been born without lateral incisors (the teeth next to the big ones, center top), I had an ortho- dontist move my teeth around so that I could wear a partial plate with two prosthetic teeth. However, the plastic holding the teeth to the partial wasn't well designed for a twelve-year-old boy's lifestyle. So, they'd inter- mittently break and need to be repaired. At the point that a third repair was required (one of the prosthetic teeth broke off), and weary of the expense, my father decided to do his own repair. As he kept a can of my sister's baby teeth on his workbench, and there was some DNA overlap between us, he decided to glue one of her baby teeth onto my partial and pass it off as repaired. My protestations—that the tooth was a different size and color than mine and that once others at school saw it I would be banished to twelve-year-old social hell—bounced off him like gnats off a windshield. So, I went to school with this freakish tooth that, to me, was akin to having an elephant's tusk protruding from my mouth. And, by the time second period rolled around, I started feeling dizzy from the smell of the epoxy fumes; by third period I experienced my first-ever "buzz," which gave me an entirely new perspective on algebra. So, whenever one of my teen clients laments sibling life I'll sometimes quip: *But,* I bet you've never had your sister's tooth glued into your mouth.

During the academic year I host a monthly television program on mental health issues entitled *Mental Health Matters*. During a recent edi- tion of the show, I asked the panel of four experts this question: "Let's say it were possible to engineer a childhood that was failure free. Would you want to do it?" All four people instantly declared "No!" As one of them put it: "An adult who has never been tested by failure—and learned the lessons failure teaches—would likely be a very vulnerable person."

Supportive Strategy

Test the Premise that Crisis = Pain + Opportunity

Your pain is the breaking of the shell that encloses your understanding.
Kahlil Gibran, *The Prophet*

Every situation, properly perceived, becomes an opportunity.
Helen Schucman

In this book I'm arguing that opportunity is pain's Siamese twin. But, you can test this premise for yourself. Write down the ten worst things that have happened to you. Do this before reading the next paragraph.

Now, for each of the ten events, do the following:

1. Rate the pain you experienced from one to one hundred, with one hundred being the greatest amount of pain that you could ever feel.

2. Ask yourself, "Are there any ways that my life is now better because I experienced that pain?"

3. Rate the value of the benefit you experienced, from one to one hundred.

I've done this exercise with many people. I typically see one of two outcomes. The first outcome is that people either make the connection between pain and opportunity, or they let me know that they already knew the connection. The second outcome is that people see very little upside from their suffering.

I've noticed that people in the first group seem to be doing better and suffer from less depression, anxiety, and stress than people in the second group. Moreover, I've never once had someone in the second group, as a function of completing a course of psychotherapy, not come to discover the opportunities that they hadn't noticed before.

If the dots connect for you, use this information in your daily life. As you experience inconveniences, surprising stresses, and legitimately painful things, give the pain its due. Notice it. Feel it. Let yourself remember that it is natural to experience it. Then, when you've given the pain its due, wonder where the gift is.

Strategy Summary

Try to look for opportunities to offer your child choices; the more choices she makes, the more she is practicing decision making. As she matures and has success, expand the range of her choices and freedom.

When your child asks to do something you're inclined to forbid, ask yourself if he would be harmed or if your resources would be unduly taxed. If not, consider it an opportunity to provide him with increased independence.

Many problems can be well addressed using the problem-solving method reviewed in this chapter. This can be put to use at work, in your marriage, with friends, and with your child.

Once you have the knack of it yourself, it's easy to help your child figure out whether his negative thoughts are true by using the thought-testing method in this chapter. If the painful thought is deemed false, you can ask your child to substitute a happy thought or to distract himself by doing something fun. If the painful thought proves to be true, you can loop into problem solving.

Opportunity is imbued within all crises. After the pain has been given its due, help your child look for the present.

The Skeptical Parent's Challenge

Parent: Problem solving? Thought testing? I'm not a psychologist. How can I be expected to help my kid with this stuff?

Author: I realize that much of this material may be new to you. However, it's been around for a long time, and—speaking from considerable experience—you don't need a psychologist to learn, apply, and coach these strategies. With a little practice, you'll get it. And, if not, it's likely there is a qualified mental health professional in your area who can help (see Chapter 10).

Parent: There are days that I do the exact opposite of what you've counseled. I solve the problems. I direct how something should be thought about. I try to keep my kid from hurting and modeling poor coping. So, you seem to be implying that I'm messing him up in more ways than I can count.

Author: All of the things you say that you do I've also done, do, and probably will continue to do in the future. I try hard to minimize them, but I get tired, distracted, and grouchy, and then parent reactively. This book is not about how to be a perfect parent. Hardly. This book is about how to parent when you are acting with intention. (See also the Introduction for a discussion on the difference between shepherding and sculpting parenting models.)

Parent: Sometimes $#@! happens, and there is no good that comes from it.

Author: I realize that many believe this. And, I can't point to a definitive research study that proves such a perspective wrong. I've just never seen an example of it. The best examples I have of the contrary perspective are parents who have had a child die. Is a greater pain possible? But, time and time again, I've seen such parents find the opportunity imbued within that pain. Certainly, every one of these parents would go back in time and save their child if they could, but, they've discovered the gifts that that vicious and cruel dragon was guarding.

Take Care of Yourself and Your Relationship with Your Significant Other

Even if you're married and both of you actively parent, the resulting exhaustion can cause you to fantasize about bigamy—not for sexual reasons, but so that there might be another adult to share the labor.

To those readers who are single parents (and in the United States alone there are about 19.3 million of you): You have—from the rest of us—our deep respect and admiration. To parent well as a single parent is to reach an incredible height of love and selflessness. In homage to what you do, I offer some potential bumper stickers:

- *Don't get into a knife fight with a single parent.*
- *DON'T HONK! I'm a single parent and it could put me over the edge.*
- *Single parents know how to party (because we never get to).*

- *I'm a single parent. Marry me, give me money, or get out of my way.*
- *My kid has a single parent. Think twice before messin' with him.*
- *Single parents don't date. We interview.*
- *Don't take it personally. I'm a single parent and too busy to return calls.*
- *Earn karma: Hug a single parent (but shower first).*
- *Single parents should have reserved parking.*
- *If you can read this you're probably not a single parent because you can focus long enough to read such a long sentence.*
- *I'm not superhuman. I'm just a loving single parent.*

The research makes it clear that our child's wellness is tied to ours. This chapter focuses on the challenges of resolving family-of-origin issues, of self-care, and of couple-care.

Resolve Old Business

If you don't believe in ghosts, you've never been to a family reunion.
Ashleigh Brilliant

Unresolved pain tends to control us, often in surprising ways. The person who comes from a painful childhood, when leaving home, often feels emancipated. "Thank God I'm out of there!" However, without having come to terms with what happened, she can be surprisingly controlled by the very history she wishes to put behind her.

How much pain did you experience growing up as a kid? If you had a happy childhood, and assuming you're an insightful person, you're blessed and may be free to chart your own course with your family or to just borrow from the one you grew up with. However, if you experienced significant abuse or neglect, or even just suffered typical slings and arrows, and you haven't done any work on understanding and healing those wounds, you may be impacted in ways you don't realize.

Rachel grew up with her two birth parents and a younger brother. Her father spent his days plumbing and his evenings drinking. When not drinking, her father was generally silent. After the first couple of drinks he'd become affectionate but in an ineffective fashion. After the next couple of drinks he'd become irritable, erupting verbally if anyone disturbed him.

Rachel described her mother as "an angel" who would tend to her and her brother's basic needs. She also did everything she could to avoid upsetting their father, including keeping the children silent and away from him.

At a young age, Rachel took over many parenting responsibilities and also avoided bringing friends to the home, because her father embarrassed her. A gifted athlete and actor, Rachel also hid her athletic and performance schedules from her parents, as she was worried that her father would show up drunk. Rachel could not wait to leave home, with her only regret being that she felt like she was abandoning her brother.

By the time she was thirty-two, Rachel was finding it difficult to maintain a romantic relationship. While she was driven, and had a successful career as an attorney, she found she was attracted to men who needed someone to rescue them. While the initial stage of the rescue would be passionate, Rachel would soon find that the man had needs she couldn't address. Alternatively, she was not attracted to men who seemed to have their act together; words like "nice" and "friend" and "boring" came to mind. This confused her so she just concluded that the problem was insurmountable. Hence she swore off dating and decided to have a child on her own.

A common way that adults try to deal with pain from the past is to bury it: "The past is the past. Leave it there," or "What good does it do to remember any of that stuff? It doesn't change a thing." The problem is that this type of pain is buried alive, not dead, and it continuously claws to get out. So, the options are to

- sedate it (e.g., abuse alcohol, work excessive hours, engage in compulsive behaviors);
- throw oneself into efforts to make sure it stays buried (e.g., avoid intimacy, restrict emotions, avoid conflict);
- act it out (e.g., repeat the original parenting script or its extreme opposite);
- unearth it, understand it, and disempower it.

How many people grow up hating a behavior in their parent only to later find themselves either showing that very same behavior or marrying someone who does? How many adults find themselves abusing or neglecting their children, even though they swore they would never do such a thing? How many parents are too lax with their kids because they were treated harshly, or enmeshed with their children because they were neglected?

Jennifer was a strong woman in a solid, twenty-year marriage. Both she and her marriage survived the death of a child, at age two, from cancer. Jennifer also had two physically healthy teenage children, although one was prone to depression and the other to bouts of anger and anxiety. Jennifer was a successful bank executive who was in a long-term recovery from cocaine dependence; in her support group she had taken on a leadership role and had "helped to save the lives of many."

Jennifer came to see me because she continued to suffer from bouts of depression even though, as she put it, her life was "fantastic." My evaluation suggested that Jennifer was dealing well with the loss of her child and that her recovery from addiction was strong.

One of six children, she described her childhood as happy. She indicated that she came from a large and traditional Polish-Catholic family. I learned that Jennifer's father was often absent from the home, working in his career as a politician. She described his interpersonal style as austere, though she knew that he loved her very much. She described her mother as a disciplinarian who was overextended taking care of the household and the children.

When I asked who met her emotional needs growing up, it was as if I asked her who provided her with the gasoline for her private jet; the question was foreign. Upon reflection, she realized that her reaction was a symptom and that she was primarily left to meet her own emotional needs growing up. Hence, her inherent sense of worthiness was fragile, even though she knew she had multiple competencies.

The result of this is that she felt fine about herself as long as her colleagues, family, and associates reflected back to her that she was doing well. But, if such reflections were absent, she felt worthless and life seemed devoid of meaning. To find peace she had to unearth the feelings of longing and emotional deprivation from her childhood that were buried alive. Once she did this, she could begin an even more successful recovery.

The Importance of Self-Care

The biggest thing I remember is that there was just
no transition. You hit the ground diapering.
Paul Reiser

Just about everything that significantly affects me affects my kids. Just about everything that significantly affects my kids affects me. This is what it means to live in a system. This is why self-care is an extremely important parenting agenda. That said, we parent-lunatics often underestimate the impact that *our* stress has on our children. For instance, and according the 2010 edition of the American Psychological Association's *Stress in America* survey, 69 percent of parents indicate that their personal stress has no more than a slight impact on their children, but 91 percent of youth indicate that they know when their parent is stressed (because of increased yelling, arguing, and complaining) and between 25 and 47 percent of tweens feel sad, worried, or frustrated secondary to their parents' stress.

When I was in training, one of the first family interviews I observed involved a family that was under a great deal of stress. The father was a responsible man who was in a job that demoralized him. The sole earner, he endured the job for his family's sake. However, he was in denial about what impact his daily imprisonment had on the family. "I'm very careful to leave work at work. I do not bring it home with me and so my kids are not affected by it."

What he learned was that there was less of him available for his family life because of what he had to endure at work. His daily grind kicked the teeth out of his spirit. True, he didn't talk about his work at home, but he didn't talk about much else, either. And while he attended family functions and extracurricular activities, he did so in a silent, yawning fashion.

Most of us have plenty of well-thought-out reasons for neglecting self-care. "I can't be happy unless my kids are happy," "I must address the business of life and my kids' needs before I can take care of myself," "It would be selfish for me to take care of myself when my family needs me."

When receiving preflight instructions on an airplane, the flight attendant asks adults traveling with children, should the oxygen masks drop, to put the mask on themselves first, before attending to their child. How helpful am I to my child if I'm passing out from lack of oxygen? I've seen many, many families where the household is going down in flames, the oxygen masks have long since dropped, but all of the oxygen is going to the children.

> Cheryl adopted her niece Julie at age one after Julie's parents died in an accident. When Julie was thirteen, Cheryl brought her to me because she was defiant. The evaluation suggested that Cheryl needed help setting up behavioral strategies for Julie. I also learned that Cheryl was depleted because she practiced little self-care and had been "running on empty" for years.
>
> She said she used to enjoy bowling and had been successful in league play but no longer had time for it. One of my recommendations was that she go back to bowling. Cheryl strongly resisted my suggestion. Cheryl thought Julie needed her at home and she'd feel guilty if she didn't accommodate Julie's needs. I finally had to challenge her (with a smile): "Cheryl, stop being so selfish! Julie needs for you to not indulge your feelings of guilt so that she can have a more effective mom. Please, go bowling!"
>
> Cheryl started going bowling and doing so also helped her to realize that she needed to upgrade her health habits, which she did. The cumulative effect was that she had much more energy available to follow through on the behavioral strategies we developed for Julie.

Materialism and Self-Care

When it comes to happiness, it is easy for my beliefs and my behavior to come into conflict. What does my *behavior* say about my formula for happiness? Does my *behavior* suggest I believe that the way to be happy is to earn more income? Is being happy about acquiring possessions? Is working lots of overtime the way to be happy? Does my *behavior* suggest that I believe the only way to have fun is to become intoxicated, to create a six-pack on my stomach, or to eliminate all signs of dirt and grime from my life? If I kept a time log of what I do, what would it suggest about my formula for happiness?

The collective attitudes about income and happiness are ironic. If you ask the average person whether the statement "Money cannot make you happy" is true or false, most will say "true." But if you ask him what sort of changes in his life would make him happier, he'll say having more money. Indeed, Dr. Frankie Laanan surveyed more than 10,000 freshmen attending community colleges about their reasons for attending school. The top one was to land a better job; a very close second was to make more money.

Money offers more choices and fewer burdens. And, wealthy people have the opportunity to spend their money in ways that promote happiness (e.g., lifting the burdens of others). But there's a fine line between having a healthy relationship with money and pursuing an agenda that does not promote, and may even interfere with, happiness. Here are three common ways that an unhealthy pursuit of money can interfere with happiness:

First, money itself doesn't seem to promote happiness once you are fed, clothed, sheltered, safe, physically healthy, and educated. For instance, research on lottery winners indicates that their level of happiness returns to whatever it was prior to their hitting the number within a year after winning. Moreover, case studies of unhappy wealthy people reveal that money not only doesn't cause happiness but makes it easier for people to make choices that interfere with happiness. In my clinical experience, those who are wealthy are easily persuaded by these arguments.

Second, people who spend too much energy guarding their money tend to shrink within themselves. If money is my backstop, I worry that my family and I will fall into an abyss if I don't have enough of it. Certainly, we do well to pursue enough money to take care of our basic needs. But if I'm already living comfortably, excessive clutching onto money can cause quite a bit of discomfort and loneliness.

Third, we buy possessions that end up owning us. Not only do these possessions consume our money but our time and energy. They need to be maintained, polished, and repaired. Imagine a man going to a novelty shop and spending half of his savings on golden, diamond-studded handcuffs. He then goes home and handcuffs himself to a tree because he hopes this will make him happy. Silly, huh? The man shackled to his tree is less free to dance, to experience the bounty imbued within creation, and to love. This is also true of us if we spend large amounts of time serving our things.

Once each year I sit on a panel of professionals who meet with undergraduates who have not declared a major. I see how confused these students feel. They not only have little idea what vocation to choose, but they also are lost regarding how to make a choice. When I've asked such students what they want, they often say that they wish to be happy. If I followed up with, "And, what does it take to be happy?" they've often said, "Have a good family and a good job." These are reasonable goals. It's just that these kids seem to have little idea what constitutes a "good job," other than a feature of it is that they can make enough money to do those things that they *really* want to do when they're not working. Many of them don't seem to realize that happiness can be engendered *because* of a vocation.

Couple-Care

All men make mistakes, but married men find out about them sooner.
Red Skelton

And when . . . Socrates was asked if one should marry . . . he answered:
"If you do not marry . . . you are lonely, your family dies out, and a
stranger inherits; if you do, you suffer perpetual anxiety, querulous
complaints, reproaches concerning the marriage portion, the heavy
displeasure of your relations, the garrulousness of a mother-in-law . . .
and no certain arrival of an heir."
Heinrich Kramer and James Sprenger, *The Malleus Maleficarum*

While it often surprises people who have never had both a child and a spouse at the same time, multiple studies indicate that having kids weakens marital satisfaction and that kids leaving home strengthens it. There are many reasons for this, but a common theme is that the presence of kids often makes parents treat their relationship like a cactus, which survives in spite of neglect. However, many committed relationships are like orchids—uniquely beautiful if maintained but quickly threatened if neglected. Show me a household where the adult committed relationship is attended to only after life's obligations have been met, and I'll show you a relationship that is either breaking down or very susceptible to such.

John and Mary came in for marriage counseling. They were arguing routinely, were not engaging in shared pleasurable activities, and were not having sex more than once or twice a year. They noted that they knew each other well when they married and used to enjoy each other a lot. But early in their marriage three major changes happened: They had a child, John launched a printing business, and Mary started a career as an educator. For years they did little to nurture their relationship, because their jobs, their kid, and their household "demanded" all of their time.

Early in their counseling, John and Mary came to understand that they needed to change their mechanics. The exercises their therapist asked them to do took a cumulative two hours each week to perform. They did them for a short while, with instant benefit. However, they found it too difficult to consistently invest in their relationship and dropped out of treatment.

John and Mary were not prepared to make the time for each other because they thought—somehow someway—they could get by just giving each other scraps of time. Five years later they divorced, after Mary found out that John was having an affair with a co-worker.

A few years ago a good friend and I took a day fishing trip. On the commute my wife called me. My friend heard me say things like "Uh huh," "fifteen minutes," "Okay," and "Later." When I hung up I said, "If this keeps up soon we'll be reduced to clicks and whistles," and I imitated a Kalahari bushman. My friend almost crashed the car from laughing, not because what I said was brilliantly comic but because he could very much relate. At that point in our history, my wife and I had left our relationship on autopilot.

Couples who fall prey to the time trap report having unexciting sex lives, do not open up to each other, argue in a caustic fashion (or maintain tense ceasefires), and spend little time together having fun. Sometimes these couples report having conversations, but they're often limited to reviewing the mundane or dividing labor.

Do we, as a society, sufficiently make clear to prospective couples how difficult long-term commitment is? Do we sufficiently articulate the sort of maintenance schedule that is called for or how to respond when the relationship breaks down? I'm estimating the answer to be "no" for three reasons.

First, nearly half of first marriages and 60 percent of second marriages end in divorce. Second, about one out of ten people report having been unfaithful to their committed partner, with the risk increasing by 1 percent for each year of marriage. Third, most couples who come to therapy seem to know very little about how to make a long-term relationship work.

An exercise I often do with couples is to ask them to fill in the grid of Chart 7.1.

To get the full effect, get out a sheet of paper, make the squares, and fill them in before reading on. (A blank form can be found at www.resilient youth.com.)

I find that a person who knows herself and her partner well can fill in each square in about the same amount of time. On the other hand, couples who are young in their relationship, or have not been tested by conflict, struggle mightily to fill in #2 and #4. And couples who come in for marriage counseling often struggle to fill in #2 and #3.

Relationship events are like a waltz. They don't exist without both people participating. Certainly, one person is usually leading the waltz, and the roles may switch, but the dance doesn't happen without both people engaging.

Were I to quickly summarize couple's counseling, I would say it's to move some of the mental energy from squares #1 and #4 to squares #2 and #3. The notion is that if I'm a person in a conflict-laden relationship, I most likely want to tell a therapist what I'm doing to invest in the relationship (#1) and what my partner is doing that is messed up (#4). However, couple's counseling tries to make me more aware of what I'm doing to contribute to the problem (#2) and to develop an appreciation for what my partner is doing that is helpful (#3).

I can't count the number of times I've seen marriages with sound foundations break up because of three interrelated misconceptions about romantic relationships. These misconceptions collectively act as a flame that can easily draw in weary moths:

The first suggests that true love is something that just "happens" to people. This myth goes that if the union is sound, positive feelings are

Chart 7.1

	What this person does to promote the health of our relationship	What this person does to interfere with the health of our relationship
Me	1	2
My Partner	3	4

strong and consistent, and if such feelings are lacking, or are replaced with negative feelings, the union is unsound.

The second misconception is that good relationships should not be extremely difficult, even some of the time. Folks subscribing to this myth say things like "This relationship is difficult." That's like saying, "This swimming is exerting." It's in the nature of swimming to be exerting, and it's in the nature of long-term romantic relationships to require back-breaking psychological labor, at least some of the time.

The third misconception is that if one has "fallen out of love" the fix is to find true love.

Jack was married to his wife, Rose, for eleven years. They had two children. Jack and Rose didn't argue much, but they were distant from each other. While they had sex a couple of times a month, it inspired as much passion as flossing their teeth. They rarely had fun together and usually did not communicate beyond discussions about the child care and how to divide labor.

Meanwhile, Jack developed a sexual attraction for a divorced woman at work. As do many in this situation, he continued to put himself in progressively riskier (and more exciting) situations with the co-worker until finally (and inevitably), they had sex. The ensuing affair was tumultuous and passionate. On the one hand, he felt crushing guilt whenever he was home and interacting with his wife and children. On the other hand, he found his wife's behavior to be even more noxious and unattractive, particularly when he compared it to the highly doting and sexualized approach that his lover took with him.

Rose didn't stand a chance in this competition. It was the long-term, poorly maintained, and "real" relationship (e.g., having to pay bills, take care of kids, divide labor) with her versus the short-term, infatuated, sometimes intoxicated and sexually charged relationship with the co-worker.

In his mind, Jack realized most of this, but he couldn't stop himself. He told Rose about the affair, asked for a divorce, and moved in with the coworker. One year later the co-worker asked him to move out: Not only had the infatuation died, but the co-worker was unwilling to live with the downside of Jack's reality (i.e., alcohol abuse, divorce conflicts, and child-rearing problems).

Of course, there is more at stake here than just our happiness. Modeling is a powerful agent for instilling attitudes in our children. Though both are important, the behaviors we model in our romantic relationships likely have a greater influence on our kids than what we say about our romantic relationships.

THE STRATEGY

Love yourself first, and everything else falls in line.
You really have to love yourself to get anything done in this world.
Lucille Ball

What may be done at any time will be done at no time.
Scottish Proverb

Here, I offer tactics for the following: recovering from old pain, finding meaning in your work, experiencing rejuvenation from recreation and investing in and maintaining your relationship with your significant other.

Heal Old Pain

Most of us become parents long before we have stopped being children.
Mignon McLaughlin

Try this exercise: Get a regular 8.5 x 11–inch sheet of paper and draw a vertical line down the center. On the left side put what you most value about your childhood. On the right put what troubled or troubles you about it. Take at least thirty minutes to complete this exercise, but the longer the better, even if it's over the course of a few days.

After you're done, see how upset you feel about the pain and ask your significant other or a trusted friend to tell you if she or he believes you are currently affected by what you've written on the right side (the latter assumes that the other person knows you well, cares for you, is insightful, and is willing to tell you things that may be challenging to hear). If you are at peace about what is on the right side of your paper, and people who know you well agree, then you're probably fine. Otherwise, a healing protocol may be in order.

Planning to resolve pain from our family of origin can feel like planning to climb an icy edifice naked with no gear. It's so, so easy to walk away from the task. But, as I argue above, the more we come to terms with such pain, the less it affects our current life and the better a parent and lover we stand to be.

An excellent way to work on such pain is to be in an effective psychotherapy. In saying this, I speak as an academic who reviews this science on a regular basis, as a practicing clinician, and as a psychotherapy client (twice). I will say much more about mental health services in Chapter 10, but here I wish to emphasize that counseling can be an excellent way of trying to unearth, understand, and disempower buried-alive pain. Important aspects of these feelings and thoughts often lie outside of our awareness and can be exceptionally challenging to understand and resolve. A skillful psychotherapist can make this investigation fruitful and life giving. As a man, I will never give birth to a child. But, as a psychotherapist, I've given rebirth to more people than I can count. The following is one example:

> Lisa was a forty-three-year-old married mother of two girls, ages ten and seven, and a boy, age twelve. She first came to see me in order to get her youngest daughter care for attention-deficit/hyperactivity disorder (ADHD) and bipolar disorder. Through the course of that successful work it became clear that Lisa was depressed and that she was unhappy in her marriage to her husband, Randy.
>
> After a few marriage-counseling sessions, we learned that Lisa was not ready to receive from Randy what she said she wanted. This caused us to suspect that buried-alive pain was dominating her, so we started individual counseling. We learned that Lisa was devastated by the loss of her father at age seven. As she remembered it, she was his princess and he was her sun and stars. While she had been close to her mother, she was her father's baby. After his death, not only did she do little grieving, but she also experienced her mother becoming emotionally unavailable (her mother struggled to support the family by working two jobs). She experienced some closeness with an aunt, but she mostly learned to live without much affection. Lisa learned that to get closer to her husband,

she would need to gain peace regarding the unresolved feelings from her childhood.

Our work took the form of her learning about, and coming to terms with, the complex array of feelings that she had for both parents. As she did so, she and her husband drew much closer, which in turn benefited their children greatly.

There are other viable ways to work on ourself that can be done in conjunction with, or even instead of, psychotherapy: support groups, self-help books, and spiritual direction, for example. It is just as important to ensure that the professionals we work with are duly qualified and practice methods that have scientific support. Because such work occurs in vulnerable areas of our lives, we do well to recognize that we can be susceptible to the influence of misguided, or even dubiously motivated, "experts."

Parents who do this kind of work are so strong. Instead of swimming in a current of pain that has usually existed for generations, such a parent finds a way to stand in the current, break the cycle of pain, and offer a new course for her children. This type of difficult work is usually a private affair that is not done to applause; this is part of what helps to make it so glorious.

Develop Self-Care through Work and Play

Nothing has a stronger influence psychologically on their environment and especially on their children, than the unlived lives of the parents.
Carl Jung, *Psychological Reflections:*
An Anthology of the Writings of C. G. Jung

My father didn't tell me how to live; he lived, and let me watch him do it.
Clarence Kelland

To parent with intention, I need to be mentally well. In this section I focus on two aspects that can make a significant contribution to that outcome: effective work and play.

The most important component in being happy is to have close and effective relationships. Car engines run on gas. Humans run on love. One way to love is to execute a vocational life that makes a positive difference, whether delivered inside or outside the home. So, I would ask: Are you doing what you can, without compromising your most important relationships, to get the most out of your vocational life? Show me a parent who sees himself as effectively making the world a better place, and I'll show you a parent who is both bringing a dynamic person to his relationship with his child and modeling an effective way of living.

Matt was a thirty-five-year-old grocery clerk who made minimum wage. His primary job was to bag groceries. While a primary vulnerability in Matt's life was his low intelligence, a primary asset was his sense of mission. Matt strived to bag groceries with excellence. He did not want customers with less strength unduly taxed, nor did he want to see the quality of the groceries diminished by the process of being bagged and transported. Thus, he was very careful. Even more importantly, Matt saw himself as having the opportunity to bring a bright moment to each customer's day. Thus, he would compliment, offer help, and otherwise charm customers. Such was his skill that regular customers would endure a longer wait in order to be in Matt's line. Matt's vocational life had meaning, though he was paid very little.

Tim was a dentist and investor who grossed three quarters of a million dollars per year. While he could have taken pride in the fact that he took great care of his patients' dental health, he did not look at things that way. Instead, he was preoccupied with income production. Tim didn't see patients walking into his office; he saw dollar signs. Thus, he endeavored to move patients through his office in a manner that best suited his bottom line. Tim did a lot of good, but this was lost on him. To the world around him, Tim was a "success." But, Tim was miserable, because he never made enough money to silence the demons that plagued him. Moreover, his family knew that he would not be available to them unless he thought he had generated enough income that week; weary of this, and angry at him for his refusal to do couple's counseling, his wife divorced him. He also became alienated from his four children during the ensuing legal battles. A few years later he was seriously contemplating suicide.

When I speak to those undeclared undergraduates I mentioned earlier, I suggest to them that the formula for getting electricity in their veins in their vocational life is to figure out what they *excel* at and then to deliver it in service to others. If you have not achieved this, then it could be very beneficial to your children for you to consider whether it might be possible and practical for you to do so. You could start by trying some of the strategies listed in Chapter 2.

Alternatively, if you hate your job but cannot make an external change, ask yourself if a different perspective or approach would be helpful. Too many of us give away our power: "I can't enjoy my job because my boss is a jerk," or "I can't get important things done because the system won't let me." Potential solutions to these sorts of toxic work environments are too varied for me to review here. But, I can suggest trying some of the techniques discussed in other parts of this book: problem solving, looking for the opportunity imbued within crises, thought testing, communicating effectively when doing conflict resolution, resolving past pain, and maintaining good self- and relationship care. If these fail to help, I recommend seeking the services of a good mental health professional.

> Jim was a psychiatrist who had a rich and rewarding vocational and family life. He also played low-stakes poker once a month, went to a weekly happy hour with co-workers, and intermittently fished and golfed with friends. All of these activities were done with the blessing of his wife, who had her own outside engagements that Jim supported. Moreover, Jim was generally in a great mood after he finished one of these activities, and his children enjoyed the stories he shared.

I would argue that children benefit if we have, and pursue, interests that exist outside of our family and vocational lives. If your vocational and family lives are rich and rewarding, this may not be critical. However, outside and effective engagements can allow you to feel revitalized, making you a better person to those you love; you will also be offering your children very valuable role modeling. Personal recreation needn't take a lot of time nor compromise other important personal, vocational, and family agendas.

If you're at a loss about where to begin, consider the list of activities in Chapter 2 and see if any of them might be fun to try, or ask a friend if you can tag along when she or he next engages in a hobby or fun activity. A new interest could end up being a gift to you, your child, and your partner.

Build a Strong Relationship with Your Partner

*Marriage makes people treat each other as articles of
property and no longer as free human beings.*
Albert Einstein

*Marriage is three parts love
and seven parts forgiveness of sins.*
Lao Tzu

You can infuse more intimacy into your relationship in a number of ways: Write a gratitude letter, do special time for couples, spice up your sex life, recreate together, do nice things for your partner, and employ discipline when attempting to resolve conflicts.

Write a Gratitude Letter

Returning to the relationship grid in Chart 7.1, reflect on what falls in square #3. Then, create a gratitude letter that incorporates those thoughts and other things that you are grateful for about your partner (be sure to address it directly to your partner and avoid using the third person). I've been asking families to do gratitude letters for years with surprising—at first to me and continuously to them—success.

We humans are often quick to tell family members when they've annoyed us, but we sometimes keep our positive thoughts to ourselves, or just take them for granted. Gratitude letters help to put us on a higher path. (See the sidebar "Write One Gratitude Letter Per Month" on page 30 for a description of the method.)

One caution: Offer the letter without an expectation of a particular response; otherwise you could end up stressing your relationship.

Have Special Time

Another way to build your relationship is to spend at least one hour per week doing special time. In the couple's version, each person shares with, attends to, and values her or his partner. Make (not find) at least one hour each week to talk about intimate matters. Ensure that each of you is not overly tired and is unplugged from technology. Also, make sure the kids are occupied, asleep, or medicated (just kidding on the latter part . . . not really . . . yes, yes, I'm just kidding!). Then, try to have a discussion about matters that are important to you. If this feels difficult, come prepared with a list of discussion starters. Here are twenty for you:

- I'm most afraid of . . .
- The three things I want to accomplish next year and in the next five years are . . .
- My best and worst memories are . . .
- The three things I both like and wish to change about myself are . . .
- My ideal vacation is . . .
- What I like most about our sex life is . . .
- The thing I most want to ask God is . . .
- If I had to be an animal instead of a person I'd be a . . .
- My favorite five movies of all time are . . .
- If I could have any superpower I'd choose . . .
- On my deathbed I'd most like to think . . .
- The one way I'd like to improve as a person is . . .
- The thing I most cherish about you is . . .
- The things that make me most sad, happy, mad, and worried are . . .
- If I had three wishes I would wish for . . . (avoid saying money or more wishes and keep it personal—no "world peace" wishes)
- The person I'd most like to meet from history is . . .
- When we retire, I'd like to . . .
- The best and worst things about my vocational life are . . .
- What I most wish for our kids is . . .
- The thing that most embarrasses me about myself is . . .

I suggest using some structure. One of you could be the speaker and the other the listener. The speaker chooses the topic and says what she wishes, striving to generate at least a couple "paragraphs" on the topic. During this part, the listener gives undivided attention. When the speaker is finished, the listener paraphrases what he heard. Then the speaker indicates whether clarifications are needed; if yes, the listener re-paraphrases. Once the speaker agrees that the listener has understood, the listener can give his reaction. Have a conversation until it runs out of steam. Then switch roles.

Remember, just like starting an exercise program, it's important to start out with easier topics and build to more challenging subjects after a few weeks, at least if you've been feeling somewhat distant from each other. Also, if the conversation starts to turn into an argument, change the topic; you can use the other hours of the week for arguments. This time is only for sharing, attending, and valuing.

(An alternative exercise would be for each of you to independently make a list of the top ten things you'd like to accomplish before you die. Then share them with each other. Suggestion: Make it a personal project to help your partner check off items on his or her list.)

During this special time it's vital that the communication be intimate. An intimate communication is honest, often feels either risky or challenging to disclose, and is something you'd be disinclined to share with an acquaintance. Communication doesn't have to feel anxious to be intimate. But if a communication feels difficult to share, then it's highly likely that it's intimate. The reason for this suggestion is that most of us can't help but feel closer to a partner who responded to an intimate communication with compassion and kindness. Of course, we all must use good judgment regarding what intimate thoughts and feelings should be shared. It would usually be a mistake to share *every* thought and feeling or to be aggressive under the flag of "I'm just being honest."

It is important that this communication contain feelings and not just thoughts or analysis. This is tricky, as the verb "feel" is often used in place of the verbs "think" and "believe." For instance: "I feel you are too hard on yourself" is really saying "I think . . ." and contains no communication about feelings. To say, "I feel sad when I see you being hard on yourself" is to share a feeling. "I feel I cannot do my job well" is really saying, "I believe . . .," while saying "I feel worried that I'm incompetent at work" is sharing a feeling. Of course, thoughts are a part of intimate communications. It's just that sharing feelings facilitates growing closer.

Here are some additional tips for special time for couples:

1. Try not to do anything else during the communication. Multitasking interferes with intimacy and being in the moment. Plus, the human experience of getting someone's undivided positive attention regarding intimate matters is becoming rarer and rarer.

2. Really listen. This means not talking, quieting your inner world,

making eye contact, and paying close attention to what is being said. You'll know you're doing a good job if time seems to fly by.

3. Anytime strong feelings are aroused in a communication with your partner, use the reflective listening strategy reviewed above and repeat back what you heard; then ask your partner to verify that you've heard correctly before responding. Often we may hear a different message from what was intended, especially when the communication is emotional and from someone we've known a long time. We "been-there-done-that" married people tend to overestimate our capacity to read our partner's mind, especially when in conflict. Taking the time to make sure that the heard message is the intended message can save a lot of time, misunderstanding, and energy.

Tricia and Greg were married for fifteen years and had a toddler. Tricia was a stay-at-home mom. Sensing that things were in a down cycle, Tricia decided to buy a sexy dress and to suggest that they go out on a date. She purchased the dress and modeled it to her husband the next morning, playfully asking, "What do you think?" Greg responded by saying something like, "I like it, but I think you look better in the black one that is similar to that one." Tricia heard this as his suggesting that he thought she looked fat. She didn't say anything but was hurt and angry. On a slow burn all day, she decided not to make Greg dinner, which was a departure from their routine.

When Greg came home he asked, "What's for dinner?" Tricia snapped, "I'm tired. Get your own dinner."

Now it was Greg's turn to be silently angry as he thought, *"Here I'm busting my hump all day for this family, and she can't be bothered to push some buttons on the microwave!"* Later that night they wanted to watch different shows on TV; in the face of that minor tension they exploded into an intense argument.

Had Tricia simply asked, in the morning, "It's important to me that you're being honest. Are you saying that I look bigger in this dress than in the other one?" Greg could have clarified by stating, "Oh no! Not at all! You look hot in both. I just like how the black contrasts with your blonde hair."

Reflective listening can spare a lot of drama in long-term relationships.

4. Maintain good body language. Make your body say to your partner that you're listening.

5. Let your partner know about any positive thoughts or feelings you're having about what she is saying. Try to avoid sharing negative thoughts or feelings (that can be done at another time). Too often in our intimate relationships we're undisciplined and say more than is advisable or make little effort to be kind in how we raise our concerns. What would happen to our work relationships if we were equally uncensored there?

6. Give the benefit of the doubt. Good intentions can create an atmosphere of openness.

7. If you're finding this is work, and you're exerting yourself when you don't feel like it, give yourself a mental pat on the back, because this means you're in the game and not moaning in the locker room.

8. If you find that you cannot do this well alone, seek a qualified relationship counselor.

Keep Your Sex Life Active

One way to do this is to try to keep your sex life mutually satisfying and interesting. To people who have never been in a long-term relationship, the phrase "boring sex" might sound like an oxymoron. However, to those of us in such a relationship, sex inevitably gets routine unless we work at it. Here are some suggestions:

- Share some of your fantasies with your partner (maybe swap notes) and try those that seem safe and consistent with your values.
- Get a book or two on creative strategies for sex.
- In terms of frequency, couples vary a lot in what is satisfying. Be open with your partner about your needs and be willing to compromise.
- It's common for one person in the relationship to be the primary pursuer of sex. For those of you who are in the pursued role, take the initiative from time to time lest you enhance your partner's risk for becoming demoralized.

Have Fun Together

Healthy couples have fun together. You certainly share enough labor, so you also need time to play. Couples who are grinding gears often do fun things only with the kids, away from their partner, or rarely. In my initial interview for couple's counseling, I always ask what first interested each person in their partner. In just about every instance I hear that the glue that first bonded the couple was doing fun things, but they later let life's obligations shove the shared fun out of their lives.

I can offer two suggestions. First, think back to what you did together for fun when you dated and try to do some of those things again, assuming they fit your current values and health status. Second, if your partner likes to do something that you don't think you'd like to do, but you've never tried it, try it! Life is like a four-star restaurant with a varied and sumptuous menu. Yet, how many of us restrict our sampling?

Trying *new* recreational activities that are safe and fit your values can be exhilarating. Granted, you won't like some of the things you try, but you'll also get surprisingly lucky from time to time (e.g., I always thought that I'd hate golf but tried it and loved it instantly. . . as much as I completely stink at it).

Do Something Nice for Your Partner

Doing nice things for your partner can also put air under the wings of the relationship. Again, it is important to do this without expecting a response.

> The distance that had evolved in her relationship with her husband, Luke, troubled Jennifer. One of Luke's complaints was that Jennifer, who was the one who made dinner each night, rarely cooked but instead used the microwave. Jennifer's perspective was that they both worked and that if cooking was important to Luke then he should do it himself. However, wanting to make a gesture, she arranged to come home early from work in order to cook a meal for the family. When Luke came home and saw what Jennifer was doing, he was delighted. But, being an emotionally reserved fellow, he only said, "Thanks for doing this," and gave her a kiss on the cheek.
>
> One of Jennifer's complains about Luke was that he spent too much time on the computer, especially after dinner. She wished to have some couple or family time after their meals. Luke's perspective was that he worked fifty to sixty hours each week and the only thing he did for himself was to go on the Internet a little each day to relax. He also pointed out that some of this computer time was spent doing work.

After the meal was finished, Luke got up and went to the computer. Jennifer was furious. She thought, "Here I busted my butt trying to do something he wanted, and he can't manage to stay away from the computer for one night!" After thinking this thought for about fifteen minutes, Jennifer went to Luke and screamed it at him.

Luke, during dinner, had privately resolved to do something nice in return for Jennifer as he felt grateful for her effort. So, he went to the computer to arrange for a weekend getaway at a local resort for couples. When Jennifer came to him and started screaming, he instantly thought, "So, she didn't make dinner just to be nice, but only so that she could control me! Forget this getaway!"

Later, he screamed this thought at her. In the ensuing argument they both deployed their most toxic weapons.

Jennifer's desire to offer a gesture was wonderful. But, it was dangerous to do it with the expectation of a response, especially because of the numerous landmines in the relationship. I would have wished for her to say to herself: "I'm going to do something healthy for our relationship because that's what I can control. I'm not going to do it with the expectation of a response because I can't control that." Certainly, if you asked my wife she could give you plenty of examples of me doing something nice with an implied contingency. All of us make these kinds of mistakes. The key is to recognize them as mistakes and to strive for a higher ground. At the end of the day, that's the best that any of us can do.

Here are ten examples of nice things to do for your partner:

1. Get some massage oils, create an area to lie down, and give your partner a lengthy massage. (If you're the one who typically initiates sex, and that's a source of tension in your relationship, be careful not to make the message sexual lest your partner conclude that you were offering the massage for selfish reasons.)

2. Draw a bath for your partner, adding special scents; light a few candles; prepare some finger food; and put on your partner's favorite music. Then tell your partner you'll keep the kids away for the next hour.

3. Get tickets to an activity that your partner loves going to but you previously had resisted attending. Then try to have fun or show interest at the event.

4. After the kids are in bed (or shipped off to someone else's house), prepare a romantic dinner for two. Cook your partner's favorite food, light candles, put up a folding table with linens to create an intimate little table for two, and put on your partner's favorite music.

5. Send your partner some balloons during the day, declaring your love and inviting her or him to lunch.

6. Make a videotape of all the things you appreciate about your partner and mail it to him or her.

7. Do a major chore that your partner usually does, telling your partner that you appreciate that he or she normally does this but that you want to provide a respite.

8. Send a card declaring your love and include a coupon for a free back massage to be performed by you.

9. Write your partner a poem. (Don't evaluate as you write. Just free associate and express positive feelings and thoughts.)

10. One day when your partner comes home weary, tell her or him that you'll cover all duties for that night and to just relax.

Work on Resolving Conflicts

> *I never mind my wife having the last word.*
> *In fact, I'm delighted when she gets to it.*
> Walter Matthau

All functional relationships experience conflict. Here are some things to keep in mind as you negotiate your path to resolution:

First, try to put off resolving conflicts until you've already invested considerable energy in nurturing the relationship. Imagine that a co-worker with whom you have a distant relationship started doing something that bothered you. Now imagine two different scenarios: In scenario #1 you bring up your concern in as straightforward and as tactful a manner as possible. In scenario #2, you invite her to lunch a couple of times, discover that you have some shared interests, and start exchanging pleasantries during the day. Then you bring up your concern. The odds are much more likely that the problem would be resolved effectively in scenario #2.

Second, when you decide to take on a problem, avoid doing it when you're angry. Few of us do things well when we're suffering from transient brain dysfunction. I know this is easier said than done, and all of us, no matter how committed to the principle, do err, but it's worth striving for.

Third, ask yourself what your role is in the difficulty. Even though your partner may be leading the dance, what missteps did you take? And, I'm not suggesting saying things like, "My mistake was imagining that you are more giving than you are." I'm talking about a real error on your part. You can own and control your missteps but not your partner's. Owning your mistakes also makes it harder for your partner to be defensive.

> Jeremy routinely complained that Deanna withheld sex. He pointed out that they were having sex twice a month, while he preferred at least twice a week.
>
> Jeremy could wax philosophic about how destructive he judged Deanna's behavior to be. I asked him, "Jeremy, how do you help her to not be available more often for sex?" Like most people who are asked that sort of question, he was surprised by it.
>
> "What do you mean 'help' her? I'm not trying to help her not to have sex!" But, he eventually joined me in the search for an answer.
>
> What he figured out was that he often approached her for sex at bedtime, which was typically preceded by either an argument or by his coming home from a late night at work as a laborer; in the latter case he had the aroma of a man who had just completed a hard day's work as a laborer. Of course, these contributions by Jeremy did not release Deanna from her contributions to the problem (i.e., having a quick trigger for saying no to sex and not letting Jeremy know about the hygiene issue). But, by doing this search, Jeremy put himself in position to make some positive changes.
>
> I worked with Deanna on her contributions, too, and before long the couple reported that they had become much better at peacefully resolving their differences.

Fourth, think of your communication method as a tool and know that you have many tools at your disposal. Most couples in distress are locked into dysfunctional modes of communication and don't view themselves as having viable choices.

Imagine you're a consultant to carpenters. One carpenter tells you that he can't manage to drive nails into lumber. You ask him to demonstrate.

You then see him take a pair of pliers out of his pocket and proceed to try to hammer a nail with the handle end. As it continues to not work, he starts exclaiming. "Stupid *&^% nail, why won't you go into the wood!" You then point out that he has a toolbox that contains some other options for the job. He eventually discovers his hammer and is off and running.

The above metaphor sounds ridiculous, doesn't it? I mean, what sort of a carpenter would use the same feckless strategy over and over again? But, that's exactly what goes on when relationships break down.

> Corrine detested the fact that Rob would not cut the grass until it got embarrassingly high. Her strategy for getting him to change that behavior was to yell at him on Saturday mornings. "Could you *please* cut the grass before the neighbors start commenting on it again!"
> I had the following conversation with her:
> Me: "Corrine, when you yell at him with those words, what is your goal?"
> Corrine (looking at me like I was asking her when she last traveled to the moon): "I'm trying to get him to get off his lazy ass and cut the grass."
> Me: "And, how well is that working?"
> Corrine: "It's not. Obviously."
> Me: "If you told me that your goal is to get stuff off your chest and that you're willing to live with the backlash, I'd say you had the right tool for the job. But, given that yelling at him is not accomplishing what you intend, can you think of another way of communicating with him about this?"

Rob was responsible for his behavior. But, by using an ineffective method for communicating, Corrine was facilitating his resistance and decreasing the odds that his ass and the grass would meet. Mostly, I don't tell couples what to say to each other to resolve their conflicts. I just encourage them to be honest appraisers of the effectiveness of their tool choice, and to keep trying different tools until they find the right one.

That said, here are some tools that can be more effective for promoting behavior change than simply stating the facts:

- Express empathy for your partner's perspective. Did you ever try to stay mad at someone who was showing you empathy? (By the way, to be empathic doesn't mean to be in agreement.)
- Engage your partner in addressing his or her concerns.

- Own and apologize for your errors without rationalization or justification.
- State your partner's position to her or him, trying to make that position sound as reasonable as possible. Then ask if you got it right. Once your partner agrees that you understand, ask to switch roles.
- Compliment your partner for what you genuinely believe are her or his good attitudes, intentions, or behaviors.
- Try the problem-solving exercise described in Chapter 6.

Follow me around for a week and you'll see me using ineffective communication tools with my wife (though she has it *way* easier in our relationship). This isn't about being a perfect communicator. It's about recognizing that if I'm disciplined, genuine, and thoughtful in how I communicate, I can often accomplish reasonable and important relationship goals.

Supportive Strategy

An Exercise in Happiness

I've adapted the following from British psychologist Dr. Robert Holden's "Happiness Walk-Through" exercise that can be found in his wonderful book *Be Happy! Release the Power of Happiness in YOU*. Complete each step before reading on if you want to receive the full value.

Step One: Make a list of the ten things that would need to happen for you to be *completely* happy; not just content, but *completely* joyful. Go ahead. Write them down before going on to Step Two.

Step Two: How many of the ten things on your list are in the future or outside of your control? Reflect on what this means about your current methods for pursuing happiness.

Step Three: Make a list of ten things *you* could do *today* to be *completely* joyful and happy, even if these involve changes in thinking.

Step Four: Reflect on this quote from a Zen master: "Searching for happiness is like looking for your horse while riding it."

Step Five: Encourage your partner to do these steps.

Step Six: You and your partner share with each other what you've taken away from this exercise. For instance:

- How could the list from Step One be used to make plans?
- How could you each support insights you garnered to promote happiness today?
- What self-help projects might you share to promote happiness?

Strategy Summary

Happiness comes not from having more, not from having less, but from wanting what you have.
Gretchen Ruben, *The Happiness Project*

If you've suffered significant pain in your childhood and have not completed a program for resolving it, consider taking steps to promote your healing. You would stand to be more effective across all of your relationships.

Investing in your relationship with your partner can be one of the most giving things you can do for your children. Try to make weekly couple time for both intimate communication and recreation. Also, do spontaneous nice things for your partner at least twice each month, vary your sex life, and try to effectively resolve disputes, not win them (the prize is an empty bag anyway).

Don't stop until the fog clears and you find meaning in your vocational life.

Try to make time to do fun things on a regular basis, either by yourself or with friends. This models a balanced lifestyle and creates synergy in your relationships with family members.

The Skeptical Parent's Challenge

Parent: I thought this was a book about parenting. Geez, why don't you suggest how to fill out my taxes while you're at it?

Author: It's remarkable how many things affect our wellness and, by extension, our ability to parent with intention. My childless twenty-something graduate students get this within a couple of months of working in our clinic. They know that if I have a child case to assign and an adult case to assign, the person who accepts the child case will usually have a lot more work to do than the person who accepts the adult case; this is because any work with a child involves working with a system (i.e., the family and the school, at least).

Parent: My partner is an ass. I've tried *everything* and nothing works; even our marriage counselor gave up on us. I'm trapped.

Author: I know how real this feels. But, you're not trapped. You have choices, and you're not alone. First, I would wonder if your partner is as permanently unreachable as you characterize. This may take consulting with another relationship counselor to find out. But, I wouldn't give up based on one failed counseling experience. If, in fact, your partner can't or is unwilling to work with you on improving your relationship, perhaps going into your own counseling would be a good idea (i.e., to become more aware of your choices and to find the strength to act upon that which you believe is advisable).

Parent: You act like all job descriptions are like Mother Teresa's. Some of us have nasty, dirty jobs that we have to do simply to keep the lights on. No glory. No meaning. Just a pathetic job working with burned-out, angry, and depressed people.

Author: I know how powerful these painful illusions can be. Sure, if my job is to cheat or to hurt people, then I'm not going to be able to feel uplifted doing it. But, if my job performs some valuable function, whether it metaphorically or literally means cleaning toilets or saving lives, it has the potential to be rich with meaning and lavish with purpose. If the counsel I offer in this book cannot get you there, please consider working with a skillful mental health professional.

Parent: You suggest that recreating away from our partner can be rejuvenating. But, my partner gets angry with me when I try to do this.

Author: Think of this as a symptom that could have many causes. Perhaps your partner wishes to be closer to you. Perhaps your partner doubts her or his own value and worries that you'll stray. Perhaps your partner wants more help around your home. It's tough to know. But, just like I would not ignore a persisting fever, I would not ignore this.

Parent: I'm a single parent. I can't get time to recreate because I'm always working, parenting, or sleeping.

Author: First, I salute you. Your selflessness and love are both beautiful. This said, and even if you have no family or friends who can help, do you realize how many single parents there are who'd like to trade babysitting services? Setting up such a network could not only solve your problem but could be the beginnings of a mission that could leave you feeling as if you have electricity coursing through your veins. (Our agitations can sometimes be a Higher Power tapping us on the shoulder and whispering: "Love, this is my mission for you.") Crisis *really* does = pain + opportunity.

Strategy Eight

Emphasize a Healthy Lifestyle

I can just hear you as you read this chapter heading: "OMG, another read about eating veggies and busting my hump on a treadmill. Puhleez." Well, I promise that I'm going to try to not insult your intelligence or encourage shame. After all, our culture is obsessed with self-help books and Web sites devoted to making obvious and idealistic recommendations. In homage to such efforts, here are my favorite potential book and Web-site titles for such projects:

Possible Book Titles
  Just Limit Yourself to the Hole in the Donut
  Don't Get Mad at Yourself, Kick Some A$$ Instead
  Y'know, Self-Pity is Not Sexy

Remember, the Only Reason Dogs Lick Themselves is Because They Can
Three Syllables to a New Body: Endure Pain
If You Can't Lose Weight, Weigh the Can't in You

Possible Web-Site Domains
   www.quiturbellyachin.com
   www.justbelikeme.net
   www.luvurselfdammit.com
   www.dontbeboring.com
   www.eatlikeagoat.org
   www.whoreallycaresbesidesu.net

Okay, now that I got that out of my system, let me turn to some real issues.

The Three Pillars of Physical Health

Research suggests that between 40 and 60 percent of our health outcomes are affiliated with the choices we make. For instance, our health habits affect our moods, concentration, motivation, and stress tolerance. Show me a child whose health habits are poor, and I'll show you a child who is likely underachieving in multiple domains and is vulnerable to an assortment of medical and psychiatric problems. The three pillars of a child's physical health are diet, sleep, and physical activity.

Diet

The evidence suggests that we have alarmingly increasing rates of childhood obesity in our country (i.e., a body mass index greater than or equal to the ninety-fifth percentile). According to a 2010 study published by the *Journal of the American Medical Association*, 10 percent of newborns and toddlers fall in the obese range, with the number rising to 17 percent in the two- to nineteen-year-old category (33 percent are at the eighty-fifth percentile or higher).

Although the numbers vary across studies, a clear consensus is that obesity exists at alarming rates in our children and contributes to a number of medical (e.g., juvenile-onset diabetes, sleep apnea), psychiatric (e.g., sadness, anxiety, low self-esteem), and behavioral (e.g., more likely to be bullied, social rejection) problems. If left unchecked, obesity may create the first generation that does not live longer than their parents.

With today's time crunch, we seem to have less time available for pro-active planning and food preparation. We rush through the grocery store (who has time to read labels?), rush through the kitchen (using buttons more than flames), and fill in the gaps with trips to the fast food res-taurant (according to the USDA, almost half of the $1.1653 billion we spent on food in 2008 was spent on food away from home). The path of least resistance leaves us offering high-processed and sugary foods that our kids are less likely to resist eating and drinking (who has time to fight about food?) and that are also cheaper than fresh food.

Besides the "what's easy and cheap" issue, we're subjected to oppres-sive amounts of marketing from manufacturers of unhealthy foods. According to the 2004 documentary *Super Size Me*, the average child views 10,000 food advertisements per year, with 95 percent of those advertis-ing unhealthy foods. And, if the marketing campaigns for unhealthy and healthy foods were combating boxers, it would be like an angry Mike Tyson fighting a fearful kindergarten girl (e.g., the combined direct mar-keting budgets for just one fast food chain and one soda company in 2001 totaled more than $2.4 billion while the marketing campaign for eating fruits and vegetables has never been more than $2 million).

What are some of the effects of these campaigns? Dr. Tom Robinson, director of the Center for Healthy Weight at Lucille Packard Children's Hos-pital, led a research team that discovered that preschoolers are more likely to rate foods as tasting better (even carrots, milk, and apple juice) when they're packaged in brand-name fast-food wrapping paper. And, Drs. Linda Adair and Barry Popkin found that fast foods comprise 20 percent of our kids' food energy intake (this percentage falls between 2 and 7 in other countries).

We parents may have health habits ourselves that promote obesity. For instance, according to a 2010 article published online by the *Journal of the American Medical Association*, a little more than one-third of adults fall in the obese range, while 68 percent of us are overweight. We may use food to numb stress and psychological pain. We may overeat because food is our primary source of pleasure, or we may find it difficult to hit the off switch once we've hit the on switch. And, we may also find it to be easier and cheaper to eat a diet high in processed carbohydrates.

Sleep

*"A slightly-sleepy sixth-grader will perform in class
like a mere fourth-grader."*
Po Bronson & Ashley Merryman, *NurtureShock*

Learning how to sleep is an important developmental task of child-hood. However, the available evidence suggests that many of us parents need help in this area as well. According to the 2008 *Sleep in America* poll conducted by the National Sleep Foundation, the average American worker is working more (averaging nine hours and twenty-eight minutes each workday) and sleeping less (averaging six hours and forty minutes on work nights) than previous generations. Quoting from the September 2006 issue of *Consumer Reports*: "Pharmacists filled 43 million prescriptions for sleep drugs in 2005; that's a 32 percent increase from 2001."

Many kids do not learn how to soothe their bodies and minds into a state conducive to rejuvenating sleep. Making things more complicated is that most of our children lobby us for later bedtimes. As a parent, it taxes me to have to remember when my kids need to get to bed and ensure that they practice a good protocol for transitioning into bed and falling asleep.

Poor sleep hygiene seems to be yet another symptom of an over-stretched and overstimulated family life. My kids may be out doing activities that interfere with getting to bed on time. Moreover, if I'm over-taxed, I'm less likely to have the energy to resist my child's efforts to stay plugged into electronic pleasures. Also, if I'm tired, I have less energy to engage in healthy behaviors. For instance, the aforementioned sleep survey indicated that 86 percent of Americans report having missed an important function in the past three months due to the consequences of poor sleep, while 20 percent indicated that sleep deprivation was interfering with their sex life.

When it comes to sleep and stress, children and teens are just like adults: Sleep and concentration tend to be among those functions first affected when stress attacks. But the effects of stress can be unpredictable; what might be an excessive dose of stress for one child may be manageable for another. The way a kid *interprets* what has happened more strongly determines the impact of stress than what has actually happened. So for a parent, a child not making the traveling soccer team may not be a big deal, and even a relief, but to the child this may equate to having her membership to her favorite peer group revoked.

According to the National Sleep Foundation 2006 *Sleep in America* poll, the sleep problems of our children, by the time they reach adolescence, are profound. Only 20 percent of adolescents get an optimal nine hours of sleep on school nights; nearly 45 percent sleep less than eight hours on school nights. Poor sleep habits adversely affect driving ability, academic performance, and ability to meet primary obligations. Moreover, it's interesting to note that this survey found that "Eighty percent of adolescents who get an optimal amount of sleep say they're achieving As and Bs in school . . ."

Recent studies indicate that children who do not get a good night's sleep are more likely to act out the next day. As one example, researcher Dr. Eeva Aronen found that forty-nine healthy seven- to twelve-year-olds were more likely to act aggressively, to have attention problems, and to have social problems in school the next day as a function of how much sleep they got the night before.

Bronson and Merryman make an effective point about the consequences of even one hour of lost sleep a night in *NurtureShock:* "Because children's brains are a work in progress until the age of twenty-one, and because much of that work is done while a child is asleep, this lost hour appears to have an exponential impact on children that it simply doesn't have on adults." Inadequate doses of sleep facilitate obesity and negative thinking, and interfere with academic and cognitive functioning (i.e., one hour of lost sleep equals a loss of seven IQ points the next day).

Physical Activity

Our kids appear to be less physically active than previous generations. For instance, according to a 2010 study funded by the Kaiser Family Foundation, our children are spending a little more than 7.5 hours per day consuming entertainment media. Quoting from the report: "Five years ago, we reported that young people spent an average of 6.5 hours (6:21) a day with media–and managed to pack more than 8.5 hours (8:33) worth of media content into that time by multitasking. At that point it seemed that young people's lives were filled to the bursting point with media. Today, however, those levels of use have been shattered."

The Third National Health and Nutrition Examination Survey investigated the health-related behaviors of 4,069 children, ages eight to sixteen, from 1988 to 1994. Researchers found that almost half of the kids did not report sweating or breathing hard five days or more each week. When looking at children ages eight to ten, they found that only 44 percent of the boys and 46 percent of the girls were active five days per week.

Likewise, in the 2007 National Youth Risk Behavior Survey, about one out of four high school students had not spent one hour in physical activity that made them breathe hard in the preceding week, and only one out of three breathed hard for one hour or more for five out of the last seven days. In this same survey, 35.4 percent of these kids watched at least three hours of TV on school days.

In my clinical practice, I find that a drop in physical activity seems to occur for at least three reasons. First, we parents are busy. It taxes us less if our kid is plugged into pleasures that he enjoys. Second, we may not believe it is safe or appropriate for our child to be outside in unsupervised outdoor play. Third, kids love their sedentary electronic pleasures, and interacting with them may organize and support relationships with friends.

Synergy is a powerful process in families. If we know our kids' competencies, we have rituals, and we make time for wellness activities, we may not have to actively think too much about how much physical activity our kids are getting. Likewise, if stress is sweeping us away, if we haven't found our child's competencies, and if we don't have rituals, our child may be more sedentary, get less sleep, and be fueled by processed carbohydrates. But, those of us in the latter category don't have to worry; all of this is fixable.

Parental Substance Abuse

The 1992 National Longitudinal Alcohol Epidemiological Survey found that 28 million children were living with a parent who abused alcohol for some period during childhood. Isn't it much easier to drink some cocktails and enter a warm haze, than to try to resolve problems? Moreover, we live in a culture accustomed to ingesting substances to manipulate brain chemistry when we're troubled. I'm not referring to well-reasoned medication interventions designed to support adaptive brain functioning, especially when they're accompanied by psychological interventions. I'm referring to when we ingest agents—sometimes prescribed and sometimes not, sometimes legal and sometimes not—to numb psychological pain or to kick-start a weary soul.

Many parents model an activating and decompression routine throughout the course of the day. We may wake up weary, not having gotten enough sleep, with a ton of things we have to do; to help us get going, we might dunk our brain in caffeine. Then, as the stress of the day mounts, we may use nicotine to steady our nerves and focus. Finally, we may complete our duties and decompress with alcohol, telling ourselves that we deserve it because we've worked our tails off. Studies on modeling in families suggest that children as young as three begin to comprehend such cycles. It's also clear that each child's risk of abusing substances—and choosing partners who abuse substances—is significantly enhanced by growing up in a household where such behaviors are ritualized.

Sometimes patterns of abuse change our brain functioning so much that we become addicted. In these instances there is an invisible member of the family that wages war on all of us. Addiction is a powerful, jealous, and intelligent monster. Its power is witnessed in the breadth and depth of the damage it inflicts (e.g., on relationships, health, financial standing, self-respect, and loved ones). Its jealousy is witnessed by the fact that it persuades its primary victim to sacrifice relationships and agendas that threaten its influence. Its intelligence is witnessed in the countermoves it makes when others who care for the primary victim try to get him to recognize the beast and its impact.

No matter how badly such a beast attacks its primary victim, the victim often drapes himself in denial: "I don't have a problem because . . . I work . . . I only drink . . . I've quit before for . . ." The beast gets its victim to focus on the symptoms that she doesn't yet have and persuades her that she will never truly relax or have fun again without it. These lies so convince the victim that it often takes a shocking event for the person to come to and realize what's going on. Short of such a realization, just about every potential benefit that might accrue to a family by practicing the strategies in this book is at risk.

THE STRATEGY

Studies indicate that modeling is a powerful agent in shaping children's attitudes and behaviors. One of my clients recently had a shocking insight when her twelve-year-old told her that he wanted to drink his beverage out of a wine glass. When asked why, he replied, "It's just cooler."

It is excruciatingly difficult for my child to engage in good health habits if I do not. How can I eat a steady diet of processed carbohydrates—which are the foods my children crave—while insisting that my children eat well? Even if I can pull this off in the short run, my children may become highly attracted to unhealthy foods. If I'm not getting sufficient physical activity, I may be lethargic and less inclined to have the energy to promote sufficient activity in my child. And, if I'm not sleeping well, I'm probably weary and less inclined to apply the sort of structure needed to get my child to sleep well. Finally, if I'm coping with my pain and stress through compulsive behaviors (e.g., shopping, gambling, TV, alcohol), I may find it most challenging to be the parent I intend to be.

In short, the strategies in this chapter are built on a foundation of good parental self-care (see Chapter 7). That said, I'm not suggesting that a parent who is not able, or prepared, to demonstrate good health habits forgo her responsibility to promote healthy behaviors in her children. For instance, even if a parent smokes, it's her responsibility to forbid such behavior in her child. Hypocrisy may damage such a parent's credibility, but, washing her hands of the responsibility is more troubling, as it puts her child's health and wellness at greater risk.

If you agree, but find yourself unable to make positive health changes on your own, join the club!

Correct Parental Performance Deficits

If my health habits are askew, a self-assessment can be very helpful. Perhaps I have a knowledge deficit, a performance deficit, or both.

A knowledge deficit means that I lack information about what constitutes a healthy diet, activity schedule, and sleep routine and/or how to implement such within my tight schedule and one-of-a kind personality. Knowledge deficits reflect gaps in my education. All I need to do is educate myself by relying on authoritative sources (e.g., a physician, a nutritionist, well-conceived Web sites).

A performance deficit means that I already know how and what to do to be well, but I don't do it. Or, once I'm provided with the relevant information, I don't apply it. With performance deficits, I find it difficult to change my habits, often for reasons that are outside of my awareness. There are many different kinds of causes for these problems: mood disorders, addiction, childhood trauma, marital disturbance, and excessive work hours, to name a few.

As a therapist I've learned that each person's performance deficits are unique to that person. For this reason, my friend's strategies for eating well may be of little help to me because his approach works for a different performance vulnerability. That said, there are two common performance deficits. First, I may find it difficult to endure the discomforts I experience when I start my wellness program. Second, I may not recognize my triggers and take adequate steps to avoid them.

Many millions of dollars of revenue are generated each year by whispering the same seductive message: *You can lose weight without discomfort.* Developing a diet and activity plan that minimizes your discomfort and maximizes your rewards is advisable, but some degree of discomfort is inevitable. Strategies listed in the following sections of this chapter are designed to help.

Many of us stop noticing what we're doing when we do unhealthy things—we disassociate. There are two ways to combat disassociation. First, we can keep a log of everything we eat. Many support associations have good methods (including electronic) for logging (e.g., I keep mine on my iPad). Second, we can keep a log of times when we eat in an unhealthy fashion. I suggest including what was going on before, during, and after the unhealthy eating, both externally and internally.

Chart 8.1 is an example of a functional behavioral analysis (FBA) chart. Completing an FBA can provide surprising insights. In the examples, the trigger each time was a three-fold combination: feeling tired after having offered sustained service to others, being upset, and not resolving the conflict. She would then use unhealthy food to medicate herself. For her to break this cycle, she would need to recognize when the antecedents were in play and either learn skills to resolve the conflict, distract herself with some pleasurable activity, or find some way to occupy her mind with something engaging (e.g., planning a vacation). If you're stuck, try an FBA like this one to see what insights you can garner.

Chart 8.1

Date and Situation	Thoughts, Feelings and Behavior	What I Ate	Postscript
6/23: After a long day with kids and work, husband and I fight.	Thoughts: He is so selfish. Feelings: Anger. Behavior: Withdrew from husband.	Small tub of gourmet ice cream.	Got sleepy and went to bed.
6/25: In the middle of a busy work day, my best friend called and canceled our day trip to the city next week.	Thoughts: It's insensitive of her to do this last minute. Feelings: Sadness, anger. Behavior: Said I didn't mind and hung up the phone.	A mini deep-dish pizza and a Diet Coke.	Finished up reports at work and went home tired.
6/26: Spent Saturday taking care of the kids and husband.	Thoughts: I never do anything for myself and they don't seem to notice that. Feelings: Exhausted, sad. Behavior: Put the kids into bed and collapsed on the sofa watching taped Oprah episodes.	Candy popcorn followed with a dish of gourmet ice cream.	Got sleepy and went to bed.

The following are a few other suggestions for overcoming performance deficits:

1. Set small and measurable daily goals. Being too ambitious is a common mistake. Remember, the goal is healthy behavior for *today*. So, each day provides the opportunity for success.

2. Find allies. It's harder to back out of a wellness plan if someone else is counting on you or you're reporting back to others.

3. Use your self-knowledge. For example, music moves me. So, my iPod touch is my most essential piece of exercise equipment. Likewise, I had a client once tell me that he paid for his karate classes six months in advance because the pain of wasting that money would be greater than the pain of "dragging my [butt] to class." You may do better if you're competing, or you're outdoors, or it's first thing in the morning. The point is to use what you know about yourself in order to avoid having to rely on white-knuckle willpower. Said another way, have your current self (the one who wants to be healthy) put things in place now that support the vulnerabilities that your future self (the one who is unmotivated or resistant) is likely to experience.

4. Realize that the toughest parts are starting and establishing a routine. Once you are in a routine, the brain's release of endorphins (natural opiates) and other benefits make it more enjoyable and, therefore, easier.

5. Get help if you can't do it on your own. People who successfully recover from behaviors they previously could not control do two things: They work on themselves (e.g., in therapy, in spiritual direction), and they surround themselves with people who are trying to overcome the same problem(s).

Promote a Healthy Relationship with Food

Reviewing what constitutes a healthy diet is beyond the scope of this book. However, here are several suggestions that apply to kids and adults:

1. Use authoritative guides for meal planning. You will do better when you emphasize what you want to eat rather than when you try to use willpower to avoid unhealthy foods. For instance, a research team led by Dr. Leonard Epstein found that individuals who were instructed to consume a healthy diet fared better than those who were instructed to avoid unhealthy foods.

2. Try to avoid relying on willpower. Avoid shopping when hungry. Avoid purchasing unhealthy foods. Stock the kitchen with organic and healthy but tasty foods easily available for when you or your child get the munchies (this is an example of your current self taking care of your future self). Avoid fasting and radical weight-loss efforts.

3. Avoid fast-food restaurants. Many of them would argue that they now have healthy choices on the menu. But how many families go to a fast-food restaurant and choose only healthy foods?

4. Avoid targeting weight as a goal, as doing so facilitates disordered eating and sets a goal that can take a very long time to reach. If you set healthy behaviors as a goal, your body will take the form that nature intended, and every day presents the opportunity to reach your goals.

5. Avoid consistent use of food as a reward, as it runs the risk of imbuing food with too much importance and is usually unhealthy (i.e., we don't say "John, you can have vegetables with your meal if you do your homework").

6. Try to condition healthy language about these matters. For example, "I need to go work off the dessert I had today," "I've been good all week, so I'm having a sundae," "Argghh. I can't believe what that idiot on the phone just said to me! Where's the chocolate?" or "I'm going to starve myself this month because I need to get in that dress for Sally's wedding."

7. Avoid "all you can eat" offers from restaurants.

8. Model good decision making when portions are huge. Too often we let a manufacturer or restaurant decide the size of a healthy portion, instead of our bodies. I could say to my child, "Wow. My stomach is full, but I'm only halfway done. If I have this wrapped up and take it home, I get two meals for the price of one!"

9. Try to model good questioning about how food is prepared (e.g., "Is the calamari fried?").

10. Reject unhealthy offerings. For a time, my family went to a restaurant that offered free kids meals on Tuesdays. My kids would order something from the kid's menu, which included a side. For weeks they would order the carrots and dip as a side. However, the waitress would always bring the fries. She finally explained to us that such a high percentage of customers ordered the fries for their kids that the kitchen stopped looking at that part of the order and just added fries.

Promote Physical Activity

To increase your child's physical activity, I recommend the following:

Limit your child's sedentary electronic pleasuring to two hours per day

This is the guideline of the American Academy of Pediatrics. If a child is doing more than that, she's probably neglecting other important developmental activities: academics, physical activity, reading, contributing to the household, socializing (face-to-face). A 2006 study that appeared in *Pediatrics* found that the academic performance of 4,508 students (grades five through eight) was significantly associated with how much leisurely screen time kids consumed on school nights. I also believe it's noteworthy that on school nights half of the excellent students watched no TV and 40 percent played no video games.

Institute sixty minutes' worth of physical activity each day

Three government agencies, the U.S. Department of Agriculture (USDA), U.S. Department of Health & Human Services (HHS), and the Centers for Disease Control and Prevention (CDC), recommend *sixty* minutes per day of physical activity for kids. If your child's school doesn't have part of this covered, you can dovetail this goal with other agendas: You can ritualize physical activity with your kid (e.g., a weekly walk around the block), you can combine physical activity with fun (e.g., swimming at a local lake), you can look for ways to incorporate physical activity into your routines (e.g., parking farther away from entrances, and taking stairs instead of elevators), and you can promote your child's competencies through physical activity; of course, the first three also promote your wellness.

Pick one day each month to have a sedentary technology holiday

During this twenty-four-hour period do not allow any electronic entertainment. Such days allow the other opportunities before you and your family to come more sharply into focus. Who knows, you may decide to try it on a weekly basis!

Create a gym space at home

If you have the means and space, having exercise equipment at home can help. In our home, my kids know that they have a weekday treadmill responsibility unless they have a team practice, a game, an active gym class, or some other activity that can substitute (they also are aware that my wife and I routinely use this same equipment—if only because they hear me wheezing). If home exercise equipment is not in the budget, get creative. Look at garage sales, call nearby universities or gyms to see if they have any used equipment, place an ad offering to take used equipment off someone's hands "for free."

Anne was a single, working mom of ten-year-old Matthew. She was a hard-working, honest woman who lived life paycheck-to-paycheck. Matthew was uncoordinated. He was also embarrassed, and believed he was disadvantaged, by the fact that he didn't have a supportive father. He had tried out for sports but would quickly become discouraged, even though his mother did all that she could to help.

Anne, however, was persistent and creative. She arranged for him to take martial arts classes, having first negotiated a reduced fee with the instructor. Simultaneously, she signed him up for the Big Brother program. Two years later, Matthew had his Red Belt and was playing organized baseball (his Big Brother routinely took him to batting cages and arranged to be an assistant coach).

To reiterate a theme of this book: How easy or difficult it is to do a given strategy depends heavily upon how many of the other strategies are already in place. So, if you're doing special time, if your child is routinely pursuing his competencies, if you're engaging in regular family rituals, and if you're employing sound behavioral techniques, you may not need to make many changes in order for your child, hit the recommended targets for physical activity and you'll probably find that there isn't excessive time available for your child to engage in sedentary electronic pleasures. However, if you find this is a fight that you can't win, perhaps it's time to get help (see Chapter 10).

Promote a Good Night's Sleep

Insomnia is a gross feeder. It will nourish itself on any kind
of thinking, including thinking about not thinking.
Clifton Fadiman, *Any Number Can Play*

Regarding the amount of sleep your child needs, these are the recommendations of the National Sleep Foundation:

Age	Number of Hours
1–3 years	12–14
3–5 years	11–13
5–12 years	10–11
Teens	8.5–9.25

If your child is consistently getting less sleep than this and she shows any of the common symptoms of sleep deprivation (i.e., irritability, lethargy, poor concentration, underachievement, and obesity), she is probably sleep deprived. Here are my suggestions for promoting healthy sleep (many of which can also work for you if you're not getting at least eight hours sleep a night):

1. Do not allow the TV to be on when your child is falling asleep. Getting interested in a program can significantly delay actual sleep time.

2. Put on some soothing music or a recording of soothing sounds (e.g., the ocean, the rain, a forest) for your child to listen to as he falls asleep. Just make sure to shut it off later.

3. Have your child take a warm shower or bath an hour or so before bedtime. This can relax her muscles and facilitate sleep.

4. Make sure that the temperature in the room is conducive to sleep. Some kids are very sensitive to this.

5. Make sure that your child's mattress is conducive to sleep; people vary regarding whether they need firm or soft mattresses. Consider replacing older mattresses.

6. Make sure that your child cannot hear sounds that might keep him awake.

7. If your child continues to struggle to fall asleep, try allowing her to listen to a book on tape at bedtime. However, try to make this either a story that she already knows or one that is not so compelling that it will keep her awake waiting for the next development in the storyline.

8. If your child tells you that his active mind impairs his ability to fall asleep, and the above strategies do not work, try a couple of different imagery interventions.

> • Ask her to imagine doing a repetitive, pleasurable activity. This can be any number of things: fishing, bowling, pitching a baseball game, shooting free throws, walking on a beach, etc. She should try to engage all of her senses: imagine the sights, sounds, smells, and touches. This is a more effective version of counting sheep. Busying the mind with non-stressful, but slightly engaging material, allows the body's fatigue to take over.
> • Ask him to imagine that it is the next day and he is very, very tired but *must* stay awake. He very much wants to sleep, but must not and cannot. Imagining himself in a class at school is often ideal. This paradoxical imagery occupies the mind so that the body can take over.

9. If your child routinely snores, inform your pediatrician; this may signal the need for a medical intervention (i.e., due to enlarged tonsils or adenoids, or sleep apnea).

If you've addressed these issues and your child is still demonstrating significant sleep disturbance, there may be value in consulting with a qualified medical or mental health professional (see Chapter 10).

Supportive Strategy

Become More Mindful

Have you heard of the mindfulness movement? It blends some of the best wellness strategies from Western and Eastern traditions. Here are three ways to try it:

1. Take ten minutes a day to do this exercise: Get in comfortable clothing, and sit in a comfortable piece of furniture in a peaceful, quiet, and comfortable room. Set a timer for ten minutes and focus your attention on only one thing while you breathe into your stomach. You can focus on a flickering candle, your breathing, or some object. Try to only notice the characteristics of whatever it is you are focusing on. If your thoughts drift, just nonjudgmentally notice that and bring them back to whatever you are focusing on. Done? You can now claim that you have meditated. Such strategies have been found to promote wellness (e.g., increase feelings of well-being, enhance affection for others) and to reduce pain (e.g., physical pain, agitated feelings).

2. The next time you are in a situation where you are made to wait, and you are agitated (e.g., in a traffic jam, in a long line at a store), try this exercise: Pick something to focus on and study its intricacies in depth. Maybe you study the details of the grass by the side of the road while stopped in traffic, the pattern of the sweater of the person in front of you in line, or the nuances of a piece of art hanging in the doctor's office. Try to notice every little feature and element, focusing

only on that object. Should you be able to focus on this task, don't be surprised if your agitation diminishes and time flies.

3. For your next meal, try to savor every mouthful and chew very slowly. Focus your mind on letting the flavors of the food resonate more deeply within you. Choosing several meals each week for this exercise can facilitate your ability to be mindful, which is the exact opposite of being disassociated.

Strategy Summary

Plan your child's diet in consultation with authoritative guides.

Limit your child's sedentary electronic pleasuring to two hours per day.

Plan for your child to sweat or breathe hard for at least sixty minutes each day.

Establish bedtime rituals and set a lights-out time that ensures that your child will get enough sleep (see the hour guidelines in this chapter).

Remember, every nickel you invest in your wellness is seven cents invested in your child's wellness.

The Skeptical Parent's Challenge

Parent: For a book that avoids lecturing, you sure sound pretty preachy in this chapter. You criticize the fast-food industry; you admonish against drinking alcohol; you challenge that it's hard for our kids to be physically well if we're not. Why don't you write your own health bible or something?

Author: I'll share with you that I struggled the most with this chapter. Were the research about these matters not so compelling, I probably would have found a way to leave it out. Moreover, I struggle with my own diet (I have a body that is intolerant of dietary lapses—I gain weight if I even smell a donut), so I understand that this content is very challenging. For all of us, though, there is no way to get around it: A neglected body means a neglected mind; thus, the more we fight the right fights, the better we do.

Parent: It's so embarrassing to do something like go to a support group, or start showing up at a gym, and only be able to do a fraction of what those around me can do. I think you underestimate this issue.

Author: Let me ask you this: What thoughts would go through your mind if you saw someone suffering from alcoholism take the step of going to a meeting for the first time? Or, what if you were at a gym and you saw someone come in, who seemed to be uncomfortable and who could only do half of what you could do? Most people would admire such a person. And, regarding that very small minority of people who may be inclined to think about you as you fear: a harsh judgment toward you has *much* more to do with that person's pain than your reality.

Parent: My kid fights me *so* hard when it comes to diet, physical activity, and sleep. She seems able to go twelve rounds with this stuff while I find it hard to go three.

Author: You're far from alone. This is a very common concern. First, I would try to condition yourself out of using the word "exercise" and into using the term "physical activity." Doing so would leave you delightfully surprised at the number of ways you could accomplish it together, without getting into power struggles about the word "exercise." Second, if you start doing the other strategies in this book you will find that you'll be able to go more rounds and your daughter will be able to go fewer, causing a victory in her favor.

Strategy Nine

Establish Collaborative Relationships with Other Important Adults

Many problems can occur when adults come together to serve children. Teachers misunderstand but try to tolerate parents and vice versa. Parents and coaches try to merge conflicting agendas. Stepparents and birth parents try to unite in a single cause, while negotiating complex family dynamics that range from effective to nightmarish. But, is there any relationship canyon vaster than the one that often exists between men and women? I thought I'd begin with a lighthearted homage to our efforts to understand each other.

Five Misunderstandings Fathers Have about Mothers

1. She is not trying to lose weight for you. She is trying to lose weight for other women. And, no, not for the reason your mind goes to.

2. When her only response is "fine" when you ask if it's okay for you to go on a weekend trip with your buds, it's not. Go on that trip only if you wish to learn more about celibacy.

3. She has *way* more energy for the toilet-seat debate than you do. And, this has nothing to do with anything rational. Just leave it down, Grasshopper (Google "grasshopper kung fu," if you must).

4. She needs to mark you. So, don't take it personally when she says, "You're wearing that?" Just go with the flow.

5. When she tells you about a problem, she usually doesn't want you to suggest how to solve it. I know, I know; this makes no sense. But, she just wants you to let her know that you understand what she's feeling and to validate it. So, teddy bear it, big guy.

Five Misunderstandings Mothers Have about Fathers

1. Yes. He knows that you are typically on a higher ground. But, hearing you occasionally say "I was wrong" or "I'm sorry" can help a lot. Go ahead, you can do it. Just practice making the words in front of a mirror.

2. He wants, y' know, *that,* way more than he may be admitting or letting on. And, it doesn't matter too much whether it comes in a box, a bag, or with a dancing bear dressed in a tutu.

3. When you cry, or are upset, he feels like it is his responsibility, and he wants to fix it. While this usually makes zero sense, and is certainly not what you are looking for, it's born out of love.

4. Don't misinterpret the fact that he and his friends tear each other down. You can generally judge the affection in his relationship with his male friends by how many insults they throw at each other. I know this is counterintuitive, but, then again, how rational is your interest in shoes?

5. Boys need toys. So, don't point out the obvious flaws in his "logical" arguments regarding why he *needs* a new iPad/drill/mitt. Just realize that he'll be better for you if he can regress and play with some new shiny whatchamacallits every now and again.

Later in this chapter I review strategies for dealing effectively with other adults who minister to your child. First, let me review some of the common problems that arise in these relationships.

Divorce and Separation

"I am" is reportedly the shortest sentence in the English language.
Could it be that "I do" is the longest sentence?
George Carlin

Few pains run deeper than those experienced when a spouse, who is one of the world's leading experts on you, rejects you. Piled onto this can be other pains resulting when your partner cheats, ruins your finances, compromises the well being of your children, abuses you, assaults you, or seriously damages your well-being through thoughtless or cruel acts.

In their book *10 Lessons to Transform Your Marriage*, international marriage experts Drs. John Gottman and Julie Gottman include a scale that ranks stresses people experience from one to one hundred. They assign divorce a seventy-three, which falls ahead of imprisonment (sixty-three) and getting fired (forty-seven). Moreover, as the divorce rate is so high, and most children do not reach age eighteen living with both birth parents, the experience of living in a realigned family is common.

Many divorced parents I've worked with seem to believe they can indulge feelings of rage and hatred for their ex without compromising their love for their child. However, any rage and hatred I harbor eats at me most of all. For this reason, there is less of me available for love and life. Remember, divorced parents are still part of the same family. Just as one person's joy and love ripple throughout the entire family, so too do painful feelings. And don't forget that a child can usually tell when a parent harbors resentment toward the other parent, even when he or she tries to hide it. And this often tears her up.

Beth and Tony had divorced five years earlier after ten years of marriage. They had one child, fifteen-year-old Darren. Beth and Tony both reported that they were happily remarried. However, they were maintaining an intense divorce war that was facilitated by their spouses and attorneys. Pending court dates were common, and Darren was kept in the loop about the issues. Both parents would make disparaging remarks about the other to Darren; moreover, both parents used Darren as a spy.

I became involved when Tony, who had physical custody of Darren, sought treatment for his defiance. I'll never forget Darren, as he had elevated his defiant behavior to an art form. My theory was that the divorce war was a major cause of his defiance. As part of my treatment plan, I asked to involve Beth. Tony resisted this, making arguments that Beth had a history of being abusive to Darren (much of this amounted to practicing discipline strategies that Tony judged to be ineffective but which were not abusive); he had gotten to the point that he viewed Beth as being evil.

All of my typical strategies for reaching such a parent failed. Finally I said something like this: "Tony, I can see that you're not hearing me. Let me put it differently. Let's say you were to take a knife and stab Darren in the shoulder. From a psychological perspective, you would be hurting him less than you are with this divorce war. You are killing the life out of him and there's nothing that can be done about that until you can snap out of this."

Because we had developed a strong relationship, he was able to hear me. Hence, he allowed me to involve Beth in the work. After about eighteen months of treatment, the parents formed a truce, and Darren's defiance abated.

Divorce stings badly, and the pain involved often overwhelms otherwise effective parents. If I have a migraine, my capacity to attend to others' needs is inversely related to the degree of my pain. However, divorce-based pain is a much more complex and toxic form of pain. With a migraine I can tell my children about the pain, how much it's bothering me, and even receive empathy. With divorce-based pain, the source of my pain is my relationship with someone deeply loved by my child. I can loathe my migraine, and share such feelings with my child, who may even join in. If I do the same regarding my ex, I'm simultaneously stabbing at my child's psyche.

Separate Households

Even in instances when divorced parents get along, stresses created by the divorced family structure may energize the obstacles that keep parents from executing the strategies in this book. For instance, maintaining adaptive rituals is more challenging when another household's needs must also be attended to. Likewise, it's more challenging to make time for special time when my child is not with me full-time. The other household may have a different philosophy about monitoring, discipline, diet, and extracurricular activities, which compromises my efforts. If we parents do not get along, things are much harder.

> Meghan and Rob were divorced for three years after ten years of marriage. They had two boys, ages eight and six. They were done with the courts and tried hard to avoid conflicts. However, they were still angry at each other over past conflicts and current misunderstandings. Their relationship was best characterized as a tense cease-fire. Meghan and Rob communicated on a "need-to-know" basis.
>
> Their eldest, Jacob, had always possessed a cheerful temperament. However, he had become sullen as a result of his parents' cold war. Jacob had several talents that became even more important to him during these years (any person benefits from possessing strong arms, but those restricted to a wheelchair benefit from them even more). One of these talents was playing baseball. His parents were able to communicate sufficiently to get Jacob to about 75 percent of his games and practices; while this was less than the other kids on the team, it was enough to get by. The team he played on made it to the playoffs, in large part because of Jacob's contributions. Unfortunately, Jacob didn't make a single playoff game, in part because the playoff schedule was announced with only one week's notice; short-term coordination of Jacob's participation required a level of communication that was beyond what his parents' cold war could tolerate.

I believe both of these parents loved Jacob more than their own life. However, their suppressed rage was blinding their ability to fully realize the impact that their animosity was having on their boy.

Blended Families

Almost one out of five kids live in a blended family. Thus, another complex issue is the relationship with a stepparent. Here I wish to review two common problems: when a stepparent is not allowed to parent and when the stepparent fuels conflict between the birth parents.

In reorganized families, there may be a rule that only birth parents are empowered to "parent." This is like asking a person to staff the oars on her side of a boat using only one arm. Not being able to parent can significantly hamper the stepparent's capacity to support the family's efficacy. Moreover, if a reorganized family is composed of children from more than one previous union, parenting can feel quite overwhelming.

A premise of this book is that we easily lose our minds when it comes to our kids. However, few adults can more quickly inspire our insanity than a stepparent who is married to our ex. "Go ahead and marry her if you actually think that's a good idea, but she better not try to tell *my* kids what to do!" While extremely understandable, such declarations are as feckless as a person standing on a beach and shouting at the ocean: "You will not take sand off this beach!"

Kids know that their birth parent can easily go nuclear if she hears about something that their stepmother did, whether real, imagined, or exaggerated. Not only does this parental behavior significantly compromise the stepparent's authority, but kids tend to use this dynamic to manipulate adults. For instance, I know one boy who brought home an uncharacteristically poor report card; he dodged his father's anger by telling him, in tears, that his stepfather had already yelled at him over it (as best as I could piece together, his stepfather merely expressed doubt that the report card represented his best effort).

Many stepparents are wonderfully intuitive and loving people who try to promote healing between their spouse and their spouse's ex. Such a person is wise enough to know that this healing promotes health and happiness in her family. Alternatively, some stepparents fan the flames of anger and hurt. In my practice, I've seen two common motivations for inciting this type of behavior. First, the stepparent may experience conflict between the divorced couple as an indication that his place is secure with his spouse. In this scenario the stepparent doubts his own appeal and interprets a cooperative relationship with the ex as a threat. Second, the stepparent may resent the resources that her family allocates to the ex's family.

Matthew and Robert were seven and nine, respectively. Their parents, Ralph and Gina, who felt hostile toward each other, were bringing them in for treatment because Matthew was depressed and Robert's grades were in decline. Their stepmother, Evanne, had no birth children of her own.

Matthew and Robert lived with Gina during the week and with Ralph and Evanne on the weekends. Evanne was angry over the size of Gina's support payments. Whenever Ralph and Evanne were not able to do something because of finances, they faulted Gina. (Evanne also wished to have more money to take care of her sick mother.) Every time Ralph expressed a negative thought or feeling about Gina, he could count on a high-five from Evanne. Likewise, should he express empathy for Gina's position, he could count on icy silence.

The three adults worked to not voice their conflicts in front of the children, but the kids knew who detested whom. Hence, when they were with Evanne and Ralph, they would make statements about how much they preferred it there and would be sure to tell them about Gina's mistakes during the week. Likewise, they would complain about Ralph and Evanne when they were with Gina. They were tearing themselves apart at the seams in order to please their parents.

Our kids very much want to please us, even if doing so means sticking a dart into their own shoulder. The trick is for us to be aware of how we sometimes inadvertently set the stage for such behaviors and to let our children know that we don't care to hear that kind of information.

Other Adult Players

Other important adults in our child's life typically include teachers, coaches, daycare providers, and anyone who monitors or provides a service for our children. Deciding how to partner and interact with these people is complicated. If we do more than our child needs, we challenge her independence and appear intrusive. If we do less than our child needs, we may set him up to needlessly falter and suffer. Making this more complex is that the middle ground is a moving target (i.e., our child is always growing, circumstances are always changing, and the competencies and motivation of the service providers vary tremendously).

If my child and I are blessed, he does well across the board. Such a child doesn't need me to interact with the adults who serve him; I may desire to be collaborative, but it isn't necessary. However, if my child is struggling, he may need me to collaborate in order to do well. The complex scientific literature on this point suggests that children who have significant vulnerabilities end up doing better when their parents collaborate. For instance, researchers Drs. Arthur Reynolds and Suh-Ruu Ou, in their review of the scientific literature on the effectiveness of early childhood interventions, concluded that the degree of parent involvement at school was one of the three primary predictors of a child's success at school.

THE STRATEGY

Divorce is inevitably painful for everyone. However, a divorced or divorcing parent can pursue a number of strategies to promote healing and to avoid needless suffering.

Promote Adult Healing

The 2000 U.S. Census indicates that more than one million kids were living with a divorced parent in the previous year, while other research has projected that a little more than one-third of children will have divorced parents by the time they're sixteen. According to a review of the scientific literature by psychologist Dr. Joan Kelly, a key modifiable predictor of how well kids adjust to a divorce is how well their parents get along. Similarly, an intervention model evaluated by researchers Dr. Sharlene Wolchik, Clorinda Schenck, and Dr. Irwin Sandler has identified four modifiable factors for promoting good adaptation of children to divorce: Mother-child relationship quality, father-child contact, effective discipline, and interparental conflict.

Clearly, child adjustment to divorce hinges heavily on parent adjustment. Here are six steps that may get you on the path to helping your kids during or after a divorce:

Step One: Acknowledge that you have suffered a wound. White whales are more common than woundless divorces, at least when children are involved. What happens if a person who has a physical wound ignores it? If it's small, it may heal on its own. But significant wounds need attention. Imagine you saw a person with a gaping wound and you said, "Hey Bill, shouldn't you take care of that wound?" and the person responded, "What wound? Oh, that? That's not really a problem. It's fine." This is how I often feel in my office when otherwise sensible parents tell me that they don't need a healing plan for their divorce wounds.

Step Two: Have the wound understood and healed, preferably in collaboration with a knowledgeable professional. A good assessment would suggest a plan for healing. However, any combination of the following may help: prayer, selected readings, support groups, improved self-care, leaning on loved ones, counseling (sometimes in combination with medication), meditation, and other strategies covered in this book. Parents who heal divorce wounds are able to be more intentional in their parenting and have more freedom to love. (See also the Supportive Strategy at the end of this chapter.)

Step Three: Resolve ongoing conflicts with your ex. If there are none, count yourself wise and lucky. Otherwise, seek the services of either a trusted third party or a mental health professional in order to accomplish peace. Imagine you walked into a home and were told that the father lived on the third floor and the mother on the second, with the children traveling in between the floors and the parents trying to communicate on an as-needed basis. Imagine how the wellness of children living in such a household could become compromised. Divorced families are still families, and peace promotes wellness within everyone.

Step Four: Avoid certain kinds of harmful (though often understandable) reactive parenting approaches. Here are some examples:

- Berating your ex within earshot of your child or using your child as a soundboard for problems you're having with your ex. Imagine each criticism as a dart you throw at your child.
- Quarreling with your ex within earshot of the child.
- Allowing your child to say negative things about your ex without challenge. Your child may be making such statements in order to please you, even though it involves sticking darts in herself. If your child is genuinely upset with your ex, arrange for her to

discuss her concerns with a neutral and mature family person (e.g., one of your ex's blood relatives) or counselor.

- Expressing nonverbal anger toward your ex within earshot of your child. This may not be a dart, but it's a hard-thrown tennis ball.
- Questioning your child about your ex. Your child may become overwhelmed playing the role of a spy.
- Disagreeing with, or qualifying, positive statements that your child makes about your ex. It can be extremely challenging to hear your child make positive comments about your ex that you know are not true. Even if these statements are inaccurate, positive illusions are an important part of a resilient mind. He'll have plenty of opportunity to reevaluate the accuracy of such statements over time.
- Trying to form a coalition with your child against your ex. In addition to the dart issue, children develop their models about how families work in childhood. Forming a coalition against a parent leads your child to conclude that whatever is gained by one family member is lost by the other.
- Threatening to limit access to your ex. This can be terrifying to a child.
- Threatening to take your ex to court within earshot of your child. This is also scary to a child. Not only are the two most important people in her life at each other's throats, but she also has to worry that one of you will seriously wound the other.
- Rejecting, or qualifying, the intermittent feelings of loss that your child expresses about your ex. Regardless of the motivation (e.g., feeling guilty that your child is going through this), such responses encourage maladaptive responses to loss.
- Staying trapped in feelings of rage or hurt toward your ex.

Step Five: Embrace the following proactive, and often healing, parenting approaches:

- Having positive conversations with your ex within earshot of your child. This is one of the biggest favors you can do for your child following a divorce.
- Complimenting your ex within earshot of your child, with honesty and sincerity. Though this may cause bile to rise up in your

throat, it's often a salve to your child's divorce wounds.

- Affirming to your child that your ex loves him. As Dr. Selma Fraiberg illustrates in her book *The Magic Years*, children think magically and in egocentric terms. They often blame themselves for their parents' divorce. Even if your ex is attentive toward your child, she may imagine that he or she is upset with her, so these affirmations can be very helpful. Likewise, if your ex is neglectful, your child is likely to conclude that this has something to do with how lovable he is. There are few things more comforting than when you affirm your ex's love for your child in these moments.
- Qualifying or disagreeing with negative statements that your child makes about your ex. If your child makes statements suggesting significant abuse or neglect, arrange for her to review this with a qualified professional. Otherwise, to support your ex to your child is to support your child.
- Putting your child's best interests above any feelings of rage or hurt that you feel toward your ex.
- Keeping your child unaware of any ongoing court battles and trying to be done with them as soon as possible.
- Allowing, and welcoming, your child to express feelings of loss pertaining to your ex. It sucks to be a kid going through a divorce. Letting your kid talk about that, and expressing empathy toward her thoughts and feelings, regardless of how doing so makes you feel inside, facilitates her adjustment.
- Providing your child with methods for coping with the divorce (e.g., readings, a child divorce support group, counseling).
- Making peace with your ex and accomplishing a personal recovery from the divorce.

Can I try to read your mind for a moment? Is part of what you are thinking going something like this: "Yes, I get it. But, my ex doesn't and far from it. So, while I'm being reasonable and supportive, he's filling my kid's mind with poison about me. So, if I do as you suggest, it is like having the judge hear only from the prosecutor and not the defense attorney!" In response, let me share a composite case from my practice:

Mary was a single twenty-eight-year-old who was a successful real estate agent. She presented for treatment because she found herself unable to work well with, or become close to, women. All her close friendships were with men, although a successful romantic relationship eluded her.

Mary reviewed her childhood, which included a painful divorce when she was eight years old. She described her mother as her preferred parent throughout childhood. Mary explained that her mom and dad had very different styles of parenting. She said that when she was at her mom's she was allowed to do as she wished. She could eat, sleep, and play as she wished; she also had no chores, and her mom "trusted" her to meet her responsibilities without monitoring. She also described her mother as being affable, unless the topic turned toward her father, at which point she would become bitter and complain about him. She would also fuel and agree with all of Mary's complaints about him; in fact, such declarations often resulted in a reward.

On the other hand, her father very rarely had an unkind word to say about her mother and insisted that Mary meet her academic, household, and self-care responsibilities. Moreover, Mary's father was actively engaged in monitoring her, especially when she was outside the home. Mary noted that her father's standards facilitated a great deal of conflict between them during adolescence, during which time she viewed her mother's residence as an oasis. However, by the time she was twenty-three, she was very close to her father, had little contact with her mother, and realized that her mother had taken the easy path.

Mary believed that her mother loved her, but also that she was ill-equipped to extend herself in selfless ways. Alternatively, she came to a view that her father was "a very strong and loving man." As she worked through her resulting anger and sadness regarding her relationship with her mother, she found herself becoming more able to draw closer to women and to have effective sexual relationships with men.

Despite what might appear to be the consequences in the short run, loving your child can *never* be the wrong choice.

Step Six: Don't punt on second down. I've seen too many divorced parents reach the conclusion that their ex spouse is beyond approach. The ex has become almost a mythic figure: the pure personification of unreasonableness, cruelty, or narcissism. Exaggerated statements represent this stance: "She can't be reasoned with," "He's not capable of considering someone else's needs," "There's no love left in her heart," or "Do you think he actually cares about the kids? No way! This is just to hurt me!"

Very rarely is a person *always* something or *never* something else. Even people who are generally unreasonable can intermittently be reasoned with. Even people who are highly narcissistic can demonstrate acts of selflessness. Sure, there are instances when people suffer brain injuries, are being ravaged by addiction, or otherwise are hurting to a degree that makes it excruciatingly difficult for them to give. However, it is also very, very easy to give up and not try all reasonable avenues for peaceful resolution. Staying in the game is an act of love.

Collaborate with School Personnel

Before I begin, here's a personal story: Early in my career I helped launch a chapter of Children and Adults with Attention-Deficit/Hyperactivity Disorder (CHADD) in the southern suburbs of Chicago. Each weekly meeting included a presentation by a local ADHD expert. During the question-and-answer portion of the presentations, parents with either metaphorical or literal clenched fists said things such as, "Those darn teachers and principals. You can't believe what they're doing!" So persuasive and passionate were their protestations that I became convinced that there was something seriously wrong with the Chicago public schools' treatment of children with ADHD.

Later in my career, I started doing in-service trainings for teachers. During the question-and-answer sessions, several teachers with either metaphorical or literal clenched fists would say things such as, "Those darn parents. You can't believe what they're doing!" It occurred to me that as long as such clenched fisting is happening, the service to children is probably being compromised.

The interventions I review below depend on two premises. First, most teachers are in the business because they wish to make a positive difference in kids' lives, not because they want to make a lot of money (if so, they've had poor career counseling). As a group, teachers are a mission-driven lot. In my experience, if a teacher is acting in an ill-advised fashion, it's usually because he's overwhelmed or because she's lost her way. Second, most parents love their kids more than their own lives. Hence, if a parent is performing in a fashion that's ill advised, it is usually because of some human condition with which it's easy to empathize. To render a harsh judgment is to miss key aspects of the big picture. To be empathic is to be objective and accurate.

Parent-Teacher Conferences

The least intensive opportunity to collaborate with teachers is the school conference. This is usually just you, and/or your spouse, and the teacher. To get as much out of the meeting as possible, I suggest doing a number of things.

First, prepare your list of questions or concerns in advance. Consult with your significant other or a good friend regarding whether your list seems reasonable. (This is another way of asking whether you are effectively controlling your understandable urge to be a lunatic.) Be sure to prepare questions about social skills, respect for the teacher, work-related performance, and grades.

Second, be a few minutes early and try to keep to the allotted time. (This says to the teacher that you are respectful of his needs, too. You can always ask for another meeting if you have more to discuss.) Upon introduction offer a big toothy smile and a firm handshake. Then display rapt attention as the teacher shares his thoughts and materials. For your first reaction try to affirm anything positive that you've noted about the teacher or your child's experience with the teacher.

Third, and if not mentioned, ask the teacher what she believes your child's strengths are. This is important to review before considering your child's opportunities for growth.

When going over opportunities for growth, try to do these five things:

1. Endeavor to keep an open mind (i.e., respecting that all of we engaged parents have the propensity to act like crazy people).

2. Avoid acting like you believe the teacher is responsible for your

child's problems. It's fine to ask a diplomatic question or two. But, if you get resistance, imagine how you would feel if a teacher, in an unsolicited fashion, implied that you had opportunities for growth.

3. Keep in mind that the teacher has a number of other children in the classroom. This will keep you from expecting too much.

4. Ask the teacher to articulate the specific ways he is hoping your child will behave, instead of phrasing the behaviors in negative terms.

5. If your child is struggling, ask if it's possible for him to make a unique and positive contribution to the class (e.g., the kid assigned to erase the boards, run messages, collect papers). This strategy, which I once heard recommend by Dr. Robert Brooks at a presentation, is good for any child, but is especially important for kids who are struggling. Our self-esteem is affected by what is mirrored in the eyes of others.

To conclude your meeting, review the things you've agreed to. It's also ideal to follow up with a brief "thank you for the meeting" note that reviews your affirmations for the teacher, what you covered, and what you've agreed to.

Daily Communication System

A more intensive strategy is to set up a daily communication system from home to school that is tied to a behavioral contract or token system (see Chapter 5). This is for instances when you need to correct behavioral problems with social skills, teacher compliance, or academic effort or per-formance. Figure 9.1 is what a log sheet might look like.

Let me offer a few instructions. Starting at the top, you don't need to put a slot for the teacher's name if your child has only one teacher. Your child, if she is old enough to do it, ought to fill in the portion above the thick line; otherwise you would ask the teacher to fill it in. The teacher should fill in the section below the thick line and only sign the paper if the top part is filled in correctly, assuming your child was the one responsible for filling it in.

I say to teachers, "It's not your job to make corrections to the top part. But, if you see errors, and have the time, we'd be most grateful if you could help correct them. That said, if you don't have the time, no problem. Just

Figure 9.1

John's Log Sheet

Date: _____ Teacher: _____

Today's Homework: _____
_____
_____

Returned Grades: _____
_____
_____

Next Quiz/Test Date: _____

Long-term Project (what it is and when it is due):_____
_____
_____

Grade for behavior toward peers: A   B   C   D   F
Grade for behavior toward teacher: A   B   C   D   F
Grade for staying on task and effort: A   B   C   D   F

Comments:_____
_____
_____
_____

_____
Teacher's Signature

don't sign it." (There are methods for responding to forgeries, but I'm loathe to review them here, because kids who are inclined to act in this way, beyond once or twice, are probably doing other things that would call for you to consult with a mental health professional.)

You and the teacher may need to talk about what the behavior grades mean. They're not like academic grades. I suggest the following:

> A = Did something extraordinarily nice or effective
> B = Behaved in an expected fashion
> C = There were a couple of small mistakes or lapses
> D = There was a moderate mistake or lapse
> F = Unacceptable behavior or performance

For prereaders, you can use happy, neutral, and sad faces to record behavioral performance. (You can find a sample form on www.resilientyouth.com)

Within the token system or contract there should be rewards for bringing the sheets home signed, for doing the homework listed on the sheets (including remediating any poor grades, studying for tests, and working on long-term projects), and for earning good behavior grades (usually one level of reward for a B and another for an A). Rewards can include chips, points, or access to a privilege. You can also set up weekend rewards based on cumulative performance during the week, as well as a monthly reward. There should also be punishments established for Ds and Fs in behavior grades; these might include withdrawal of chips/points, a time-out, or the suspension of a privilege.

I would start out having these sheets come home daily. It's easier to reduce the frequency of reporting than it is to increase it. If the sheets come home consistently positive for two to three weeks, you could consider, in consultation with the teacher(s), going to a weekly report. Once you get four to six weeks of positive weekly reports you could consult with the teacher about whether to discontinue the reports altogether.

If these methods do not work, you probably need the help of a child clinician. In these instances a capable expert will likely wish to schedule a school staff meeting (these are more elaborate than a parent-teacher conference).

If your child is struggling with some other adult—a daycare supervisor or a coach—these same strategies can work. Start out with a conference. If that doesn't resolve matters, go to a log sheet. In instances when you can observe the interactions (e.g., your child's behavior at soccer events), you can be the one to code the log sheets, first asking your child how she might evaluate her performance.

Hunter was a ten-year-old boy who lived to play basketball. He played whenever he could. At the end of the recreation league's regular season, an additional brief season was added for those boys who wished to continue playing into the spring (these were usually boys who preferred basketball over baseball). Hunter lobbied his parents to agree to the extended basketball season in lieu of baseball. They agreed.

The assigned coach and Hunter did not mesh. The coach did not know Hunter, but he did know most of the other boys on the team from past, shared experiences. He was a "my way or the highway" type of coach who had his favorites going into the season. As Hunter bristled, the coach bristled back, and Hunter played less.

Hunter's dad arranged to consult with the coach, using strategies similar to the ones I reviewed earlier. This consultation generated specific behaviors that the coach was looking for Hunter to display. These behaviors were then turned into a log sheet that generated points for Hunter. He was told that once he accrued a predetermined number of points, he would be granted the video game of his choice, as long as it had an acceptable rating (the coach was unaware of this program).

Hunter became more successful, in the coach's eyes, overnight (not because the coach changed but because Hunter stopped acting in ways that made it harder to see his athletic ability). In the next few weeks he became a regular starter; by the end of the season he seemed to have favored status with the coach.

Supportive Strategy

Practice Forgiveness

Forgiveness, whether it is unilateral or collaborative, private or interactive, promotes healing. To require that the other person apologize, or feel remorseful, is to give that person too much control over our wellness. To not forgive is to stay trapped in pain and anger. To be released from this trap, try these four steps:

1. Pick someone toward whom you hold a grudge or harbor a hurt.

2. Fully reflect on the ways in which that person harmed you. Take time to be fully aware of your pain. Journaling can help. Talking to a close friend, loved one, or therapist can help, too. There is no time-line for this. Explore the wound(s) fully. Once you find you're not unearthing new material, consider the next step.

3. Put yourself in the other person's shoes. What human condition explains that person's behavior toward you? Try to understand the other person; if you subscribe to a spiritual model, its tenets may work synergistically with this effort. This step *does not* minimize nor justify what was done to you. Your pain is real and needs to be both respected and given its due. Again, don't rush this step.

4. Forgive that person as thoroughly as you can, endeavoring to be compassionate, loving, and kind. (As I indicated above, this can be done privately or collaboratively, depending on what's best for you, the other person, and the situation.) Be patient with yourself. Full forgiveness sometimes takes time and comes in waves.

Of all the supportive strategies I've shared, this is the one that's most challenging and complex, so you may—if you're like many of us—need help.

Strategy Summary

If you're divorced from your child's other birth parent, one of the biggest presents you can give your child is to make peace both with your ex and within yourself.

Create positive synergy with your child's teacher(s) and others who serve your child. Often this can be facilitated by approaching them with the same skill, understanding, and tact that you would wish to be used with you if your roles were reversed.

Intervene sooner rather than later when there is a problem. Establish specific behavioral targets in collaboration with key players, a method for tracking the goals, rewards for compliance, and punishments for non-compliance.

The Skeptical Parent's Challenge

Parent: You stress that I should do all that I can to promote my child's relationship with my ex. *But*, mine drinks daily and gets verbally abusive. How do I support that?

Author: This is an excellent point. And sadly, a common problem. I'm not suggesting that a child be put in the care, or even in the presence, of an abusive or neglectful parent. In these situations it would be especially important to engage the services of an appropriately trained mental health professional.

Parent: My ex and his wife routinely allow my child to do things that I don't think are healthy. Are you saying that I should not try to find out about these things or do nothing about them?

Author: The Serenity Prayer comes to mind: "God grant me the serenity to accept the things I cannot change; the courage to change the things I can; and the wisdom to know the difference." If there is tension between you and your ex and you try to control how your ex parents your child, you're not likely to improve the situation and may actually worsen it. I know this is maddening, but it's more maddening to try to do something not within your power. Again, involving a mental health professional in these matters can be most helpful.

Parent: My kid's teacher is a harsh perfectionist. You seem to be suggesting that I should ignore that and even try to charm him.

Author: I know it can sound like I'm suggesting puckering up, but I'm not. Nor am I suggesting that you be passive. I'm suggesting you try to empathize with the teacher's goals (not methods, but goals), consult in the way I've described, and encourage your child to see this as an opportunity to learn how to deal effectively with such styles. However, if these interventions do not work *and* your child is being harmed, then a consultation with both a child mental health professional and the school principal would be in order.

Parent: I hate daddy ball! It is unacceptable for parents to favor their own kids when their talents do not call for it. You seem to be suggesting I should just tolerate it.

Author: I hear you. It's very frustrating to experience this. But, don't we all experience versions of daddy ball from time-to-time in our adult lives? As a kid and an adult, the choices are avoidance, rage, passive acceptance, or effective coping. I hope I've illustrated what the latter can look like.

Get Help if Your Child is Demonstrating Problems You're Unable to Fix

The child's sob in silence curses deeper than
the strong man in his wrath.
Elizabeth Barrett Browning, *The Cry of the Children*

Children endure much needless suffering. It doesn't take much for kids to develop mental or behavioral disorders. Kids exposed to four or more adverse events experience a ten-fold increased risk of maladjustment. Children experiencing at least three adverse events are one-hundred times more likely to meet diagnostic criteria for depression, while about one-third of children exposed to a serious trauma develop PTSD.

Alternatively, children can suffer from mental illnesses even when faced with ordinary stress. For instance, a child with a family history of certain disorders (e.g., ADHD, bipolar disorder) can start to show symptoms within the confines of typical family life. Taken all together, it appears that about 10–20 percent of U.S. children meet the criteria for a behavioral or mental disorder. *However, only about 20–30 percent of these kids receive effective care.* And, even when kids get care, they've often already been suffering for years.

Let me cherry-pick some findings from the relevant research literature:

- A study of four thousand kids investigated by child welfare found that only 25 percent of the kids with mental health needs had received care in the previous year.
- A study of kids enrolled in a special education program found that 50 percent of the kids with ADHD had unmet needs for mental health services.
- A study of 776 teenagers suffering from depression found that they were no more likely to be referred for care than nondepressed kids. A different study found that 75 percent of depressed kids go undiagnosed; and, that even when kids are accurately diagnosed, only about 20 percent of them get specialty care. Perhaps this contributes to the fact that suicide is the third leading cause of death among those fifteen to twenty-four years old and the fifth leading cause of death among those five to fourteen years old.
- Seventy-one percent of adults don't perceive a child who is demonstrating daily symptoms as having a clinical problem, and one-third of adults believe that ADHD improves on its own.

Quoting from researchers Dr. Sheryl Kataoka, Lily Zhang, and Dr. Kenneth Wells: "We found that only 21 percent of the children who need a mental health evaluation receive services. This suggests that about 7.5 million children have unmet needs."

When I'm giving a talk for parents, I sometimes begin by putting my hand on my cheek and saying: "I must apahligize. My tuuth is really thore and sthwollen. So sthorry if I sthound wierd. It's been this way for two months. I was thinkin' maybe I should get it looked at. I don't know. Maybe I will, maybe I won't. We'll thsee." I'm hoping parents think: *What is he doing? Doesn't he know we have professionals called dentists?* Or, *What century does he live in? Doesn't he know it's stupid to suffer like that?*

The impairment children experience from mental pain stands to be much more damaging than dental pain. Yet, most kids hurting in this way don't get effective mental health care. This suffering is unnecessary, beneath us, and too often affiliated with tragic outcomes (e.g., depression has a higher mortality rate than cardiac disease).

Common Childhood Behavioral Disorders

According to authors Drs. Judith Rapoport and Deborah Ismond, children and teens are eligible for forty-two different diagnoses within our primary and current diagnostic system for psychological disorders (i.e., the *Diagnostic and Statistical Manual of Mental Disorders—Fourth Edition*; the DSM is currently under revision so the number of categories may change in the DSM-V). Let me review three of the more common categories.

Anxiety Disorders

Anxiety disorders are the most common type of psychological disorder in children, with about 10–20 percent of U.S. kids suffering from one. Dr. Aaron Beck, one of the founders of cognitive-behavioral therapy, has suggested that all anxiety disorders have at their core one of two fundamental fears: fear of a physical death and fear of a social death. Most anxious kids with whom I've worked have irrational fears of either being harshly judged or having harm befall them or loved ones. While there are twelve different ways to diagnose anxiety in kids, here are some of the more common conditions:

Generalized Anxiety Disorder (GAD) is characterized by excessive worrying that causes physical symptoms. It can seem that as soon as one worry is resolved, two new ones replace it.

Panic Disorder involves intense and impairing anxiety attacks, sometimes even without the child knowing why. A child may feel like she is having a heart attack or going crazy.

Obsessive-Compulsive Disorder involves a child having intrusive and painful thoughts (e.g., our house will blow up) that he can only diminish by doing rituals that have no logical purpose (e.g., turning a light switch on and off ten times before leaving a room). In typical cases, the rituals take an hour or more per day to perform.

Social Phobia is characterized by excessive fears about interacting with others. The child worries that she will say or do something that will lead to horrible social consequences. Hence, she avoids relating to others in certain circumstances; the more severe the pain, the more restrictive the social circumstances in which the child is willing to engage.

Posttraumatic Stress Disorder is discussed in Chapter 4.

Mood Disorders

At any given time, about 3 percent of kids and about 8 percent of teenagers are clinically depressed. However, when you broaden the lens and ask how many experience a major depressive episode by age eighteen, the numbers rise to about one in three females and one in five males. Add to these figures the incidence rates of the other mood disorders and you can see that we parents do well to learn to recognize the signs of these maladies. The following is a brief description of the more common mood disorders in youth:

Major Depressive Episode requires that one of two symptoms be present for at least two weeks: either the child doesn't enjoy things or his mood is either sad or irritable most of the time. Other possible symptoms include sleep and appetite disturbance, lethargy, low self-esteem, hopelessness, and concentration problems.

Bipolar Disorder is a very complex disorder, especially when it has an onset in childhood. Typically the child experiences either rapid alternations between depression and mania or experiences them both together. Manic episodes can be manifested by euphoria or extreme rage, both of which cause the child to behave in destructive ways. Significant disruption in the child's ability to think is a hallmark symptom (e.g., believing they have extra special powers). He may also experience hallucinations.

Dysthymic Disorder is akin to a persisting fever in the child's mood. To meet current criteria a child must be sad or irritable, for most of the day, on most days, for a year or longer. Other related symptoms are listed above, under Major Depressive Episode.

Attention Deficit and Disruptive Behavior Disorders

What's the best way for a child to get needed mental health services? Annoy an adult. While most of the kids with ADHD or disruptive behavior disorders (DBDs) do not get care, this group's capacity to stress adults sometimes quickens their access to it. The following are summaries of the three primary types of disorders in this category:

Oppositional Defiant Disorder (ODD) involves resisting adult commands and having problems regulating anger. These symptoms may be manifested at home, at school, or both.

Conduct Disorder (CD) can emerge if ODD is not treated, or some kids skip past ODD right into CD. These children typically have the same problems as children with ODD, but they also do some of these: violate laws, damage property, and hurt animals or people.

Attention-Deficit/Hyperactivity Disorder involves impaired attention and/or hyperactivity and impulsivity. There are currently three types of ADHD: Predominantly Inattentive (significant attention problems without significant hyperactivity/impulsivity), Predominantly Hyperactive/Impulsive (opposite of the inattentive type), and Combined (both types of symptoms are present to a significant degree). When people talk about ADHD, they usually mean the Combined type, which comprises about 75 percent of these children. The impairing symptoms must be manifested both at home and at school for at least six months. If another medical or psychiatric problem can account for the symptoms, the ADHD diagnosis is withheld.

Other Categories

There are many other categories of mental health disorders in children. Children with eating disorders may binge eat, starve themselves, or try to make food leave their bodies quickly. Children with pervasive developmental disorders may have difficulty forming effective relationships, show unusual preoccupations, and struggle with language. Though more common in adolescence, children can sometimes abuse substances. They can also have problems toileting, forming attachments, distinguishing reality from fantasy, responding effectively to stress, and learning academic material. Moreover, most kids who meet the criteria for one problem often suffer from at least one other problem as well. This is complicated business that requires expert assistance.

Ease Needless Suffering

Although many of the disorders listed above are serious, many of them can be treated effectively in a relatively short period of time. Getting help need not be complicated or painful—and is usually a lot less stressful than living with an untreated mental health problem.

Think of your child's mental health as you would your child's dental health. If your child is experiencing mild to moderate emotional, cognitive, or behavioral symptoms that have lasted for two weeks or longer, do as you would if your child had mild to moderate dental pain that persisted for two weeks. If the symptoms are serious (e.g., he is suicidal, she cannot get on the school bus), do as you would if your child started suddenly sobbing that her tooth hurt a great deal. Responding in this way will significantly decrease the odds that your child will be one of the millions of children in the United States who suffer needlessly.

THE STRATEGY

In the little world in which children have their existence, whosoever brings them up, there is nothing so finely perceived and so finely felt as injustice.
Charles Dickens, *Great Expectations*

Whenever I give a talk on the power of clinical psychology to heal needless suffering, I inevitably get a few people coming up to me afterward asking for my business card so that they can arrange for me to evaluate their child. They usually seem very eager and interested. However, I rarely get a call sooner than six months. I often imagine such parents picking up the phone and—like an adolescent calling someone for a first date—punching six numbers and then hanging up. There is something very intimidating about arranging for a child's psychological pain to be understood and healed. My clinical experience is that parents delay because they worry that their child will experience self-esteem damage. Or, a lack of knowledge about what will happen promotes ambivalence, fear, misunderstanding, or denial. I address both concerns in what follows.

ODD: A Case in Point

I'd like to elaborate on ODD to make a point about how far many of us need to travel to become more effective in supporting our kids' mental health.

As hurtful as it can be, ODD is one of the most easily treated disorders in childhood. The treatment of choice for ODD is behaviorally oriented family therapy. When I deliver this treatment, it averages eight sessions past the evaluation phase, as long as the child has no other significant problems and the parents are able to parent with intention. Assuming no other complications are present, it's very successful in the majority of instances (i.e., the child complies with adult directives at least 85 percent of the time within fifteen seconds, the child completes at least 85 percent of his academic work, and each parent-child combination is spending at least one hour per week doing special time). Alternatively, if a child receives individual therapy, or no treatment, the symptoms can go on for years. In summary: A very impairing disorder is, in the large majority of instances, quickly cured as long as it is properly tended to. Given this reality, can you appreciate the frustration I feel when I have experiences like this one:

> A few years ago I attended a parent-teacher conference for one of my kids. The business of the conference was concluded with extra time on the clock. So, I asked the teacher how often she has to deal with defiant children. She said every year it seems like she has a couple of defiant kids in her class, and they represent an enormous challenge. I then asked if she ever refers the kids for care. She said that her pattern had been to refer them for individual counseling with the school counselor, though she noted that this often did not seem to work. I took the opportunity to give her an overview of the best treatment for ODD. This very experienced and competent teacher said that she had never heard that information before.

Find a Good Clinician

The first question to ask yourself is, *"What type of professional can do this work?"* That's a difficult question to answer, but effective child mental health professionals have some common characteristics (it may be difficult for you to discern some of these, but the more of them that you can discern, the better the match you may have):

- The clinician has a great capacity for empathy (i.e., is able to understand, and even feel, another person's experience and then effectively communicate that back to the person).
- The clinician is intelligent. Good clinicians are bright enough to be able to synthesize the research literature with your child's and family's story. A clinician can be of average intelligence and be effective if the problem(s) he treats are similar to ones he himself has conquered (e.g., an addictions counselor who is in an effective recovery).
- The clinician is motivated because she truly cares. In the era of managed cost, this attribute is especially important. Good clinicians are tenacious when it comes to chasing down healing for your child.
- The clinician is psychologically minded.
- The clinician is open and flexible. Effective clinicians must be able to revise their opinions when contradictory evidence appears. Likewise, the clinician needs to make adjustments based upon your priorities and values. Sure, she owes it to you to offer her recommendations and the reasons behind them. But, if you disagree, a skilled clinician ought to be able to discuss what adjustments are possible and how they might affect the prognosis.
- The clinician is culturally competent. Being culturally competent doesn't necessarily mean that the therapist has worked with many people in your demographic category (though such would be a plus); it does mean that he understands that race and culture matter and is open to exploring how such interacts with the care.

The above characterizations are based primarily on my opinion and experience, as the empirical literature along these lines is hardly conclusive. As one researcher declared, "When the data are lacking, opinion prevails."

Here are a few thoughts about professional clinician education and training:

- Education is extremely important. While state credentialing categories and degree program requirements vary quite a bit for clinical psychologists, counselors, psychiatrists, social workers, and psychiatric nurses, the more years of quality training a clinician has, the better.
- Experience is very important. The more a skilled clinician practices his craft, the more he learns and refines. I'm better now than I was five years ago; I hope I'll be able to say the same thing five years from now. No one is so experienced as to not have significant opportunities for growth.
- Licensure is critically important. When a state grants a license to a clinician, it means that the person passed a review of credentials. While states vary in terms of what they require and to which professions they grant licenses, these reviews ensure that the clinician meets basic educational and experiential requirements. Be sure to look for evidence of current state licensure or certification in the clinician's waiting room, search for it online, call the relevant board and ask for verification, or ask the clinician for the documentation.
- Continuing education is very important. It's fair to ask prospective therapists how many years' worth of *supervised* clinical training she had during her graduate training or since (not counting years doing exclusively medical treatments), how many years she has been in practice, how she continues to educate herself, and whether she is licensed to practice in your state. Review the person's resumé (many clinicians put them on their Web sites). While not required to demonstrate competence, evidence of peer validation (e.g., board certification, publications, being elected to professional offices) can be comforting.

Last, a good approach to finding a competent clinician is to ask people for referrals: trusted confidants; your child's pediatrician; local parent support organizations; faculty within university psychology, psychiatry, counseling, or social work departments; a school counselor. You might then call the names you've been given and inquire about evaluation procedures, openings, and financial arrangements; these conversations can also give you a "feel" for it.

The Effectiveness of Child Psychotherapy

I need to explain two terms: effect size and meta-analytic studies. Effect size is a way for researchers to measure the impact of a clinical intervention. A .5 effect size is considered moderate; the child is not out of the woods yet, but the treatment is showing measurable benefit: Maybe a depressed child is starting to sleep well for the first time in months or a defiant child behaves well at school for a couple of weeks. A .8 effect size would be considered, according to one researcher, "whopping"; maybe that depressed child displays no observable signs of depression for two weeks or that defiant child behaves well at school and at home for a month.

A meta-analytic study is one that combines the results from several studies to try to reach more far-reaching conclusions about an important question.

In a 2005 article published in *American Psychologist*, researchers Drs. John Weisz, Irwin Sandler, Joseph Durlak, and Barry Anton reviewed the evidence on the effectiveness of talking psychotherapies for youth. Their findings suggest a good news/bad news story. I'll share the good news now and get to the bad news later.

The article indicates that there are more than 1,500 outcome studies on child and adolescent psychotherapy. The effect sizes from meta-analytic studies were reported to be as follows (remember, .5 = moderate and .8 = whopping):

Composition of Meta-Analytic Study	Effect Size
75 studies on children aged 12 and younger	.71
A collection of studies of youth aged 4–18	.79
106 studies of children aged 4–18	.79
223 studies of youth aged 4–18	.88
150 studies of youth aged 2–18	.71

Quoting the authors: "The average treated child was functioning better after treatment than more than 75 percent of control group children. The effects fall within range of what has been found in meta-analyses of predominantly adult psychotherapy."

While minority youth tend to be underserved even more than Caucasian children, available evidence is that the effect sizes for their outcome studies average around .44. While this figure is smaller than the statistics indicated above, this area of investigation is burdened by a lack of well-constructed studies. The authors of this review, Drs. Stanley Huey and Antonio Polo, concluded: "In summary, the psychotherapy outcome literature leaves room for considerable optimism regarding treatments for ethnic minorities."

In summary, 20–30 percent of all children meet the criteria for a diagnosable psychological disorder (make that 24–42 percent if you add kids who are experiencing psychological impairment but their pain doesn't rise to the level required for a primary diagnosis), but only about 20–30 percent of them get effective care, even though we often know how to cure or effectively manage the problem(s). Is this acceptable?

Get a Good Evaluation

Let's say you decide to have your child evaluated by a mental health professional. What might you expect? (The following is based on the assumption that potential medical causes for your child's symptoms have been ruled out.)

First, a skilled clinician will explain, up front, her goals and methods for the evaluation. Typically, the primary goals would be to generate a model that explains the symptoms your child is experiencing and to develop a plan for healing, which should involve either a cure (e.g., in the case of ODD) or effective management (e.g., in the case of ADHD). Desirable methods for reaching these goals include the following:

A family interview

(It's generally difficult to competently complete such a family interview in less than ninety minutes.) Any assessment of your child is really an assessment of his world, a critical part of which is your family. Thus, it makes sense to interview some key players. Clinicians can have equally valid preferences for whom they interview. But, for me, a minimal list includes the child of concern and the adults who live with the child. If there's a birth parent outside the home, I strive to get that person's input as well, though the point at which I do so varies. I also try to include any stepparents who live outside the home. A good interview would survey at least the following areas:

- The symptoms of concern
- Your child's and family's strengths
- Stress experienced by family members and your child
- Your child's psychiatric history, if there is one
- Your family psychiatric history, both formal (i.e., those who received treatment) and informal (i.e., family members who might have benefited from treatment but did not pursue it)
- Your child's and family's history for substance use
- Details about current and past family functioning
- Your child's academic performance
- Your child's social and extracurricular engagements
- Your child's medical and developmental history

A child interview

Your child is an expert on her inner world, so it's important for the clinician to meet alone with her, as there may be important details that your child doesn't want you to know, no matter how close you are. Depending on the age of your child, some portion of the time may be spent observing play. (I usually do this in a fifty-minute appointment.)

A review of relevant records

This would certainly include school records, but often includes— if they exist and are relevant—medical, psychiatric, welfare, and legal records. I would worry about the accuracy of the diagnostic impression if the clinician doesn't review key records, at least if they're available.

The completion of behavior rating scales and/or psychological testing

What child isn't depressed, anxious, hyper, or something *some* of the time? For this reason, competent clinicians do not diagnose a condition before establishing that the symptoms exist to an unusual degree (i.e., typically at or above the ninety-third percentile, when compared to children of the same sex and approximate age).

A feedback session

The following are advisable components:

- A review of your child's and family's strengths. Your child and family have many more strengths than symptoms.
- A review of the diagnostic impression. This should include how the clinician arrived at the diagnosis, the nature of the diagnosis (e.g., the criteria, known causes, prevalence rates, and prognosis), the next most likely diagnostic model (should the selected model prove to be incorrect), and an opportunity for you to ask questions. (This is also a good time to ask for reading materials that elaborate on the diagnosis or the recommendations.)
- A review of the recommendations for either interventions and/or additional assessments. Recommendations for interventions would typically include an overview of the evidence supporting them.

Thus, a quality assessment would ask you, other parents, parent figures, your child (if his reading skills are sufficient), and your child's teachers to fill out questionnaires that would allow comparisons to a large group of children who are doing well. The effective clinician may also give you questionnaires asking about your child's strengths, your child's developmental history, your family's psychiatric history, your psychological wellness, and other relevant content. Finally, the evaluator may suggest psychological testing, which involves additional measures.

Unfortunately, there is an Achilles' heel in our system of measurement. The norms allow us to compare your child to children of the same sex and age group. But, if your child is racially or culturally diverse, we often cannot reliably account for that (i.e., the best measures include ethnically diverse samples, but typically not to a degree that allows for comparisons based on race and culture). This said, a skilled child clinician would know how to partner with you in making indicated adjustments.

If the process goes well, you will leave feeling as if you had looked into the clinician's brain and understood her impression, why she arrived at her impression, as well as her plan for healing your "baby" as quickly and as thoroughly as possible. You should also find that the clinician is respectful, skilled, and caring.

What Happens in Effective Psychotherapies?

In the aforementioned study in *American Psychologist*, there was also bad news: "Studies of treatment as usual in settings in which therapists were able to use their clinical judgment to deliver treatment as they saw fit, not constrained by evidence-based interventions or manuals, and in which there was a comparison of their treatment to a control condition . . . have found effect sizes ranging [at] about zero . . . indicating no treatment benefit."

This suggests that when a clinician practices without being duly influenced by the scientific literature, there is a high risk that the benefits won't exceed what a placebo can accomplish. This finding matches my experience.

Types of Talking Psychotherapy for Children

Many types of therapies exist, and, like medications, they have variable track records across different diagnostic categories. Many children with ADHD respond well to tailored doses of methylphenidate. On the other hand, it's probably not going to help much with PTSD (I say "probably" because just about anything can help with just about anything some of the time). So it is with child psychotherapies.

Thus, be wary of the child psychiatrist with a generalist practice who prescribes methylphenidate to every kid she treats. Likewise, question the child psychologist with a generalist practice who treats every child with play therapy.

That point made, let's review four major types of child therapy:

Cognitive-Behavioral Therapy (CBT)
I hope that by the time my kids have kids, cognitive-behavioral strategies will be routinely taught in schools. CBT teaches a child a collection of methods for manipulating her mood and coping with stress. Some of these strategies are cognitive (e.g., thought testing), some are behavioral (e.g., making yourself do fun things even when feeling sluggish), and some are both (e.g., problem solving).

CBT is usually a structured approach, though skilled therapists deliver it flexibly based on a child's and a family's needs. Handouts and between-session work are common. CBT can be delivered in groups of children, to a family, or to an individual child. Unless they are directly involved in the sessions, parents are usually brought in intermittently so that they may be trained to coach the skills at home.

It's not unusual for CBT to take between twelve and eighteen sessions; however, it can take longer or be briefer. CBT can be especially helpful for anxiety and mood disorders, though there are several other symptoms for which it may also be helpful.

Behaviorally Oriented Family Therapy (BOFT)

Sometimes this approach is called parent training, but I don't care for that term. Parent training implies that parents lack basic skills. There is certainly a place for treatments that teach parents such skills. However, BOFT assumes that parents already possess basic parenting skills but that their child needs supercharged, nonintuitive interventions in order to thrive.

The parents I have delivered this treatment to typically have other children in the home who are responding quite well to their parenting. However, they also have at least one child who is not responding to their best efforts. BOFT can be the answer in these instances.

For younger children, the therapist may meet only with the parents. This can be counterintuitive to some parents, who say, "Hey, my child has the symptoms, not me." While that's true, parents are in the best position to reengineer their child's environment so that compliance leads to a lavish banquet and defiance leads to a walk in the desert.

It's not unusual for this approach to take between eight and fifteen visits, though it can take longer.

Play Therapy (PT)

Play therapy is the most difficult of these therapies to describe (and learn). PT attempts to have the child represent her inner world through play. Invariably, the source of the child's pain is played out. The therapist then tries to help the child resolve the pain through interventions in the play. Most play therapies are unstructured and often take longer than behavioral approaches (i.e., a minimum of six months is common and one to two years would not be unusual), though not always. Please keep in mind that any effective longer term care is done collaboratively, with full informed consent, so that it does not occur unless a parent believes it has value.

Play therapy can be especially useful for children who are highly traumatized, whose verbal skills are compromised, or in instances when behavioral interventions have failed or have been ruled out. There are also short-term approaches that endeavor to train parents how to conduct therapeutic play at home (e.g., Filial Play Therapy).

Psychoeducational Interventions (PI)

The goal of psychoeducational interventions is to educate the parent(s) about the disorder(s) in question. There are several advantages. First, some disorders promote significant parent-child alienation. Understanding the nature of the attacking illness can help a parent to replace anger with empathy, which aids in the healing process.

Second, the treatment for some disorders requires a marathon mentality: Parents need to coordinate long-term medication treatments, bring a new set of school teachers on board each year, and consider new developmental hurdles in relation to the disorder (e.g., readiness for a sleepover at another child's home, preparedness to go on an out-of-town class trip). Having good information increases the chances that a parent will stay on her game and comply with the most important treatment recommendations.

Third, as with all professions, child clinicians' skills vary. An educated parent is in a better position to know whether a clinician's approach is ill advised, pedestrian, or state of the art.

The length of these programs varies considerably, but six to twelve sessions would not be unusual (when I offer this service I often piggyback it onto some of the other therapies I've listed above). It is also common to need additional doses as a child matures and issues change.

Other Psychotherapies

Many other types of talking interventions exist, including support groups, family and individual therapy, and interpersonal therapy, though some of these may not be offered until a child reaches adolescence. There are also treatment models that weave together different kinds of interventions (e.g., multisystemic therapy). When your therapist recommends an approach, a fair question would be, "What scientific evidence supports using this approach with my child?" Don't worry if she needs to get back to you. She may know that the recommended approach is indicated but not have the specific evidence on the tip of her tongue. I would only worry if the therapist acts defensively or tries to fault your question. Also, keep in mind that certain childhood disorders are not as well understood (e.g., Reactive Attachment Disorder), so your therapist may need to extrapolate heavily.

Set Measurable Goals

After following the assessment procedures I reviewed above, many effective child therapists set *measurable* goals. This accomplishes at least two things. First, it becomes clear whether the interventions are working. This supports either confidence in the approach or suggests a need to reassess and adjust. Second, these goals suggest when the work can be considered completed, as no one's life is ever problem free (though booster sessions may be advisable). Here are sample measurable goals:

- Ben will comply with parental directives at least 85 percent of the time within fifteen seconds for a period of at least three weeks.
- Jenna will raise her hand at least twice each day in class and will not make any anxiety-based requests to go to the school nurse for a period of three weeks.
- Robert will sleep at least nine hours a night and eat at least three meals a day for a period of at least three weeks.
- Michele will have a dry bed for a continuous period of four weeks.

I have two caveats about treatment planning. First, these goals are not to-do lists. It would be easy for an achievement-oriented parent (like me) or child (like my eldest) to sally forth and will these outcomes without making the underlying changes that promote lasting change. So, it's good to set the goals and then forget about them. Second, your therapist's default style may not be to set measurable goals. However, she ought to be open to your suggesting such and partnering with you along these lines.

What about Medications?

Medication treatments can be helpful. For example, in just about every instance of ADHD, bipolar disorder, and schizophrenia, it's a good idea to at least consider the value of pharmacotherapy. You can always find examples of kids with such problems who are doing well without medications, but skilled clinicians propose intervention plans that stand the best chance of healing an afflicted child as quickly and as thoroughly as possible.

Medications can also be helpful in the treatment of anxiety disorders, mood disorders, and in cases when talking treatments leave impairing symptoms unresolved (e.g., debilitating anger). The main thing is to find a clinician, or treatment team, who can teach you about the pros and cons of medication treatments with regard to your child's unique problem(s), including whether it's advisable to try talking treatments first.

The one thing that is not indicated, in the vast majority of instances, is to use medication alone or to use a medication trial as the primary assessment tool. In a managed-cost era it may be cheaper in the short run to over-rely on medication, but the best care typically includes talking treatments as well. Keep in mind that fiscal pressures may be a factor in some practices and that some competent prescribers may know very little about talking treatments. This is part of the reason why it's advisable for you to become an expert in the research attached to your child's diagnosis/diagnoses.

Cost of Mental Health Services

Like all parents, my husband and I just do the best we can, and hold our
breath, and hope we've set aside enough money to pay for our kids' therapy.
Michelle Pfeiffer

Many parents wonder about cost. First of all, many—if not most—health insurance plans cover mental health services for children. As of January 2010, the Mental Health Parity and Addiction Equity Act (MHPAEA) became active. This law requires health insurance companies, when they cover mental health services, to not cover them to a lesser degree than traditional medical services. However, if you do not have health insurance that covers what your child needs or you have other reasons why you must pay out of pocket and can't afford the fees, here are other possibilities:

1. It may be advisable to consult with an attorney who is knowledgeable about mental health services. For instance, you may qualify, based on your child's diagnosis/diagnoses and/or your family income, for government support (i.e., health insurance, payments secondary to a finding of a disability, transportation, and respite).

2. Visit your local community mental health center (CMHC). While the quality of care can vary in CMHCs, you can move around within the system to find a good fit. Many of these centers offer sliding scales or payment plans.

3. Find out whether a local university offers a graduate program in psychology or a related mental health field. If so, they may have a training clinic. At these clinics, graduate students provide care under the supervision of faculty. Typically, the enthusiasm and motivation of the therapist is high, the design of the assessment and intervention plan is state of the art, and the fees are very low.

4. Many charitable organizations offer evaluation and counseling services by licensed or certified providers on a sliding scale (e.g., Catholic Charities, Jewish Social Services).

5. Mental health professionals tend to be a mission-driven lot. While I'm unclear how often asking for a reduced fee up front would work, if the clinician has completed an evaluation and gotten to know you and your child, he may be willing to reduce his fee if you have cause to ask.

Supportive Strategy

Pursue Your Own Therapy

If you accept the premise that the most concise way to judge a person's mental health is to assess that person's capacity to love, then a personal therapy can be one of the best presents you can give to those in your life.

Albeit sometimes in a faulted or incomplete way, I have done or am doing every primary and supportive strategy in this book, including this one. So far I've completed two psychotherapies. I went to therapy the first time, for three years, during graduate school. I initially did this because my mentors emphasized how any therapist worth his fee has gone through his own therapy. And while I entered therapy primarily for that reason, I'm convinced that I would not be married to my wife of twenty years were it not for that therapy (which is actually why I won't give my wife the contact information of that therapist).

I got into my second therapy so that I might more fully realize my professional and personal missions. While life was going very well, I *knew* I could be getting more out of it; my only regret is that I didn't start it sooner.

Many of the recommendations I offer for finding a therapist for your child work for you, too. Why not consider going into counseling if you have obstacles within yourself that keep you from enjoying every little bit of this lush and wonderous world in which we live? How would you compare what you have to lose with what you have to gain? After all, blink three times and you, like the rest of us, will be greeting death and looking back at your life wondering what it has all meant.

Strategy Summary

If your child is suffering from mild to moderate problems for a period of two weeks or longer, or if she has serious problems, use the ideas listed in this chapter to find a lean–mean–healing–machine to help you to help your "baby."

Expect an expert therapist to explain her goals and methods, to do a thorough interview, to create in you a sense that she cares, to collect relevant records, and to complete some sort of measurement that allows her to compare your child to his peers.

Expect an expert therapist to explain his diagnostic impression and how he arrived at it, to provide a summary of the relevant research on the problem(s) in question, to offer a plan of healing that is evidence based and tailored to your family's unique situation, culture, and values, and to establish measurable goals for the intervention plan. You might also ask for suggestions for reading about your child's problem(s) or care.

Assuming you comply with what is recommended, expect either results or a change in approach. And, if you find compliance too difficult, expect to be able to have a frank discussion with the clinician about other approaches or choices.

The Skeptical Parent's Challenge

Parent: I took my child to see a therapist for a year. All she did was ask him to play, and nothing got better; plus, she charged me an arm and a leg.

Author: It would be very frustrating to pay for an expensive service and see no significant changes. However, it's tough for an outsider to know what went wrong. All I can do is suggest two things. First, we know that child psychotherapy can often bring about significant healing for a wide array of child problems. Second, as in any profession, an array of talent exists among providers. I hope you can use the guidelines in this chapter to find someone who is a better fit. After all, would any of us stop taking our child to see dentists if the treatment offered by the first one didn't work?

Parent: I don't want some stranger telling me how to raise my kid, or blaming me for her problems, no matter how subtly or cleverly.

Author: I believe those are fair expectations. No competent child clinician should try to replace your role as a parent or get into the blame game. It isn't practical or advisable for a therapist to act like a parent, and blaming suggests an incomplete understanding. This is a partnership, with both you and the clinician providing critically important contributions to understanding and healing. If it goes well, you ought to believe that you are *both* working together toward goals that you *both* believe have value and using methods that make sense to you *both*. I would not settle for less as a parent, strive for less as a clinician, or expect less from a trainee.

Parent: I hesitate to take my child to a mental health professional, as I don't want him to think he's screwed up. He gets enough negative feedback from the world as it is.

Author: Over the years I've found that this is the number-one reason parents hesitate to bring their kid in for a mental health evaluation. Many people can relate to what you are saying. I have two responses. First, skilled child clinicians have procedures in place for assessing and emphasizing strengths. Second, this type of care, if competently executed, stands to significantly reduce the number of failures and amount of pain in your child's life; of course, this does a great deal to promote your child's self-esteem.

Parent: I brought up the idea to my kid of seeing a counselor. He objected. What's the point of taking him in if he refuses to participate?

Author: Most kids are either neutral or opposed to the idea of seeing a mental health professional (in my experience kids who want to come in are either especially insightful or especially lonely). A child therapist working with kid resistance is like a mason working with mortar—it's part of the job. In my own practice I find that the large majority of kids who initially reject the idea of coming in can be effectively engaged. I tell parents: It's your job to get him in my office. It's my job to deal with him once he's here.

Before I say good-bye, and to give those of you who do not yet have teenagers an early present (as well as to channel the stress I experience from having 2.0 teenagers at home), I'll share one more list: The top ten things you can threaten to do to your teen, in front of her friends, if she refuses to meet an important obligation.

1. Dance (I like to model making a lasso over my head with one hand and smacking my backside with the other).
2. Kiss 'em (if you're a mom, wear bright red lipstick and fill in just a little outside your lip line).
3. Use his or her pet baby name (I just got my car washed because I agreed to delete one of my teenager's examples from this text—this is probably part of the reason why, when I'm in the nursing home, the staff will find balloons tied to my ears after my children have visited).
4. Hold her hand.
5. Wear high waters with pastel-colored socks and squeaky shoes.
6. Hum songs.
7. Make a T-shirt with her baby picture blown up and a caption that reads "(her name) is the cutest baby in (name of your state)."
8. Ask, "How come it smells like updog?" When someone asks, "What's updog?" You answer, "Not much. What's up with you?" Then belly laugh.
9. Ask, "Would you guys like to have a root-beer float party this weekend?"
10. Suggest to the friends that they use your child as a role model for how to live a virtuous life.

Well, it's time to say good-bye, and I'm not very good at that. But, before I go I want to leave you with a final thought, a truth I frequently see in my work with parents. That truth is that you are a beauteous beauty. Parenting is tough, fatiguing, and endless. Yet, you do it, sometimes stumbling and bumbling, sure. But you're in the game, and you stay in the game, even though you are often left weary and exhausted beyond description. This love of yours, this sublime selflessness, is more exquisite and precious than anything hanging in the Louvre. I hope you can allow yourself that and feel uplifted by the meaning of what you are accomplishing. May God bless you.

Your Servant,
David

❖ References

I will continue to provide resources and services through the primary Web site supporting this book (www.resilientyouth.com), my blog (www.hecticparents.com), and my Twitter page (www.twitter.com/HelpingParents).

Two types of information follow. "References" refer to the scholarship or literature that was either cited in the text or that supports the strategies and recommendations included in the book. "Further Reading or Viewing" refers to additional material that is related to the chapter's content. (Any Web sites that follow are also listed on www.resilientyouth.com, where they are easy to copy and paste into your browser's address bar.)

Introduction

References

Alvord, M. K. & Grados, J. J. 2005. Enhancing resilience in children: A Proactive approach. *Professional Psychology: Research and Practice, 36,* 238-245.

Armstrong, N. I., Birnie-Lefcovitch, S., & Ungar, M. T. 2005. Pathways between social support, family well being, quality of parenting, and child resilience: What we know. *Journal of Child and Family Studies, 14,* 269-281.

Bonanno, G. A. 2004. Loss, trauma, and human resilience: Have we underestimated the human capacity to thrive after extremely aversive events? *American Psychologist, 59,* 20-28.

Bonanno, G. A., Galea, S., Bucciarelli, A., & Vlahov, D. 2006. Psychological resilience after disaster: New York City in the aftermath of the September 11th terrorist attack. *Psychological Science, 17,* 181-186.

Brooks, R. B. 2006. The Power of parenting. In Goldstein, S., & Brooks, R. B. (Eds.). *Handbook of Resilience in Children.* New York: Springer.

Cowen, E. L. 1994. The Enhancement of psychological wellness: Challenges and opportunities. *American Journal of Community Psychology, 22,* 149-179.

Fraenkel, P. 2003. Contemporary two-parent families: Navigating work and family challenges. In Walsh, F. (Ed.) *Normal Family Processes: Growing Diversity and Complexity* (3rd Ed.). New York: Guilford Press.

Holder, M. D., & Coleman, B. 2007. The Contribution of temperament, popularity, and physical appearance to children's happiness. *Journal of Happiness Studies, 9,* 279-302.

Levitt, S. D., & Dubner, S. J. 2009. *Freakonomics.* New York: Harper Perennial.

Lyubomirsky, S., Sheldon, K. M., & Schkade, D. 2005. Pursuing happiness: The Architecture of sustainable change. *Review of General Psychology, 9,* 111-131.

Maziade, M., Caron, C., Cote, R., Merette, C., Bernier, H., Laplante, B., Boutin, P., & Thivierge, J. 1990. Psychiatric status of adolescents who had extreme temperaments at age 7. *The American Journal of Psychiatry, 147,* 1531-1536.

Rosenfeld, A. & Wise, N. 2000. The Overscheduled Child: Avoiding the Hyper-parenting Trap. New York: St. Martin's Griffin.

Shriver, M. & Center for American Progress. 2009. *The Shriver Report: A Woman's Nation Changes Everything*. Retrieved from www.awomansnation.com/shriverReport.pdf.

Sroufe, L., A. 2002. From infant attachment to promotion of adolescent autonomy: Prospective, longitudinal data on the role of parents in development. In Borkowski, J. G., Ramey, S. L., & Bristol-Power, M. (Eds). *Parenting and the Child's World: Influences on Academic, Intellectual, and Social-Emotional Development. Monographs in Parenting.* Mahwah, NJ: Lawrence Erlbaum Associates Publishers.

Steel, P., Schmidt, J. & Shultz, J. 2008. Refining the relationship between personality and subjective well being. *Psychological Bulletin, 134,* 138-161.

Tschann, J. M., Kaiser, P., Chesney, M. A., Alkon, A., & Boyce, W. T. 1996. Resilience and vulnerability among preschool children: family functioning, temperament, and behavior problems. *Journal of the American Academy of Child and Adolescent Psychiatry, 35,* 184-192.

Werner, E. 2006. What can we learn about resilience from large-scale longitudinal studies. In Goldstein, S., & Brooks, R. B. (Eds.). *Handbook of Resilience in Children.* New York: Springer.

Chapter 1

References

Albom, M. 2002. *Tuesdays with Morrie: An Old man, a Young Man, and Life's Greatest Lesson.* New York: Broadway Books.

Barkley, R. 1997. *Defiant Children: A Clinician's Manual for Assessment and Parent Training* 2nd Edition. New York: Guilford Press.

Bronson, P. & Merryman, A. 2009. *NurtureShock*. New York: Hachette Book Group.

Brooks, R. B. & Goldstein, S. 2002. *Nurturing Resilience in our Children: Answers to the Most Important Parenting Questions*. Burr Ridge, IL: McGraw-Hill.

Covey, S. 2004. *The 7 Habits of Highly Effective People*. New York: Free Press.

Csikszentmihalyi, M. 2001. *Flow: The Psychology of Optimal Experience*. New York: Harper Perennial.

Csikszentmihalyi, M. 2004. in Montana PBS (producer). *Introducing Positive Psychology: Signature Strengths, Flow and Aging Well.*

Fergusson, D. M. 2003. Resilience to childhood adversity: Results of a 21 year study. In Luthar, S. S. (Ed.). *Resilience and Vulnerability: Adaptation in the Context of Childhood Adversities*. New York: Cambridge University Press.

Fromm, E. 1956. *The Art of loving*. New York: Harper & Row.

National Sleep Foundation 2008. *Sleep In America Poll*. Retrieved from www.sleepfoundation.org/article/press-release/sleep-america-poll-summary-findings.

Oswald, A. 2002. Are you happy at work? Job satisfaction and work-life balance in the US and Europe. www.andrewoswald.com.

Rideout, V. J., Foehr, U. G., & Roberts, D. F. 2010. *Generation M2. Media in the Lives of 8-18-Year-Olds*. Kaiser Family Foundation. Retrieved from www.kff.org/entmedia/upload/8010.pdf.

Zisser, A., & Eyberg, S. M. 2010. Parent-child interaction therapy and the treatment of disruptive behavior disorders. In Kazdin, A. E., & Weisz, J. R. (Eds.). *Evidence-Based Psychotherapies for Children and Adolescents (2nd Ed.)*. New York: Guilford Press.

Further Reading and Viewing

To read more about the power of gratitude

Emons, R. A. 2007. *Thanks!: How Practicing Gratitude Can Make You Happier*. New York: First Houghton Mifflin.

Books that support the spirit of special time
> Bolin, D. 1993. *How to be Your Daughter's Daddy: 365 Ways to Show Her You Care.* Colorado Springs, CO: Pinon Press.
> Bolin, D. & Sutterfield, K. 1993. *How to Be Your Little Man's Dad: 365 Things to Do with Your Son.* Colorado Springs, CO: Pinon Press.
> Cohen, L. J. 2002. *Playful Parenting.* New York: Ballentine Books.

Web sites offering creative ideas for fun activities with kids
> familyfun.go.com/playtime
> www.creativekidsathome.com
> www.creativekidscrafts.com/ideas.html

Web sites devoted to promoting and supporting fatherhood
> ririanproject.com/2007/10/25/the-7-habits-of-highly-successful-fathers
> www.fatherhood.org

YouTube videos that can help you to remember how much you love your child
> www.youtube.com/watch?v=sHPZBCJ-LaE
> www.youtube.com/watch?v=RS4wljFuh3Y

Chapter 2

References

Blechman, E. A., McEnroe, M. J., Carella, E. T. & Audette, D. P. 1986. Childhood competence and depression. *Journal of Abnormal Psychology, 95,* 223-227.

Bouffard, T., Marcoux, M. Vezeau, C. & Bordeleau, L. 2003. Changes in self-perceptions of competence and intrinsic motivation among elementary schoolchildren. *British Journal of Educational Psychology, 73,* 171-186.

Brooks, R. B. & Goldstein, S. 2002. *Raising Resilient Children: Fostering Strength, Hope, and Optimism in Your Child.* Burr Ridge, IL: McGraw-Hill.

Brooks, R. B. & Goldstein, S. 2002. *Nurturing Resilience in Our Children: Answers to the Most Important Parenting Questions.* Burr Ridge, IL: McGraw-Hill.

KidsHealth 2006. *Kidspoll—Are Kids Too Busy?* Retrieved from www.nahec.org/KidsPoll/busy/Busy_Summary_of_Findings.pdf.

Holden, R. 2007. *Happiness Now! Timeless Wisdom for Feeling Good Fast.* New York: Hay House.

Lyubomirsky, S. 2008. *The How of Happiness: A New Approach to Getting the Life You Want.* New York: Penguin.

Masten, A. S., & Coatsworth, J. D. 1998. The Development of competence in favorable and unfavorable environments. Lessons from research on successful children. *American Psychologist, 53,* 205-220.

Milun, K. & Hanson, R. 2007. *Little League Baseball Needs to be Reclaimed for the Commons.* Retrieved from onthecommons.org/content.php?id=1064

Mruk, C. J. 2006. *Self-esteem Research, Theory, and Practice: Toward a Positive Psychology of Self-Esteem* (3rd Ed.). New York: Springer Publishing Company.

Obach, M. S. 2003. A longitudinal-sequential study of perceived academic competence and motivational beliefs for learning among children in middle school. *Educational Psychology, 23,* 323-338.

Peterson, C. & Seligman, M. 2004. *Character Strengths and Virtues: A Handbook and Classification*. New York: Oxford University Press.

Rath, T. 2007. *StrengthsFinder 2.0: A New and Upgraded Edition of the Online Test from Gallup's Now, Discover Your Strengths*. Washington, D.C.: Gallup Press.

Seligman, M. 2004. In Montana PBS (Producer). *Introducing Positive Psychology: Signature Strengths, Flow and Aging Well*.

Shields, D., Bredemeier, B. L., LaVoi, N. M., Power, F. C. 2005. The Sport behavior of youth, parents and coaches: The Good, the bad and the ugly. *Journal of Research in Character Education, 3*, 43-59.

Thompson, R. A. 2006. (2nd Ed.) *Nurturing Future Generations: Promoting Resilience in Children and Adolescents Through Social, Emotional and Cognitive Skills*. New York: Routledge.

Twenge, J. M. & Foster, J. D. 2010. Birth cohort increases in narcissistic personality traits among American college students, 1982-2009. *Social Psychological and Personality Science, 1*, 19-25.

Vatterott, C. (2009). *Rethinking Homework: Best Practices that Support Diverse Needs*. Alexandria, VA: ASCD.

Wendy, J., McGue, M. & Iacono, W. G. 2005. Disruptive behavior and school grades: Genetic and environmental relations in 11-year-olds. *Journal of Educational Psychology, 97*, 391-405.

Werner, E. 2006. What can we learn about resilience from large-scale longitudinal studies. In Goldstein, S., & Brooks, R. B. (Eds.). *Handbook of Resilience in Children*. New York: Springer.

Further Reading and Viewing

Books and Web sites that can aide in forming a mission statement
Covey, S. 2004. *The 7 Habits of Highly Effective People*. New York: Free Press.
Covey, S. 1999. *The 7 Habits of Highly Effective Families*. New York: Simon & Schuster, Ltd.
www.franklincovey.com/mission_builder/Mission_Statement_Builder.pdf
singleparents.about.com/od/familyrelationships/qt/mission_state.htm
www.homeschool.com/articles/Stephen_Covey

A Book that can aide in discovering your child's competencies
Fox, J. 2008. *Your Child's Strengths: Discover Them, Develop Them, Use Them*. London: Penguin Books.

Web sites that may be helpful as you try to identify and support competencies in your children
www.authentichappiness.com: VIA Survey of Character Strengths and the VIA Strength Survey for Children.
www.strengthsfinder.com: StrengthsFinder 2.0 test (you will need to purchase an access code).
www.ted.com/talks/kiran_bir_sethi_teaches_kids_to_take_charge.html: Case study video of the power that flows from the realization of competencies.

Web sites that can help to promote academic competence
www.freerice.com: This Web site offers an engaging–and sometimes addictive–vocabulary task. It's a way to grow your child's vocabulary, and yours, while having fun. And, they purport to donate rice to combat world hunger.

kids.nationalgeographic.com/kids: *National Geographic Kids.*
www.kidsdiscover.com: From the magazine *Kids Discover.*

Two movies, both true stories (one dramatized and one a documentary), demonstrating the power of competencies in children
Briski, Z., & Kauffman. (Directors). 2005. *Born Into Brothels: Calcutta's Red Light Kids* [Motion Picture]. United States: Red Light Films.
Zaillian, S. (Director). 1993. *Searching for Bobby Fischer* [Motion Picture]. United States: Mirage Entertainment.

A provocative and important movie about the unhelpful pressures that are often placed on our children
Abeles, V. & Congdon, J. (Directors). 2009. *Race to Nowhere* (Motion Picture). United States: Reel Link Films.
A YouTube video that witnesses the power of a well executed mission www.youtube.com/watch?v=6QpTSztA1cM

Chapter 3

References
Center for Marriage and Families at the Institute for American Values. 2005. Family structure and children's educational outcomes. Retrieved from center.americanvalues.org/?p=28.
Centers for Disease Control and Prevention 2008. The Youth risk behavior surveillance system (YRBSS): 2007. Retrieved from www.cdc.gov/mmwr/PDF/ss/ss5704.pdf.
Centers for Disease Control and Prevention 2002. The Youth risk behavior surveillance system (YRBSS): 2001. Retrieved from www.cdc.gov/mmwr/PDF/SS/SS5104.pdf.
Ginsburg, K., Durbin, D. R., Garcia-Espana, J. F., Kalicka, E. A. & Winston, F. K. 2009. Association between parenting styles and teen driving, safety-related behaviors and attitudes. *Pediatrics, 124,* 1040-1051.
Guttmacher Institute 2010. *Facts on American Teen's Sexual and Reproductive Health.* Retrieved from www.guttmacher.org/pubs/FB-ATSRH.pdf.
Harvard Family Research Project. 2008. *Highlights From the Out-of-School Time Database.* Cambridge, MA: Harvard Family Research Project.
Hinshaw, S. P., & Lee, S. S. 2002. Conduct and oppositional defiant disorders. In Mash, E. & Barkley, R. (Eds). *Child Psychopathology* (2nd Ed.). New York: Guilford Press.
Kerr, D. R., Capaldi, D. M., Pears, K. C., & Owen, L. D. 2009. A Prospective three generational study of fathers' constructive parenting: Influences from family of origin, adolescent adjustment, and offspring temperament. *Developmental Psychology, 45,* 1257-1275.
King, R. 2001. Psychosocial and Risk Behavior Correlates of Youth Suicide Attempts and Suicidal Ideation. *Journal of the American Academy of Child & Adolescent Psychiatry, 40,* 837-846.
Long, T. J., & Long, L. 1983. Latchkey children. In Katz, L. G. (Ed.). *Current Topics in Early Childhood Education.* Norwood, NJ: Ablex Publishing Co.
National Institute on Drug Abuse. 2010. *NIDA Infofacts: High School and Youth Trends.* Retrieved from www.drugabuse.gov/pdf/infofacts/HSYouthTrends09.pdf.
Indiana State University. 2008. National Survey of Student Engagement 2008 results. Retrieved from nsse.iub.edu/NSSE_2008_Results/docs/withhold/NSSE2008_Results_revised_11-14-2008.pdf.

Patterson, G. R., & Stouthamer-Loeber, M. 1984. The correlation of family management practices and delinquency. *Child Development, 55,* 1299-1307.

Richardson, J. L., Dwyer, K., McGuigan, L., Hansen, W. B., Dent, C., Johnson, C. A., Sussman, S. Y., Brannon, B., & Flay, B. 1989. Substance use among eighth-grade students who take care of themselves after school. *Pediatrics, 84,* 556-566.

Santelli, J. S., Lindberg, L. D., Abma, J., McNeely, C. S. & Resnick, M. 2000. Adolescent sexual behavior: Estimates and trends from four nationally representative surveys. *Family Planning Perspectives, 32,* 156-194.

Wolak, J., Mitchell, K., & Finkelhor, D. 2007. Unwanted and wanted exposure to online pornography in a national sample of youth Internet users. *Pediatrics, 119,* 247-257.

Further Reading and Viewing

To learn more about both the power of gratitude and specific techniques for executing it
Emmons, R. A. 2007. *Thanks! How Practicing Gratitude Can Make You Happier.* New York: Houghton Mifflin Company.

Web sites that help with monitoring
Programs that offer Internet site blocking services (and sometimes more than that)
www.freeverse.com/mac/product/?id=5003
www.webwatchernow.com
www.cybersitter.com
www.spector.com: A program for monitoring how a computer is used.
www.familysafemedia.com: A Web site that offers multiple resources to support a parental monitoring agenda.

Web sites that provide you with information to make informed choices about media
www.tvguidelines.org
www.esrb.org/about/resources.jsp
www.netalert.gov.au
www.nichd.nih.gov/publications/pubs/upload/adv_in_parenting.pdf: *National Institute of Health's offering Adventures in Parenting: How Responding, Preventing, Monitoring, Mentoring, and Modeling Can Help You Be a Successful Parent.*
While not really a resource to read or view, sometimes we parent-lunatics all need PEACE AND QUIET when we're trying to read or view something. To that end, I find the noise canceling headphones sold by Bose to be very effective: www.bose.com

Chapter 4

References

American Psychological Association. 2010. *Stress in America Survey.* Retrieved http://www.apa.org/news/press/releases/stress/national-report.pdf.

American Psychiatric Association. 1994. *Diagnostic and Statistical Manual of Mental Disorders.* (4th Ed.). Washington, D. C.: American Psychiatric Association.

Barnes, L., Plotnikoff, G., Fox, K. & Pendleton, S. 2000. Spirituality, religion and pediatrics: Intersecting worlds of healing. *Pediatrics, 106,* 899-908.

Barnett, R. C., & Hyde, J. S. 2001. Women, men, work, and family. *American Psychologist, 56,* 781-796.

Center for Marriage and Families. 2005. *Family Structure and Children's Educational Outcomes.* Retrieved from www.americanvalues.org/pdfs/researchbrief1.pdf.

Children's Defense Fund. 2005. *State of America's Children.* Retrieved from www.childrensdefense.org/child-research-data-publications/data/state-of-americas-children-2005-report.pdf.

Davison, K. 2009. Helping families and communities reverse the trend of childhood obesity. Presentation at State Leadership Conference, American Psychological Association, Washington, D.C.

Eisenberg, M., Olson, R., Neumark-Sztainer, D., Story, M. & Bearinger, L. H. 2004. Correlations between family meals and psychosocial well-being among adolescents. *Archives of Pediatric and Adolescent Medicine, 158,* 792-796.

Fiese, B. H., Tomcho, T. J., Douglas, M., Josephs, K., Poltrock, S., & Baker, T. 2002. A Review of 50 years of research on naturally occurring family routines and rituals: Cause for celebration? *Journal of Family Psychology, 16,* 381-390.

Fletcher, K. 2007. Post Traumatic Stress Disorder. In Mash, E., & Barkley, R. (Eds.). *Assessment of Childhood Disorders* (4th Ed.). New York: Guilford Press.

Fletcher, K. 2002. Childhood Post Traumatic Stress Disorder. In Mash, E. & Barkley, R. (Ed.). *Child Psychopathology* (2nd Ed.). New York: Guilford Press.

Grant, B. F., Dawson, D. A. 1997. Age at onset of alcohol use and its association with DSM-IV alcohol abuse and dependence. Results from the National Longitudinal Alcohol Epidemiologic Survey. *Journal of Substance Abuse, 9,* 103-110.

Hill, P., & Pargament, K. 2003. Advances in the conceptualization and measurement of religion and spirituality: Implications for physical and mental health research. *The American Psychologist, 58,* 64-74.

Kataoka, S., Zhang, L. & Wells, K. B. 2002. Unmet Need for Mental Health Care Among U.S. Children: Variation by Ethnicity and Insurance Status. *American Journal of Psychiatry, 159,* 1548-1555.

Kelly, J. 2000. Children's Adjustment in Conflicted Marriage and Divorce: A Decade Review of Research. *Journal of the American Academy of Child and Adolescent Psychiatry, 39,* 963-973.

Kilmer, R. P., Cowen, E. L., Wyman, P. A., Work, W. C. & Magnus, K. B. 1998. Differences in Stressors Experienced by Urban African American, White, and Hispanic Children. *Journal of Community Psychology, 26,* 415-428.

Kiser, L. 2007. Protecting Children from the Dangers of Urban Poverty. *Clinical Psychology Review, 27,* 211-225.

McIntosh, S., & Mata, M. 2008. Early Detection of Posttraumatic Stress Disorder in Children. *Journal of Trauma Nursing, 15,* 126-130.

Nansel, T., Overpeck, M., Pilla, R. S., Ruan, W. J., Simmons-Morton, B., Schmidt, P. 2001. Bullying Behaviors Among US Youth: Prevalence and association with psychosocial adjustment. *Journal of American Medical Association, 285,* 2094-2100.

National Institute of Health. 2008. National diabetes statistics, 2007. Retrieved from diabetes.niddk.nih.gov/DM/pubs/statistics/DM_Statistics.pdf.

National Institute on Alcohol Abuse & Alcoholism. 1998. Drinking in the United States: Main Findings from the 1992 National Longitudinal Alcohol Epidemiologic Survey (NLAES). *U. S. Alcohol Epidemiological Data Reference Manual, 6.* Retrieved from pubs.niaaa.nih.gov/publications/manual.htm.

Nonnemaker, J. M., McNeely, C. A. & Blum, R. W. 2003. Public and Private Domains of

Religiosity and Adolescent Health Risk Behaviors: Evidence from the National Longitudinal Study of Adolescent Health. *Social Sciences & Medicine, 57,* 2049-2054.

Parke, M. 2003. *Are Married Parents Really Better for Children? What Research Says About The Effects of Family Structure on Child Well-Being.* Center for Law and Social Policy. Retrieved from bit.ly/a4HLfd.

Popenoe, D. 1998. *We Are What We See: The Family Conditions for Modeling Values for Children.* University of Wisconsin-Madison General Library System. Retrieved from parenthood.library.wisc.edu/Popenoe/Popenoe-Modeling.html.

Resnick, M. D., Bearman, P. S., Blum, R. M., Bauman, K. E., Harris, K. M., Jones, J., Tabor, J., Beuhring, T., Sieving, R. E., Shew, M., Ireland, M., Bearinger, L. H. & Udry, J. R. 1997. Protecting Adolescents From Harm: Findings from the National Longitudinal Study on Adolescent Health. *Journal of the American Medical Association, 278,* 823-832.

Silverman, W., Ortiz, C. D., Viswesvaran, C., Burns, B. J., Kolko, D. J., Putnam, F. W. & Amaya-Jackson, L. 2008. Evidence-based psychosocial treatments for children and adolescents exposed to traumatic events. *Journal of Clinical Child and Adolescent Psychology, 37,* 156-183.

Social Security Administration. 2000. *Intermediate assumptions of the 2000 Trustees Report.* Washington, D.C.: Office of the Chief Actuary of the Social Security Administration.

United States Census Bureau. 2008. *Living Arrangements of Children: 2004.* Retrieved from www.census.gov/prod/2008pubs/p70-114.pdf.

United States Department of Health & Human Services 2008. *Child Abuse and Neglect Fatalities: Statistics and Interventions.* Retrieved from www.childwelfare.gov/pubs/factsheets/fatality.pdf.

Walsh, F. 2006. *Strengthening Family Resilience* (2nd Ed.). New York: Guilford Press.

Werner, E. 2006. What can we learn about resilience from large-scale longitudinal studies. In Goldstein, S., & Brooks, R. B. (Eds.). *Handbook of Resilience in Children.* New York: Springer.

Wyman, P.A., Sandler, I., Wolchik, S., & Nelson, K. 2000. Resilience as cumulative competence promotion and stress protection: Theory and intervention. In Cicchetti, D., Rappaport, J., Sandler, I., Weissberg, R. P. (Eds.). *The Promotion of Wellness in Children and Adolescents.* Washington, D. C.: Child Welfare League of America.

Further Reading and Viewing

Books to help forge family rituals

Cox, M. 2003. *The Book of New Family Traditions: How to Create Great Rituals for Holidays & Everydays.* Philadelphia, PA: Running Press.

Gaither, G., & Dobson, S., Hartman, C. 2004. *Creating Family Traditions: Making Memories in Festive Seasons.* New York: Multnomah Books.

Web sites to promote rituals

casafamilyday.org/familyday: This Web site promotes an annual family meal day.

www.parenting.com/activity-parties-article/Activities-Parties/Games/14-Ideas-for-Camping-Out-In-Your-Backyard?cid=tweet: This Web site provides opportunities to create precious memories in your back yard.

parenting247.org/article.cfm?ContentID=688&strategy=2&AgeGroup=1: From the University of Illinois extension.

simplemom.net/the-importance-of-family-rituals: Practical suggestions.

www.drma.com/article_FamilyRituals.php: More clever ideas.

Chapter 5

References

Barkley, R. 1997. *Defiant Children: A Clinician's Manual for Assessment and Parent Training* (2nd Ed.) New York: Guilford Press.

Baumrind, D. 1991. The Influence of parenting style on adolescent competence and substance use. *Journal of Early Adolescence, 11,* 56-95.

Baumrind, D. 1971. Current patterns of parental authority. *Developmental Psychology, 4,* 1-103.

Brooks, R. B. 2006. The Power of parenting. In Goldstein, S., & Brooks, R. B. (Eds.). *Handbook of Resilience in Children.* New York: Springer.

Christophersen, E. R., & Mortweet, S. L. 2001. *Treatments That Work with Children: Empirically Supported Strategies for Managing Childhood Problems.* Washington, D. C.: American Psychological Association.

Greene, R. 2007. *The Explosive Child.* New York: Harper Collins.

Goleman, D. 1997. *Emotional Intelligence.* New York: Bantam.

Fonagy, P., Target, M., Cottrell, D., Phillips, J., & Kurtz, Z. 2002. *What Works for Whom: A Critical Review of Treatments for Children and Adolescents.* New York: Guilford Press.

Gershoff, E. T. 2002. Corporal punishment by parents and associated child behaviors and experiences. A Meta-analytic and theoretical review. *Psychological Bulletin, 128,* 539-579.

Huebner, A., & Howell, L. 2007. Examining the relationship between adolescent sexual risk-taking and perceptions of monitoring, communication, and parenting styles. *Journal of Adolescent Health, 33,* 71-78.

Kahn, J. H. & Garrison, A. M. 2009. Emotional self-disclosure and emotional avoidance: Relations with symptoms of depression and anxiety. *Journal of Counseling Psychology, 56,* 573-584.

Kerr, D. C, Capaldi, D. M., Pears, K. C., & Owen, L. D. 2009. A Prospective three generational study of fathers' constructive parenting: Influences from family of origin, adolescent adjustment, and offspring temperament. *Developmental Psychology, 45,* 1257-1275.

Lamborn, S. D., Mounts, N. S., Steinberg, L., Dornbusch, S. M. 1991. Patterns of competence and adjustment among adolescents from authoritative, authoritarian, indulgent and neglectful families. *Child Development, 62,* 1049-1065.

Nelson, B. 2003. *The 1001 Rewards & Recognition Fieldbook: The Complete Guide.* New York: Workman Publishing.

Querido, J. G., Warner, T. D., & Eyberg, S. M. 2002. Parenting styles and child behavior in African American families of preschool children. *Journal of Clinical Child and Adolescent Psychology, 31,* 272-277.

Shucksmith, J., Hendry, L. B., & Glendinning, A. 1995. Models of parenting: Implications for adolescent well-being within different types of family contexts. *Journal of Adolescence, 18,* 253-270.

Simons, R. L., Simons, L. G., Burt, C. H., Brody, G. H., & Cutrona, C. 2005. Collective efficacy, authoritative parenting and delinquency: A Longitudinal test of a model integrating community-and family-level processes. *Criminology, 43,* 989-1029.

Skinner, B. F. 1972. *Beyond Freedom and Dignity.* New York: Bantam.

Steinberg, L., Blatt-Eisengart, I., & Cauffman, E. 2006. Patterns of competence and adjustment among adolescents from authoritative, authoritarian, indulgent and neglectful homes: A Replication in a sample of serious juvenile offenders. *Journal of Research on Adolescence, 16,* 47-58.

Steinberg, L., Elmen, J. D., & Mounts, N. S. 1989. Authoritative parenting, psychosocial maturity and academic success among adolescents. *Child Development, 60,* 1424-1436.

Tanaka, M., Fukuda, S., Mizuno, K., Kuratsune, H., & Watanabe, Y. 2009. Stress and coping styles are associated with severe fatigue in medical students. *Behavioral Medicine, 35,* 87-92.

Further Reading and Viewing

To consider how to further use acts of kindness in your life

Ferrucci, P. 2007. *The Power of Kindness. The Unexpected Benefits of Leading a Compassionate Life.* New York: Penguin.

Lyubomirsky, S. 2008. *The How of happiness: A New Approach to Getting the Life You Want.* New York: Penguin.

Books to help with discipline strategies

Barkley, R. A., & Benton, C. M. 1998. *Your Defiant Child: Eight Steps to Better Behavior.* New York: Guilford Press.

Kazdin, A. E. 2009. *The Kazdin Method for Parenting the Defiant Child.* New York: Mariner Books.

Some Web sites focusing on discipline

www.keepkidshealthy.com/cgi-bin/extlink.pl?l=http://www.aacap.org/publications/facts-fam/discplin.htm: From the American Academy of Child and Adolescent Psychiatry.

singleparents.about.com/od/discipline/tp/disciplinestrat.htm: From About.com.

www.ces.purdue.edu/providerparent/Guidance-Discipline/MakingDiscPositive.htm: From Purdue University.

Other helpful Web sites

www.resilientyouth.com: Sample contracts and token systems supporting this book.

www.apahelpcenter.org: A Web site from the American Psychological Association that contains an abundance of self help resources, including for parents.

www.psychologycanhelp.com: Also from the Pennsylvania Psychological Association that tries to do the same thing as the previous site.

Chapter 6

References

Allen, J. P., Hauser, S. T., Bell, K. L., & O'Connor, T. G. 1994. Longitudinal assessment of autonomy and relatedness in adolescent-family interactions as predictors of adolescent ego development and self-esteem. *Child Development, 65,* 179-194.

Beck, A. T., & Emery, G. 1985. *Anxiety Disorders and Phobias: A Cognitive perspective.* New York: Basic Books.

Bernard, B. 1991. *Fostering Resiliency in Kids: Protective Factors in the Family, School and Community.* Portland, OR: Northwest Regional Educational Laboratory.

Brooks, R. & Goldstein, S. 2002. *Raising Resilient Children: Fostering Strength, Hope, and Optimism in Your Child.* Burr Ridge, IL: McGraw-Hill.

Brooks, R. & Goldstein, S. 2002. *Nurturing Resilience in Our Children: Answers to the Most Important Parenting Questions.* Burr Ridge, IL: McGraw-Hill.

Clark, K. E., & Ladd, G.W. 2000. Connectedness and autonomy support in parent–child relationships: Links to children's socioemotional orientation and peer relationships. *Developmental Psychology, 36,* 485-498.

Coloroso, B. 2002. *Kids Are Worth It: Giving Your Child the Gift of Inner Discipline.* New York: Harper Paperbacks.

Endler, N. S., & Parker, J. D. 1994. Assessment of multidimensional coping: Task, emotion, and avoidance strategies. *Psychological Assessment, 6,* 50-60.

Friedberg, R. D., McClure, J. M., & Garcia, J. H. 2009. *Cognitive Therapy Techniques for Children and Adolescents.* New York: Guilford Press.

Fristad, M.A., Goldberg-Arnold, J.S. 2003. Family interventions for Early-Onset Bipolar Disorder. In Geller, B., & DelBello, M. P. (Eds.). *Bipolar Disorder in Childhood and Early Adolescence.* New York: Guilford Press.

Fukunishi, I., Hosaka. T., Negishi, M., Moriya, H., Hayashi, M. & Matsumoto, T. 1997. Avoidance coping behaviors and low social support are related to depressive symptoms in HIV-positive patients in Japan. *Psychosomatics, 38,* 113-118.

Greene, R. 2007. *The Explosive Child.* New York: HarperCollins.

Lyubomirsky, S. 2008. *The How of Happiness: A New Approach to Getting the Life You Want.* New York: Penguin.

Myers, D. G. & Diener, E. 1995. Who is happy? *Psychological Science, 6,* 10-19.

Peterson, C., Maier, S. F., Seligman, M. 1995. *Learned Helplessness: A Theory for the Age of Personal Control.* New York: Oxford University Press.

Rideout, V. J., Foehr, U. G., & Roberts, D. F. 2010. *Generation M2: Media in the Lives of 8-18-Year-Olds.* Kaiser Family Foundation. Retrieved from www.kff.org/entmedia/upload/8010.pdf.

Tugade, M. M., & Frederickson, B. L., 2004. Resilient individuals use positive emotions to bounce back from negative emotional experiences. *Journal of Personality and Social Psychology, 86,* 320-333.

Walsh, F. 2006. *Strengthening Family Resilience* (2nd Ed.). New York: Guilford Press.

Werner, E. 2006. What can we learn about resilience from large-scale longitudinal studies. In Goldstein, S., & Brooks, R. B. (Eds.). *Handbook of Resilience in Children.* New York: Springer.

Further Reading and Viewing
YouTube Videos illustrating crisis = pain + opportunity
www.youtube.com/watch?v=OEdVfyt-mLw
www.youtube.com/watch?v=6MPRReU8Vyc

Helpful Web sites
www.phac-aspc.gc.ca/dca-dea/pubs/ffc-ief/book5-eng.php#attachment: From the Public Agency of Canada, an electronic book on self-esteem.
www.resilientyouth.com: Blank problem-solving form and completed samples.

Helpful books on related content
Coloroso, B. 1994. *Parenting Through Crisis: Helping Kids in Times of Loss, Grief and Change.* New York: Collins Living.
Gibran, K. 2003. *The Prophet.* Waterloo, ON: Laurier Books.

Chapter 7

References

Alexander, P. C. 2009. Childhood trauma, attachment, and abuse by multiple partners. *Psychological Trauma: Theory, Research, Practice and Policy, 1,* 78-88.

American Psychological Association. 2010. *Stress in America Survey.* Retrieved http://www.apa.org/news/press/releases/stress/national-report.pdf.

Brickman, P., Coates, D., & Janoff-Bulman, R. 1978. Lottery winners and accident victims: Is happiness relative? *Journal of Personality and Social Psychology, 36,* 917-927.

Covey, S. 2004. *The 7 Habits of Highly Effective People.* New York: Free Press.

Cowan, P. A., Cohn, D. A., Cowan, C. P., & Pearson, J. L. 1996. Parents' attachment histories and children's externalizing and internalizing behaviors: Exploring family systems models of linkage. *Journal of Consulting and Clinical Psychology, 64,* 53-63.

Diener, E., Suh, E. M., Lucas, R. E., & Smith, H. L. 1999. Subjective well-being: Three decades of progress. *Psychological Bulletin, 125,* 276-302.

Diener, E., Horwitz, J., & Emmons, R. A. 1985. Happiness of the very wealthy. *Social Indicators Research, 16,* 263-274.

Faragher, E. B., Cass, M. & Cooper, C. L. 2005. The Relationship between job satisfaction and health: A Meta-analysis. *Occupational and Environmental Medicine, 62,* 105-112.

Giblin, P., Sprenkle, D. H., & Sheehan, R. 1985. Enrichment outcome research: A Meta-analysis of premarital, marital and family interventions. *Journal of Marital and Family Therapy, 11,* 257-271.

Gilbert, D. 2005. *Stumbling on happiness.* New York: Vintage Books.

Glenn, N. D. & McLanahan, S. 1982. Children and marital happiness: A Further specification of the relationship. *Journal of Marriage and the Family, 44,* 63-72.

Guttmacher Institute. 2000. Odds of spousal infidelity are influenced by social and demographic factors. *Family Planning Perspective, 32.* Retreived from www.guttmacher.org/pubs/journals/3214800.html.

Hahlweg, K., & Markman, H. J. 1988. Effectiveness of behavioral marital therapy: Empirical status of behavioral techniques in preventing and alleviating marital distress. *Journal of Consulting and Clinical Psychology, 56,* 440-447.

Halford, W. K., Sanders, M. R., & Behrens, B. C. 2000. Repeating the errors of our parents? Family-of-origin spouse violence and observed conflict management in engaged couples. *Family Process, 39,* 219-235.

Hetherington, E. M. & Elmore, A. M. 2003. Risk and resilience in children coping with their parents' divorce and remarriage. In Luthar, S. S. (Ed.). *Resilience and Vulnerability: Adaptation in the Context of Childhood Adversities.* New York: Cambridge University Press.

Jack. L. A., Dutton, D. G., Webb, A. N. & Ryan, L. 1995. Effects of early abuse on adult affective reactions to exposure to dyadic conflict. *Canadian Journal of Behavioral Science, 27,* 484-500.

Laanan, F. S. 2000. Community college students' career and educational goals. *New directions for community colleges, 112,* 19-33.

Lyubomirsky, S. 2008. *The How of Happiness: A New Approach to Getting the Life You Want.* New York: Penguin.

Myers, D. G. 2000. The Funds, friends, and faith of happy people. *American Psychologist, 55,* 56-67.

Mengel, M. B. 1987. Physician ineffectiveness due to family-of-origin issues. *Family Systems Medicine, 5,* 176-190.

Shedler, J. 2010. The Efficacy of psychodynamic psychotherapy. *American Psychologist, 65,* 98-109.

Twenge, J. M., Campbell, W., K., & Foster, C. A. 2003. Parenthood and marital satisfaction: A Meta-analytic review. *Journal of Marriage and Family, 65,* 574-583.

United States Census Bureau. 2008. *Living Arrangements of Children: 2004.* Retrieved from www.census.gov/prod/2008pubs/p70-114.pdf.

Further Reading and Viewing
Holden, R. 2009. *Be Happy: Release the Power of Happiness in You.* Carlsbad, CA: Hay House, Inc. This book contains multiple exercises to promote happiness.

Sometimes laughter is the best medicine
www.parentinghumor.com

Some of my favorite humorous YouTube videos on parenting and childhood
www.youtube.com/watch?v=A0ZpuA8_YYk
www.youtube.com/watch?v=1Nn9dd6FfE8
www.youtube.com/watch?v=X1glBETaSvc
www.youtube.com/watch?v=crQ7Y2alDxI

Dr. Lyubomirsky's software application for promoting your happiness
www.signalpatterns.com/iphone/livehappy_std.html

Books that contain exercises to promote wellness in a couple
Bloomfield, H., Vettese, S., & Kory, R. 1992. *Lifemates: The Love fitness program for a lasting relationship.* New York: Signet.
Gottman, J. M., Gottman, J. S. & Declaire, J. 2007. *Ten Lessons to Transform Your Marriage: America's Love Lab Experts Share Their Strategies for Strengthening Your Relationship.* New York: Three Rivers Press.

Books that I've found helpful for self and relationship care (that are not mentioned elsewhere)
Brown, H. J., Jr. 1991. *Life's little instruction book: 511 reminders for a happy and rewarding life.* Nashville, TN: Rutledge Hill Press.
Carlson, R. 1997. *Don't Sweat the Small Stuff...And It's All Small Stuff.* New York: Hyperion.
Nelson, T. 2008. *Getting the Sex You Want: Shed Your Inhibitions and Reach New Heights of Passion Together.* Beverly, MA: Quiver.
Williamson, M. 1993. *A Return to Love: Reflections on the Principles of a Course in Miracles.* New York: HarperCollins.

Web sites that may be of value
health.howstuffworks.com/human-nature/emotions/happiness/being-happy/10-tips-from-happy-people.htm: Commentary on how adults can be happy.
health.howstuffworks.com/human-nature/emotions/happiness/being-happy/5-ways-to-maximize-happiness.htm: Commentary on how adults can be happy.
www.how-to-meditate.org/breathing-meditations.htm: A useful site for learning how to meditate.
psychcentral.com/blog/archives/2009/09/26/bounce-6-steps-to-become-more-resilient/: Counsel on some key happiness strategies.

www.givesmehope.com: Inspirational stories.

www.learningmeditation.com: To learn to meditate.

www.parenting.com/article/Mom/Health--Fitness/21-Ways-to-Enjoy-Being-a-Mom: Ideas for moms to get some air under their wings.

Chapter 8

References

Aronen, E. T., Paavonen, E. J., Fjallberg, M. F., Soininen, M., & Torronen, J. 2000. Sleep and psychiatric symptoms in school-age children. *Journal of the American Academy of Child and Adolescent Psychiatry, 39,* 502-508.

Adair, L. S., & Popkin, B. M. 2005. Are child eating patterns being transformed globally? *Obesity Research, 13,* 1281-1299.

Binkley, J. K. 2005. *The Effects of demographic, economic, and nutrition factors on the frequency of food away from home.* Retreived from purl.umn.edu/19502.

Bronson, P. & Merryman, A. 2009. *NurtureShock.* New York: Hachette Book Group.

Centers for Disease Control and Prevention. 2010. *Physical Activity for Everyone: How Much Physical Activity Do Children Need?* Retrieved from www.cdc.gov/physicalactivity/everyone/guidelines/children.html.

Centers for Disease Control and Prevention. 2008. The Youth risk behavior surveillance system (YRBSS): 2007. Retrieved from www.cdc.gov/mmwr/PDF/ss/ss5704.pdf.

Consumer Reports. 2006, September. Sleepless in…well, everywhere. (Have you heard?). *Consumer Reports,* 48-51.

Crespo, C. J., Smit, E., Troiano, R. P., Bartlett, S. J., Macera, C. A. & Andersen, R. E. 2001. Television watching, energy intake, and obesity in US children. Results from the third National Health and Nutrition Examination Survey, 1988-1994. *Archives of Pediatrics & Adolescent Medincine, 155,* 360-365.

Eisenberg, M. E., Neumark-Sztainer, D., & Story, M. 2003. Associations of weight-based teasing and emotional well-being among adolescents. *Archives of Pediatric and Adolescent Medicine, 157,* 733-738.

Epstein, L. H. 2003. Development of evidence-based treatments for pediatric obesity. In Kazdin, A. E., & Weisz, J. R. (Eds.). *Evidence-Based Psychotherapies for Children and Adolescents.* New York: Guilford Press.

Epstein, L., H., Gordy, C. C., Raynor, H. A., Beddome, M., Kilanowski, C. K., & Paluch, R. 2001. Increasing fruit and vegetable intake and decreasing fat and sugar intake in families at risk for childhood obesity, *Obesity Research, 9,* 171-178.

Ferber, F. 1985. *Solve Your Child's Sleep Problems.* Tyler, Texas: Fireside Books.

Fredrickson, B. L., Cohn, M. A., Coffey, K. A., Pek, J., & Finkel, S. M. 2008. Open hearts build lives: Positive emotions, induced through loving-kindness meditation, build consequential personal resources. *Journal of Personality and Social Psychology, 95,* 1045-1062.

Hutcherson, C. A., Seppala, E. M., & Gross, J. J. 2008. Loving-kindness meditation increases social connectedness. *Emotion, 8,* 720-724.

Institute of Medicine of the National Academies 2006. Report Brief: Progress in preventing childhood obesity: How do we measure up? Retrieved from www.iom.edu/Reports/2006/Progress-in-Preventing-Childhood-Obesity--How-Do-We-Measure-Up.aspx.

National Sleep Foundation. 2009. *How Much Sleep Do We Really Need?* Retrieved from www.sleepfoundation.org/article/how-sleep-works/how-much-sleep-do-we-really-need.

National Sleep Foundation 2008. *Sleep in America Poll.* Retrieved from www.sleepfoundation.org/article/press-release/sleep-america-poll-summary-findings.

National Sleep Foundation 2006. *Sleep in America Poll.* Retrieved from www.sleepfoundation.org/sites/default/files/Highlights_facts_06.pdf.

Ogden, C. L., Carroll, M. D., Curtin, L. R., Lamb, M. M., & Flegal, K M. 2010. Prevalence of high body mass index in US children and adolescents, 2007-2008. *Journal of the American Medical Association, 303,* 242-249.

Patrick, H., & Nicklas, T. A. 2005. A Review of family and social determinants of children's eating patters and diet quality. *Journal of the American College of Nutrition, 24,* 83-92.

Puhl, R. M., & Latner, J. D. 2007. Stigma, obesity, and the health of the nation's children. *Psychological Bulletin, 133,* 557-580.

Rausch, S. M., Gramling, S. E., & Auerbach, S. M. 2006. Effects of a single session of large-group meditation and progressive muscle relaxation training on stress reduction, reactivity, and recovery. *International Journal of Stress Management, 13,* 273-290.

Robinson, T. N., Borzekowski, D. L., Matheson, D. M., & Kraemer, H. C. 2007. Effects of fast food branding on young children's taste preferences. *Archives of Pediatric & Adolescent Medicine, 161,* 792-797.

Sadeh, A., Gruber, R., & Raviv, A. 2003. The effects of sleep restriction and extension on school-age children: What a difference an hour makes. *Child Development, 74,* 444-455.

San Jose Mercury News & Kaiser Family Foundation. 2004. *Survey on Childhood Obesity.* Retrieved from www.kff.org/kaiserpolls/upload/Survey-on-Childhood-Obesity-Summary-and-Chartpack.pdf.

Snell, E. K., Adam, E. K., & Duncan, G. J. 2007. Sleep and the body mass index and overweight status of children and adolescents. *Child Development, 78,* 309-323.

Schroeder, S. A. 2007. We can do better–Improving the health of American people. *New England Journal of Medicine, 357,* 1221-1228.

Sharif, I., & Sargent, J. D., 2006. Association between television, movie, and video game exposure and school performance. *Pediatrics,* 118, 1061-1070.

Stanford University. 2007. *Building "Generation Play": Addressing the Crisis of Inactivity Among America's Children.* Standford, CA: Stanford University.

Strauss, R. S., Rodzilsky, D., Burack, G., & Colin, M. 2001. Psychosocial correlates of physical activity in healthy children. *Archives of Pediatric & Adolescent Medicine, 155,* 898-902.

United States Department of Agriculture. 2010. *Food CPI and Expenditures.* Retrieved from www.ers.usda.gov/Briefing/CPIFoodAndExpenditures.

United States Department of Health and Human Services. 2005. *Dietary Guidelines for Americans.* Retrieved from: www.health.gov/dietaryguidelines/dga2005/document/default.htm.

Whitlock, E. P., Orleans, C. T., Pender, N. & Alan, J. 2002. Evaluating primary care behavioral counseling interventions: An Evidence-based approach. *American Journal of Preventive Medicine, 22,* 267-284.

Further Reading and Viewing

A Book to promote mindfulness
Kornfield, J. 2008. *The Wise heart: A Guide to the Universal Teachings of Buddhist psychology.* New York: Bantam.

An iPhone/iTouch/iPad application to help with becoming more mindful
www.mentalworkout.com/store/be-happy-now/iphone.

Web sites to aid with health
www.mypyramid.gov. US Department of Agriculture's meal planning site. Near the top of the page click on the MyPyramidPlan link. You can then enter the sex, age, height and weight of every member of your family in order to receive a daily and weekly diet outline.
www.nhlbi.nih.gov/health/public/sleep/healthy_sleep.pdf: *To help with sleep (see the Web sites above as well).*
www.healthierus.gov: *A general clearinghouse for health related topics.*
http://apps.nccd.cdc.gov/dnpabmi/Calculator.aspx: CDC's BMI calculator.

Web sites to combat childhood obesity
www.nhlbi.nih.gov/health/public/heart/obesity/wecan: *National Institute of Health*
www.bam.gov: *Center for Disease Control (cartoon based).*
www.cdc.gov/healthyweight/children/index.html: *Center for Disease Control (tips for parents)*
www.letsmove.gov: *Obama administration.*http://brightbodies.org/index.html: Yale University School of Medicine.
www.nfl.com/play60: *National Football League.*

A clever book for helping you to serve healthy meals for your kids
Lapine, M. C. 2007. *The Sneaky Chef: Simple Strategies for Hiding Healthy Foods in Kids' Favorite Meals.* Philadelphia, PA: Running Press.

Recommended Documentaries about food
Kinner, R. (Director). 2009. *Food, Inc.* [Motion Picture]. United States: Magnolia Pictures.
Spurlock, M. (Director). 2004. *Super Size Me* [Motion Picture]. United States: Kathbur Pictures.

Chapter 9

References
Amato, P. R. 1994. Children's adjustment to divorce: Theories, hypotheses, and empirical support. *Journal of Marriage and the Family, 55,* 23-38.
Emery, R. E. 1982. Interparental conflict and the children of discord and divorce. *Psychological Bulletin, 92,* 310-330.
Fraiberg, S. H. 1959. *The Magic Years: Understanding and Handling the Problems of Early Childhood.* New York: Charles Scribner's Sons.
Gottman, J. M., Gottman, J. S. & Declaire, J. 2007. *Ten Lessons to Transform Your Marriage: America's Love Lab Experts Share Their Strategies for Strengthening Your Relationship.* New York: Three Rivers Press.
Hopper, C., & Jeffries, S. 1990. Coach-parent relations in youth sport. *Journal of Physical Education, Recreation and Dance, 61,* 18-22.
Kelly, J. 2000. Children's Adjustment in Conflicted Marriage and Divorce: A Decade Review of Research. *Journal of the American Academy of Child and Adolescent Psychiatry, 39,* 963-973.
Reynolds, A. J., Ou, S.-R. & Topitzes, J. W. 2004. Paths of effects of early childhood intervention on educational attainment and delinquency: A Confirmatory analysis of the Chicago child-parent centers. *Child Development, 75,* 1299-1328.
Reynolds, A. J., & Ou, S.-R. 2003. Promoting resilience through early childhood intervention. In Luthar, S. S. (Ed.). *Resilience and Vulnerability: Adaptation in the Context of Childhood Adversities.* New York: Cambridge University Press.

Thompson, R. A. 2006. *Nurturing Future Generations: Promoting Resilience in Children and Adolescents through Social, Emotional and Cognitive Skills* (2nd Ed.). New York: Routledge.

United States Census Bureau. 2008. Living arrangements of children: 2004. Retrieved from www.census.gov/prod/2008pubs/p70-114.pdf.

Wolchik, S. A., Schenck, C. E. & Sandler, I. N. 2009. Promoting resilience in youth from divorce families: Lessons learned from experimental trails of the New Beginnings Program. *Journal of Personality, 77,* 1833-1868.

Further Reading and Viewing

A book to support forgiveness work
Enright, R. D. 2001. *Forgiveness is a Choice: A Step-By-Step Process for Resolving Anger and Restoring Hope.* Washington, D. C.: American Psychological Association.

Sometimes we lunatic-parents, and those who serve children, could use inspiration
video.google.com/videoplay?docid=-5784740380335567758#
www.ted.com/talks/shukla_bose_teaching_one_child_at_a_time.html.

Books for facilitating divorce adjustment (the first is for parents, the second for kids)
Ricci, I. 1997. *Mom's House, Dad's House: Making Two Homes for Your Child.* New York: Fireside Books.
Ricci, I. 2006. *Mom's House, Dad's House: For Kids.* New York: Fireside Books.

Chapter 10

References
American Foundation for Suicide Prevention. 2010. *Facts and Figures. National Statistics.* Retrieved from www.afsp.org/index.cfm?fuseaction=home.viewpage&page_id=050fea9f-b064-4092-b1135c3a70de1fda.

American Heart Association. 2010. *Heart Disease and Stroke Statistics: Our Guide to Current Statistics and the Supplement to Our Heart & Stroke Facts.* Retrieved from bit.ly/93nqPM.

American Psychiatric Association. 1994. *Diagnostic and Statistical Manual of Mental Disorders.* (4th Ed.). Washington, D. C.: American Psychiatric Association.

Burns, B., Phillips, S. D., Wagner, H. R., Barth, R. P., Kolko, D. J., Campbell, Y. & Landsverk, J. 2004. Mental health need and access to mental health services by youths involved with child welfare: A National survey. *Journal of the American Academy of Child & Adolescent Psychiatry, 43,* 960-970.

Bussing, R., Zima, B. T., Perwien, A. R., Belin, T. R., & Widawski, M. 1998. Children in special education programs: Attention Deficit Hyperactivity Disorder, use of services, and unmet needs. *American Journal of Public Health, 88,* 880-886.

Christophersen, E. R., & Mortweet, S. L. 2001. *Treatments that Work with Children: Empirically Supported Strategies for Managing Childhood Problems.* Washington, D. C.: American Psychological Association.

Cohen, J. 1988. *Statistical Power Analysis for the Behavioral Sciences* (2nd Ed.). Hillsdale, NJ: Lawrence Erlbaum Associates.

Cohen, P., Kasen, S., Brook, J. S., & Struening, E. L. 1991. Diagnositc predictors of treatment patterns in a cohort of adolescents. *Journal of the American Academy of Child and Adolescent Psychiatry, 30,* 989-993.

David-Ferdon, C. & Kaslow, N. J. 2008. Evidence-based psychosocial treatments for child and adolescent depression. *Journal of Clinical Child and Adolescent Psychology, 37,* 62-104.

Fletcher, K. 2007. Post Traumatic Stress Disorder. In Mash, E., & Barkley, R. (Eds.). *Assessment of Childhood Disorders* (4th Ed.). New York: Guilford Press.

Fletcher, K. 2002. Childhood Post Traumatic Stress Disorder. In Mash, E. & Barkley, R. (Ed.). *Child Psychopathology* (2nd Ed.). New York: Guilford Press.

Giled, S., & Cuellar, A. E. 2003. Trends and issues in child and adolescent mental health. *Health Affairs, 22,* 39-50.

Goodyer, I. M., Cooper, P., Vize, C. M., & Ashby, L. 1993. Depression in 11-16-year-old girls: The Role of past parental psychopathology and exposure to recent life events. *Journal of Child Psychology & Psychiatry & Allied Disciplines, 34,* 1103-1115.

Huey, S. J., & Polo, A. J. 2008. Evidence-based psychosocial treatments for ethnic minority youth. *Journal of Clinical Child & Adolescent Psychology, 37,* 262-301.

Kazak, A. E., Hoagwood, K., Weisz, J. R., Hood, K., Kratochwill, T. R., Vargas, L. A., & Banez, G. A. 2010. A Meta-systems approach for evidence-based practice for children and adolescents. *American Psychologist, 65,* 85-97.

Jellinek, M. S., Murphy, J. M., Little, M., Pagano, M. E., Comer, D. M., & Kelleher, K. J. 1999. Use of the Pediatric Symptom Checklist to screen for psychosocial problems in pediatric primary care. A National feasibility study. *Archives of Pediatrics & Adolescent Medicine, 153,* 254-260.

Kataoka, S., Zhang, L. & Wells, K. B. 2002. Unmet Need for Mental Health Care Among U.S. Children: Variation by Ethnicity and Insurance Status. *American Journal of Psychiatry, 159,* 1548-1555.

Keller, M. B., Lavori, P. W., Wunder, J., Beardslee, W. R., Schwartz, C. E., & Roth, J. 1992. Chronic course of anxiety disorders in children and adolescents. *Journal of the American Academy of Child and Adolescent Psychiatry, 31,* 595-599.

Lavigne, J., Arend, R., Rosenbaum, D., Binns, J. J., Christoffell, K. K., Burns, A., & Smith, A. 1998. Mental health service use among young children receiving pediatric primary care. *Journal of the American Academy of Child and Adolescent Psychiatry, 37,* 1175-1183.

Pescosolido, B., Jensen, P. S., Martin, J. K., Perry, B. L., Olafsdottir, S.. & Fettes, D. 2008. Public knowledge and assessment of child mental health problems: Findings from the national stigma study-children. *Journal of the American Academy of Child & Adolescent Psychiatry, 47,* 339-349.

Rapoport, J. L., & Ismond, D. R. 1996. *DSM-IV Training Guide for Diagnosis of Childhood Disorders.* New York: Routledge.

Rutter, M., Cox, A., Tupling, C. Berger, M., & Yule, W. 1975. Attainment and adjustment in two geographic areas: I–The Prevalence of psychiatric disorders. *The British Journal of Psychiatry, 126,* 493-509.

Silverman, W., Pina, A. A., & Viswesvaran, C., 2008. Evidence-based psychosocial treatments for phobic and anxiety disorders in children and adolescents. *Journal of Clinical Child and Adolescent Psychology, 37,* 105-130.

Silverman, W., Ortiz, C. D., Viswesvaran, C., Burns. B. J., Kolko, D. J., Putnam, F. W. & Amaya-Jackson, L. 2008. Evidence-based psychosocial treatments for children and adolescents exposed to traumatic events. *Journal of Clinical Child and Adolescent Psychology, 37,* 156-183.

Simon, G. E., & VonKorff, M. 1998. Suicide mortality among patients treated for depression in an insured population. *American Journal of Epidemiology, 147,* 155-160.

Tillman, R., Geller, B., Bolhofner, K., Craney, J. L., Williams, M. & Zimerman, B. 2003. Ages of onset and rates of syndromal and subsyndromal comorbid *DSM-IV* diagnoses in a prepubertal and early adolescent bipolar disorder phenotype. *Journal of the American Academy of Child & Adolescent Psychiatry, 42,* 1486-1493.

VanFleet, R. 2005. *Filial Therapy: Strengthening Parent-Child Relationships Through Play (2nd Ed.).* Sarasota, FL: Professional Resource Press.

Weisz, J. R., Sandler, I. N., Durlak, J. A., & Anton, B. S. 2005. Promoting and protecting youth mental health through evidence-based prevention and treatment. *American Psychologist, 60,* 628-648.

Further Reading and Viewing

Helpful Web Sites

www.effectivechildtherapy.com: Created by both the Association for Behavioral and Cognitive Therapies and the Society of Clinical Child and Adolescent Psychology, this Web site reviews evidence based psychological treatments for children and adolescents.

www.mentalhealth.com: A clearinghouse for helpful information on problems with mental health.

www.nimh.nih.gov/health/index.shtml: The National Institute of Mental Health's site listing educational resources for mental health issues.

http://cdc.gov/mentalhealth/The Centers for Disease Control's electronic clearinghouse for mental health information.

Resource directories for finding a therapist (sites vary regarding what steps they take to establish the credentials of the individuals listed)

www.abpp.org/i4a/member_directory/feSearchForm.cfm?directory_id=3&pageid=3288&showTitle=1: To find a board certified clinical psychologist.

http:// locator.apa.org: The American Psychological Association's psychologist locator.

www.aacap.org/cs/root/child_and_adolescent_psychiatrist_finder/child_and_adolescent_psychiatrist_finder: The American Academy of Child and Adolescent Psychiatry's psychiatrist locator.

www.nbcc.org/directory/FindCounselors.aspx: Directory of the National Board for Certified Counselors.

www.mhw.com

www.psychologytoday.com

psychologyinfo.com/directory/state-links.html

Web Sites for learning more about Mental Health Parity

www.apa.org/helpcenter/parity-law.aspx

www.cms.gov/HealthInsReformforConsume/04_TheMentalHealthParityAct.asp

Books for kids on a wide assortment of mental health issues

www.imaginationpress.com: *American Psychological Association's publishing division.*

David J. Palmiter earned his PhD in Clinical Psychology from George Washington University in 1989 and his diplomate in Clinical Psychology from the American Board of professional psychology in 1996. David is a tenured Professor of Psychology at Marywood University where he also directs an outpatient mental health training clinic. He has a private practice in Clarks Summit, Pennsylvania, serves on the board of directors of both the Pennsylvania Psychological Association and the Pennsylvania Psychological Foundation, and is a state public education coordinator for the American Psychological Association.

Dr. Palmiter has written more than 30 professional publications, has given over 160 professional workshops on child clinical psychology across the country, and has more than 200 media credits, including for outlets such as *O Magazine, U.S. News and World Report, Parenting, Los Angeles Times,* and *Woman's Day.* His professional writing has won a national award, his media work a state award, and his work within psychology a university award.

Dr. Palmiter lives with his wife of twenty years, Lia; their 3.0 children, Morgan, Gannon, and Lauren; and their neurotic Portuguese water dog, Dakota, in Clarks Summit, Pennsylvania. Dr. Palmiter's blog is www.hecticparents.com. His Web site to support this book is www.reslient youth.com, and his primary Web site is www.helpingfamilies.com. He can also be found on Twitter (@helpingparents), LinkedIn, and Facebook.

Also Available from Sunrise River Press

Answers to Anorexia

A Breakthrough Nutritional Treatment That Is Saving Lives

James M. Greenblatt, MD This new medical treatment plan for anorexia nervosa is based on cutting-edge research on nutritional deficiencies and the use of a simple but revolutionary brain test that can help psychiatrists select the best medication for an individual. Anorexia is a complex disorder with genetic, biological, psychological, and cultural contributing factors; it is not primarily a psychiatric illness as has been believed for so long. Dr. Greenblatt has helped many patients with anorexia recover simply by correcting specific nutritional deficiencies, and here he explains which nutrients must be supplemented as part of treatment. He finally offers patients and their families new hope for successful treatment of this serious, frustrating, and enigmatic illness. Softbound, 6 x 9 inches, 288 pages. Item # SRP607

Taking Antidepressants

Your Comprehensive Guide to Starting, Staying On, and Safely Quitting

by Michael Banov, MD Antidepressants are the most commonly prescribed class of medications in this country. Yet, consumers have few available resources to educate them about starting and stopping antidepressants. Dr. Michael Banov walks the reader through a personalized process to help them make the right choice about starting antidepressants, staying on antidepressants, and stopping antidepressants. Readers will learn how antidepressant medications work, what they may experience while taking them, and will learn how to manage side effects or any residual or returning depression symptoms. Softbound, 6 x 9 inches, 304 pages. Item # SRP606

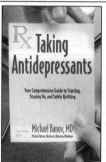

A Practical Guide to Hip Surgery

From Pre-Op to Recovery

M.E. Hecht, MD This book tells you everything you need to know before you undergo hip replacement or resurfacing surgery, directly from an orthopedic surgeon who has performed countless hip surgeries and has undergone a double hip replacement herself! Dr. M.E. Hecht tells you step by step what you'll need to do to before the day of your surgery, and then walks you through the procedure itself so that you know exactly what to expect. Sharing from her own experience as a hip surgery patient, she also discusses issues that can arise during the first few days through first months of your recovery, and includes handy checklists to help you organize and plan for your post-surgery weeks so you can focus on recovering as quickly and smoothly as possible. This book is a must-read before you undergo surgery, and will prove to be a trusted and essential resource during and after your hospital stay. Softbound, 6 x 9 inches, 160 pages. Item # SRP612

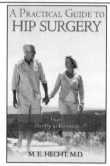

How to Manage Your Depression through Exercise

The Motivation You Need to Start and Maintain an Exercise Program

Jane Baxter, PhD Research has proven that exercise helps to lessen or even reverse symptoms of depression. Most depressed readers already know they need to exercise, but many can't muster the energy or motivation to take action. *How to Manage Your Depression through Exercise* is the only book on the market that meets depressed readers where they are at emotionally, physically, and spiritually and takes them from the difficult first step of getting started toward a brighter future. Through the Move & Smile Five-Week Activity Plan, the Challenge & Correct Formula to end negative self-talk, and words of encouragement, author Jane Baxter uses facts, inspiration, compassion, and honesty to help readers get beyond feelings of inertia one step at a time. Includes reproducible charts, activities list, positive inner-dialogue comebacks, and photos illustrating various exercises. Softbound, 6 x 9 inches, 224 pages. Item # SRP624